The Gebusi

FIFTH EDITION

The Gebusi

Lives Transformed in a Rainforest World

FIFTH EDITION

BRUCE KNAUFT

with Anne-Sylvie Malbrancke

WAVELAND

PRESS, INC.

Long Grove, Illinois

For information about this book, contact:
    Waveland Press, Inc.
    4180 IL Route 83, Suite 101
    Long Grove, IL 60047-9580
    (847) 634-0081
    info@waveland.com
    www.waveland.com

Photo Credits

Eileen Cantrell: pp. 4, 11, 23, 37, 53, 54, 93, 98, 101, 125 (left), and color inserts 1, 3, 5.
Anne-Sylvie Malbrancke: pp. 40, 104, 106, 165, 213 (top), 227 (right), and color insert 20.
Latham Wood: back cover, pp. 32, 147, 221, 230, and color insert 14.
Bruce Knauft: all photos not otherwise listed above.

To Yuway and all Gebusi—
Past, Present, Future

About the Authors

Bruce Knauft is Samuel C. Dobbs Professor at Emory University in Atlanta. He has published numerous journal articles and two substantial monographs about the Gebusi of Papua New Guinea: *Good Company and Violence* (University of California Press, 1985) and *Exchanging the Past* (University of Chicago Press, 2002). Dr. Knauft is a widely known scholar of Melanesia, and his books include *From Primitive to Post-colonial in Melanesia and Anthropology* (University of Michigan Press, 1998) and *South Coast New Guinea Cultures* (Cambridge University Press, 1993). He has also written extensively about contemporary directions in cultural anthropology, including his books *Genealogies for the Present in Cultural Anthropology* (Routledge, 1996) and *Critically Modern* (edited, Indiana University Press, 2002).

During the past 15 years, Professor Knauft has engaged with action anthropology, including project activities and scholarly programs he has directed in West Africa, East Africa, Inner Asia, South Asia, and the Himalayas. He has mentored a broad range of students who have conducted fieldwork in diverse world areas and who are now professionals in their own right. He enjoys teaching undergraduates and regularly teachers Introduction to Cultural Anthropology. The present book was written especially with undergraduates and a larger general audience in mind. Professor Knauft has remained keenly interested in the Gebusi people of Papua New Guinea since his first fieldwork among them in the 1980s, and he most recently worked with them again in 2016 and 2017, accompanied by coresearcher Anne-Sylvie Malbrancke. He also has significant interest in Tibetan Buddhism, the anthropology of development, and the political economy and class structure of racism, sexism, and political polarization in the contemporary US.

Professor Knauft's CV, selected papers, photos, online teaching modules, videos of him with Gebusi, and music links are available on his website at bruceknauft.com.

Anne-Sylvie Malbrancke is a former literature student from École Normale Supérieure. She transitioned to anthropology upon meeting Maurice Godelier in 2009, who provided her full access to his fieldwork material gathered among the Baruya of Papua New Guinea during the 1960s and 1970s. She then conducted her own doctoral fieldwork in New Guinea with the descendants of Godelier's informants among the Baruya (2013–2014) and wrote her dissertation on cultural change, with special emphasis on the ways Baruya women engage with "modernity." She subsequently accompanied Dr. Knauft on two successive field seasons in 2016 and 2017 among the Gebusi. In late 2017 she started shooting a series of documentaries, *Rituals of the World* (15 episodes), which aired on the Franco-German cultural channel Arte in 2020. The author of several theoretical articles, Dr. Malbrancke has also published a book relating her experiences on television shoots and exploring the rituals depicted: *Rituels du monde* (éditions Dépaysage, 2020). She is now in the process of shooting another series of documentaries for Arte that also focus on rites of passage: *Vivre*.

Contents

Part Two   Radical Change

Part Three   Blurring the Past in the Present

Preface

BACKGROUND

Anthropology is little without powerful portrayals of peoples and cultures across the world. These change over time. As such, we are pushed to stretch our understanding of others and, in the process, to reconsider our own beliefs and values. Over the years, a number of short books have exposed students to cultural diversity and the richness of human experience. These often take the form of short ethnographies—book-length descriptions of the people and culture considered. Within this genre, *The Gebusi* is distinctive in three connected ways. First, I have written this work without the formality of academic scholarship. This is not to dismiss professional writing. But having published some 1,500 pages of description and analysis concerning the Gebusi and related peoples in Melanesia (see "About the Author"), I here write more concisely, personally, and lyrically—for a larger and more general audience. *The Gebusi* is based on what I hope is detailed and rigorous scholarship, but it portrays Gebusi and my experience with them in more evocative and engaging ways.

Second, as a teacher of undergraduates, I have enjoyed writing this book to dovetail with topics and issues covered in many cultural anthropology courses and textbooks. This aspect of *The Gebusi* was important to me from the start but has evolved further in the book's present edition.

Third, as described below, the fifth edition of *The Gebusi* includes a dialogue of juxtaposition between my own voice and that of French anthropologist and Gebusi coresearcher Anne-Sylvie Malbrancke, providing a fresh window of critical reinterpretation in ethnographic portrayal and analysis.

THE FIFTH EDITION

This version of *The Gebusi* is different enough from previous editions as to be not just an updated but a deeply reframed work, including in relation to front-burner issues in contemporary cultural anthropology. These include the role and subject-position of the researcher, gender, postcoloniality, ethnicity, race, cultural change, government imposition and corruption, and political economy; these issues are more deeply engaged here than in previous editions of *The Gebusi*.

In the summers of 2016 and 2017, I returned to the Gebusi for four months with young French anthropologist Dr. Anne-Sylvie Malbrancke, who has previous fieldwork experience in Papua New Guinea among the Baruya of the Eastern Highlands. In the present book, Malbrancke's contributions provide a second voice, a countervoice, which complements and at times either reinforces or questions my own as original author. In the mix, issues of gender are recontextualized with much greater awareness of women's perspectives; dramatic cases of sorcery inquest, punctuated by the execution of a sorcery suspect, are documented; and matters of government graft and corruption are focused on, including in relation to issues of postcolonialism, ethnicity, and race.

Anthropologists talk much about bringing multiple perspectives of authorship and subject position to their work. This edition of *The Gebusi* engages this possibility by providing independent perspectives of a young French female anthropologist that complement my own as a senior American male ethnographer. The question of subjectivity and of subject position and the politics of representation are front and center in the present work—not as an abstract or theoretical exercise but in the concrete juxtaposition of different authorial voices. We make no particular judgment about or interpretation of this juxtaposition; rather, we leave it to readers, including students, to discuss and debate this issue. In some parts of the book, our authorial juxtaposition is more fleeting or intermittent; in other sections, it is more sustained. The last half of chapter 3, the entirety of chapter 4, and a major section of chapter 11 are written by Malbrancke.

All passages written by Dr. Malbrancke are here flagged with an "Anne-Sylvie" boldface heading, slight left indent, and ragged right margins.

The fifth edition of *The Gebusi* has retained the tone, content, and overall structure of previous versions; its changes can be easily incorporated in syllabi by instructors who have used previous editions. Though some small examples and incidents have been condensed or omitted vis-à-vis the fourth edition, the present work can be productively read as before. The main exception here is that the previous chapter 4, concerning Gebusi kinship, marriage patterns, social organization, and structural patterns of violence, has now been entirely replaced by Malbrancke's description of events relating to the execution of Powa, a sorcery suspect, which took place in 2016. To accommodate instructors who wish to retain my previous description and analysis of Gebusi kinship and social structure, the full content of the previous edition's chapter 4 is posted online at bruceknauft.com → Gebusi.

It is noteworthy that passages written by Dr. Malbrancke were originally formulated quite independently of the present book. Based on her field diaries, these passages were penned on her own initiative as part of a separate manuscript, *Papuan Chronicles,* that she wrote in French and has since generously translated into English. I did not request, comment on, or review this work prior to embarking on the fifth edition of *The Gebusi*—by which time her manuscript was finished on its own terms. As such, Malbrancke was not considering *The Gebusi* when writing up her chronicles. Yet, we found a riveting juxtaposition between her memoirs and the fifth edition of *The Gebusi* that I had already been planning to write. Given this, and with Malbrancke's full agreement and support, I have had the privilege to choose significant sections of her work and edit them to provide a second authorial voice that dovetails with the book's content while also reframing it through her vantage point. Though I have much to say about recent developments among Gebusi, the present edition foregrounds Malbrancke's own perspective on these matters, except in the final chapter.

Insofar as Dr. Malbrancke and I are collegial friends who refer to each other by our first names, we retain this usage throughout the book as well.

For students: "Updates" at the end of most chapters enable the book to be read as a story of cultural change throughout, topic by topic and chapter by chapter. As with previous editions, chapters conclude with

"Broader Connections" bullet points. These highlight and link the material in the chapter with major concepts taught in introductory anthropology courses, with key anthropological terms appearing in boldface. The author's website, bruceknauft.com → Gebusi, contains a large range of topically linked photographs and clips of Gebusi music, an index of boldface terms, videos from and about fieldwork, notes and references to *The Gebusi* fifth edition, and the index to the present book.

For instructors: The fifth edition provides links to eight online teaching modules about Gebusi that include video segments recorded in the field: "What Is Anthropology?" "Studying Culture," "Language," "Subsistence Livelihood," "Social Organization and Kinship," "Gender," "Sexuality," and "Development and Underdevelopment." Go to bruceknauft.com → Gebusi, or search for "Gebusi videos" in YouTube.

THE GEBUSI

Who are the Gebusi? When I first lived among them, they were a small ethnic group of some 450 forager-horticulturalists living in longhouses in the deep interior rainforest of Papua New Guinea, which is located just north of Australia in the South Pacific. At that time, Gebusi life was rife with dramatic practices of sorcery and ritual, body art and divination, feasting and camaraderie, violence, and alternative sex practices. When I studied with the Gebusi again in the late 1990s, they had largely transformed into a Christian people of about 615 who frequented the local market, attended government development meetings, played in the regional sports league, attended the local church, and whose children attended the local government school. They had by then become engaged with other ethnic groups in a regional process of nation-building, and they had given up many previous beliefs and practices. In 2008 and since, Gebusi, now more than 1,200 strong, have weathered an economic collapse of the local cash economy. Government services have been withdrawn, and the local airstrip is closed. In the bargain, however, Gebusi have rediscovered and rejuvenated much of their previous culture.

In all, our knowledge of the Gebusi spans a great arc of social and cultural transformation—from remote isolation in the early 1980s, to active engagement with national and global lifestyles, to the resurgence of many previous cultural practices. Their development dramatically illustrates a range of key issues in the anthropological understanding of social development, globalization, inequity, marginalization, and changes in gender relations as well as the elaboration and reinvention of indigenous traditions over time.

To me, and I think to Dr. Malbrancke, Gebusi are amazing people—funny, funky, high spirited, at turns both relaxed and intense. I hope you will agree that they are as wonderful as they are different, from a Western perspective. I am privileged to be able to work with Gebusi, a range of whom have become my deep friends for many years. I also feel fortunate to have the opportunity to convey significant and vivid aspects of their lives as well as parts of my own when working among them.

Personal names used in the text are in most cases actual names, used with permission. In a few cases we have used pseudonyms, including when a depiction is potentially unflattering or embarrassing in a modern context and the person is still alive. Quotations taken from my Gebusi field notes and from Dr. Malbrancke's translated manuscript have been lightly edited from the original to make them clearer or more compact.

ACKNOWLEDGMENTS

Bruce: It is hard to express the personal and professional debt that I feel toward my Gebusi friends and acquaintances; they are now so many and so varied that it is hard to know how and in what order to name them. My debt to Gebusi women, through the work of Dr. Malbrancke, and to Dr. Malbrancke herself, is key to this fifth edition of *The Gebusi*. I am thankful for help from former officials and staff at Nomad Station and in Kiunga, and to the Catholic Church in both these locations. Especially in remote regions, field research is difficult if not impossible without financial assistance from funding agencies. I gratefully acknowledge support for my field research among Gebusi from the US National Science Foundation, the US National Institutes of Mental Health, the US Department of Education, the Wenner-Gren Foundation, the Carnegie Corporation of New York, the Harry Frank Guggenheim Foundation, and Emory University.

Thanks go to numerous persons who have read and commented on various drafts and editions of this book, and especially Tom Curtin, Senior Editor at Waveland. I thank Eileen Cantrell for her photos of Gebusi during

1980–1982 and her information about women's lives and experiences during that time. I owe a special debt to my undergraduate and graduate students at Emory University. They have given me the courage not simply to teach anthropology from the heart but to go back to the field—and learn it all over again! My debt to Anne-Sylvie in the reformulation of this fifth edition of *The Gebusi* is so deep and strong that it is hard to express, including in relation to our collegial friendship both during and since our fieldwork together. This book is dedicated to the spirit of my friend Yuway, and to the past, present, and future of the Gebusi.

Anne-Sylvie: Debt is a central notion in anthropology and a concept we acutely feel every day—be it in the field or back home as we write up stories of events we experienced thanks to the depth of generosity and warmth people have shown us. It would take the space of this whole book to thank all Gebusi properly. I like to think they would enjoy these pages, as their stories live on and reach new horizons. I hope someday I can bring them a copy myself.

My gratitude toward Bruce, who sat on my thesis committee and challenged me to engage with my own research in a deeper and much more elaborate manner, is equally hard to measure and to express. I cannot thank him enough for giving me the chance to return to Papua New Guinea, to fully understand how little I had understood. My intellectual debt, however, does not come close to the debt of friendship I owe him.

I would like to thank my colleagues at CREDO in Marseilles, and especially Maurice Godelier, whose intellectual support has been key to my own trajectory. My deepest gratitude goes to The Harry Frank Guggenheim Foundation, who funded both of our Gebusi fieldtrips and trusted us to advance research concerning their violence reduction.

Finally, I would like to thank you, anthropology student or reader, for you are contributing to the continuing importance of this science of understanding, which the world needs now more than ever.

Entry

Anne-Sylvie
> We flew over the largest uninhabited stretch of tropical forest in the
> world, a green, luscious coat of uniformity.*

Bruce, 1998: It looks so grand from a thousand feet up, glowing, green, and vast. The broccoli tops of the trees stretch out as a vast carpet, an emerald skin shielding worlds of life within. You look down to see two blue-brown ribbons of water etching through the forest canopy. You follow them through the window of your tiny plane as they snake toward each other and merge in gentle delight. Below, in the nestled crook of these two rivers, you look closer, to where the green shifts from dark to bright, from old forest to new growth that gets cut but always sprouts anew. Inside this lime-green patch you see a score of white squares arranged in two neat rows, standing firmly as if at attention. Ten line up evenly on one side while their partners face them across the lawn, their metal roofs glinting in the hot sun. You recall how these structures were built long ago by the first Australian officers, so colonial and rugged, who trekked in across muddy rivers and swamps. Alongside these structures, a long rectangle field lies flat, its grass kept short and trim. Your plane will swoop down on it, the gilded spine of that book you have come so far to read. But its substance is

*Anne-Sylvie's entries are from her fieldwork conducted in 2016 and 2017.

not what you thought it would be, not text at all. As you descend, its meaning becomes the faces that line the airstrip, bright and eager as their skin is dark. They watch expectantly as you land. You open the door to a searing blast of heat and humanity. Welcome to Nomad Station.

Anne-Sylvie

The sensations of fieldwork work in millimeters: individually they might not build pyramids, but their implacable multitude turns them into an army of bullet ants, and all combined, they create the poignant and sometimes excruciating tapestry that is "the field." Taken on its own, a slow canoe ride in the rain would almost be fun—an adventure. A long sweaty walk through the rainforest would be exciting. Dirt, leeches, unfiltered water, falling in the forest, and hearing our carriers laughing at this sight—all of this would just be the expected lot of any expedition extracting you from a comfort zone that you'll quickly return to when it all stops. If only it all stops. If only. As the evening draws in and the sun goes down, it is time to laugh it off, maybe wine it off. Then those niggly bits will remain "bits," small things to overcome and keep at bay, a safe distance from which to enjoy the show that our life momentarily provides. But when the show goes on, and you are starring in it, your only horizon expands within that new world, a world that ranges from unknown disorders to creepy creatures.

Introduction
In Search of Surprise

Like most anthropologists, I was unprepared for what I would find. I had been married just a few months when I flew with my wife Eileen across the Pacific. We were going to live for two years in a remote area of the rainforest north of Australia, in the small nation of Papua New Guinea. I was 26 years old and had never been west of Oregon. I had no idea what changes lay in store either for me or for the people we were going to live with.

Deep into the 20th century, the large and rugged tropical island of New Guinea harbored people who had had little contact with outsiders. In the area where we were going, the first influence of Westerners did not take place until the 1960s. The 450 people whom we encountered had a name and a language that were not yet known to anthropologists. As individuals, the Gebusi (geh-BOO-see) were amazing—at turns regal, funny, infuriating, entrancing, romantic, violent, and immersed in a world of towering trees, heat and rain, and mosquitoes and illness. Their lives were as different from ours as they could be. Practices and beliefs that were practically lore in anthropology were alive and well: ritual dancers in eye-popping costumes, entranced shamans, all-night songfests and divinations, rigid separation between men and women, and striking sexual practices. A mere shadow to me at first, the dark side of Gebusi lives also became real: death

Bruce in 1980 with Soliabo, a senior man who is attempting to understand what writing is.

inquests, sorcery accusations, village fights, and wife beating. In the past, cannibalism had been common (I discovered that a woman from our village had been eaten a year and a half prior to our arrival). As I eventually realized, the killing of sorcery suspects had produced one of the highest rates of homicide ever recorded in the record of humanity.

Living and working with the Gebusi turned our own lives into something of an extreme sport. But in the crucible of our experience, Gebusi became not only real but also, despite their violence, quite wonderful. With wit and passion, they lived rich and festive lives. Vibrant and friendly, they turned life's cruelest ironies into their best jokes, its biggest tensions into their most elaborate fantasies. Humor, spirituality, deep togetherness, and raw pragmatism made Gebusi for the most part great fun to be with. I have never felt more included in a social world. And what personalities! To lump them together as simply "Gebusi" would be as bland as to describe Beyoncé, Donald Trump, Meryl Streep, and Bart Simpson as simply "American." The Gebusi were not just "a society" or "a culture"; they were an amazing mix of unique individuals.

Anthropology is little if not the discovery of the human unexpected. You might imagine the first time I tried to translate a Gebusi spirit séance from a tape recording I had made of it. I sat with Gebusi men in all seriousness as the track played. They were astonished at first to hear their own voices—but they quickly shifted from amazement to hilarity. At my prompting, they attempted, word by laborious word, to explain the humor I had recorded. It was tough, as I had no interpreters and was learning the Gebusi language "monolingually." As it turned out, their spiritual poetry had as little relation to their normal speech as the sentences of an anthropology textbook have to hip-hop. Gleefully, the men responded to my confusion by repeating yet again the bawdy jokes I had recorded. Unable to turn nighttime humor into daytime clarity, I realized that the best thing to do was to laugh along with them and enjoy their camaraderie. Seeing our strange interaction, the women said many of the songs were "no good" or "rotten."

Mostly, Gebusi were not just jovial but considerate and quick to apologize. I came to like most of them a lot, and over time, I grew to appreciate their culture—including their rituals, beliefs, and customs. But I remained keenly aware of my own ethics and values. What was I supposed to do with my morality when it collided with theirs, including in areas of gender, sex, and violence?

Cultural anthropology is likewise driven by the dilemma of competing desires. We want to appreciate the cultures we study, to understand them on their own terms and in their own context. Why should Western ways of life be thought superior? But anthropologists are also mindful of problems and inequities in the societies they study. Many of these injustices are fueled if not caused by outsiders. During centuries of colonialism, Westerners exploited and enslaved people across the world, including in North and South America, the Pacific, Africa, and significant parts of Asia. Many indigenous peoples have been subordinated, stigmatized, or killed on grounds of cultural, racial, or religious difference. At the same time, the historical legacy of such injustice often articulates with inequalities within societies that cannot, over time, be explained by external intrusion or imposition. Among Gebusi, oppression of women and violence against suspected sorcerers grated roughly against the splendors of Gebusi ritual performance and festivity. These paradoxes cannot be easily attributed to the impact of outside influence or domination.

Opposing trends underscore the challenge anthropologists face as we investigate problems and suffering: how do we reconcile the wonder of cultural diversity with difficulties caused by subjugation or violence, sometimes in the heart of the lives we study? During fieldwork, ethnographers frequently experience social life through the crosshairs of ethnocentrism, sexism, racism, religious intolerance, ageism, or other forms of discrimination. In the mix, we become more aware of the ethical standards we ourselves hold—as well as the risk of projecting these too easily onto others. This is a real dilemma I have felt when working with Gebusi.

Ultimately, Gebusi surprised me beyond the delightful "good company" of their social life and the unfortunate violence of their sorcery beliefs and gender practices. My biggest surprises have come each time I have returned to live and work with them again. Not knowing what lies in store, I brace myself, quell expectations, and try to take new conditions on their own new terms.

Anne-Sylvie

Going back to the field suddenly reactivates embedded memories, those thousands of thorns we so conveniently block out as we dream about our next fieldwork from our comfy armchair. Returning to the field, I experience again that deeper feeling, that moment, as when I first hear the sound of tropical birds. "Ah yes, that. I forgot. I'm here." "There" has become "here," once again. A deep frisson sends an electric shock down my spine.

Bruce: Over time, momentous changes have rocked Gebusi. Modern development has come and then largely gone, including government and market intrusion, Christianity, and hopes for business based on money. In this mix, some traditional Gebusi customs seem to have died out for good, but many others have continued or been revived and rejuvenated in new guises.

By the time of the approaching 2000 millennium, a decade and a half after my first fieldwork, my old community had picked up and moved—lock, stock, and barrel—from deep in the rainforest to the outskirts of the government airstrip at Nomad. Previously isolated, they were now part of a large multiethnic community of persons speaking five different languages. They became Christian and went to church. Their children went to school. Their women went to market. Sweet potatoes were now a starch staple, and new crops such as manioc, peanuts, squash, and pineapple were grown for sale as well as for consumption. Gebusi considered themselves citizens of the nation of Papua New Guinea.

Since the mid-2000s, however, Gebusi have again changed radically. Due to inefficiency and graft, the Nomad airstrip has effectively been closed. Government officials have gone, the health clinic is shut, the market is desultory, church attendance is down, schooling is compromised and sometimes nonexistent, and the local cash economy has all but entirely collapsed. Increasingly, Gebusi have been forced to return to their gardens and to the forest.

Anne-Sylvie

Nomad Station used to be a buzzing center back in the 1990s, full of activity and complete with a school, a medical dispensary, a regular market, government representatives, a jail, and even a post office doubling as a bank. Then, as years went by, against all ideas of linear progress, people started deserting the place. Money dried up, stores shut down, and unoccupied buildings gradually turned into ruins as state workers relocated to the town of Kiunga. There they could still collect the regular salary they were paid to administer services in the bush. In 2016 the station was almost dead, the buildings mostly broken down and uninhabited.

Bruce: Amid the vacuum of external connection in recent years, Gebusi, amazingly, have rejuvenated many of their traditional customs— and have become much more in charge of their own lives and society. If Gebusi during my first fieldwork seemed uncommonly "traditional," and if they became surprisingly "modern" by 2000, since then they have creatively interwoven both these legacies. In the mix, crucially, they have kept control of their own land, maintained a thriving rainforest livelihood, and increased their population without pushing on the limits of their territory.

Gebusi don't and can't reflect the lives of people elsewhere. But they do illustrate how society and culture change over time. Like Gebusi, people around the world become modern by both retaining and reshaping their unique identity, drawing on the past while creatively casting it into the future. As an anthropologist, I see culture as the diverse colors that refract through a prism of ongoing experience. By considering these refractions, we understand how people across the globe share a modern world while retaining and expanding their distinctiveness.

Exemplars in this regard, Gebusi provide a good framework for considering topics covered in anthropology courses. These include distinctive features of livelihood or subsistence; how people organize into groups; dynamics of economic exchange, distribution, and consumption; the politics of leadership, conflict, and violence; religious beliefs and spiritual practices; issues of sexual and gendered diversity; the construction of ethnicity and race; the impact of colonialism and nationalism; the role of the anthropologist; and, through it all, the dynamics of sociocultural change. Rather than describing Gebusi in general terms, I present them as individuals whose lives have unfolded across decades along with my own. My goal as author, and with Anne-Sylvie as my interlocutor and intermittent coauthor, is for Gebusi to come alive for you: for you to get a sense of Gebusi over time and in the present—and to connect this striking story with trends in cultural anthropology.

Update: See a video clip of the author's continuing surprise and uncertainty traveling to the Gebusi in 2013 on Bruce Knauft's website (online Gebusi video #1 = "Preface") or search for "Gebusi videos" in YouTube.

BROADER CONNECTIONS
Cultural Anthropology

- Through **fieldwork** and the writing of **ethnography, cultural anthropologists** become highly engaged with and attuned to **cultural diversity.**
- Cultural diversity leads anthropologists to appreciate **cultural relativity,** the value of each culture on its own terms.
- Anthropologists are also attuned to **social inequality,** including how differences of sex, gender, age, ethnic identity, religion, and other factors lead some people to dominate and subordinate others.
- Some aspects of social inequality derive from external constraint or coercion, including **colonialism, imperialism,** or **nationalist domination.**
- Other aspects of social inequality may derive from **internal social discrimination or stigma,** including as informed by long-standing beliefs and practices.
- In current practice, most cultural anthropologists appreciate **cultural relativity** *and* critique **social and cultural inequity.**
- Collectively, changes among Gebusi illustrate the relationship between **traditionalism, globalization,** and how people become **modern.**
- Because people such as Gebusi draw upon larger influences in their own unique way, they become "locally modern" or "alternatively modern" in their own way.

- A key concern for modern livelihoods is their **economic and environmental sustainability.** Gebusi are fortunate to have land, substance, and customs that provide for a thriving and sustainable livelihood.
- Because **cultural change** is not easily predictable, it is especially interesting, surprising, and exciting—and key to helping us understand our current human world.
- Like peoples across most developing countries, Gebusi have recent histories that combine strong traditions based on indigenous customs with the desire to participate in and benefit from modern activities and institutions.

A Gebusi boy, Gwabi, in traditional dress, 1981. →

Part One

Wealth in Tradition

Chapter 1

Friends in the Forest

The bananas were piled up, hot and grimy. Steam floated up from them—as if the air around us could have gotten any hotter. Some were stout as well as long, but most were slender, and a few were quite tiny. But their variety in dozens was a mystery to us then. Though all of them had been carefully scraped, long strands of soot and globs of charcoal remained from their time in the fire.

What to do with this mound of starchy bananas, presented to us so formally in that first village? Kukudobi villagers had probably not seen a white person for years before Eileen's and my arrival; the country had become nominally independent, and Australian patrol officers had left in 1975. Against this backdrop, our arrival caused quite a hubbub, a tempest in the forest. Women and children fled while men gasped with curious excitement. Emerging from the forest, the four local men who helped carry our supplies took the lead and we followed them ("When in Rome . . .") into the central longhouse. As we sat down cross-legged, a flood of unknown villagers did likewise all around us.

They must have done the cooking quickly or already known about our coming, since it wasn't long before the smoldering mound of starch was brought on a palm leaf platter and laid with gusto directly in front of me. Suddenly I was the focus of great public scrutiny. Short men with bamboo tubes through their noses looked on from all around. I was too embarrassed to check with anyone about what to do. Everything was heat and stickiness. I took one of the sooty bananas and began to munch on it, trying to show appreciation. The bananas were dry (technically they were "plantains"), but I forced myself to chew through one and pick up another. The people around started to grin as I swallowed their food. Progress was slow, however, and, judging from the size of the platter, ultimately hopeless. Using my hands, I signaled that the pile of food was large, my stomach was small, and many people could certainly be fed. What a relief when they broke into pleasant conversation and stretched out their arms, sharing the bananas throughout the longhouse. I had apparently passed my first test.

Anthropologists often talk about "The Gift," especially in Melanesia. How people produce things through hard work and sweat, infuse them with hope and good intention, and then just give them away speaks volumes about human connection. Gifts are at once a social economy and a materialized emotion. As Marcel Mauss suggested, gifts reflect and reinforce social bonds between givers and recipients. In American society, gifts at Christmastime convey meanings that reflect who we are most connected to, the strength and character of the relationship, and sometimes, as well, what we project or anticipate we will get in return.

As in many societies, Gebusi believe gifts should be given to visitors who are peaceful. Their most basic gift was the fruit of their most regular work as well as their primary source of nutrition: starchy cooked bananas. Well beyond food, however, material exchange creates social connection. Gebusi define their relationships by the things they give or don't give to others. In short order during my first fieldwork, I established a "gift-exchange name" with each man in the village—derived from something that was given or shared between us. Gusiayn was my "bird egg;" Iwayb was my "Tahitian chestnut." Based on gifts I myself gave, Yuway became my "fishing line" and Halowa my "salt." These names have endured between us now for many years. To have a social relationship and to have something memorably shared are one and the same among Gebusi.

Anne-Sylvie

Gift-exchange names are a clever and poetic means of embodying memories. Gebusi consider it impolite to call someone by his or her name. Killing a lizard and eating it together; gifting cooked pumpkin or weaving someone a net bag; catching the glimpse of a bird of paradise in the sky at the same time; all these moments are shared experiences that can meaningfully mark the starting point of a relationship and remind people of its origin. A night of drunken partying led Bruce and Anagui to become "Marley fo' life" to one another, as they listened to Bob Marley while under the influence of lord knows what exactly. John and Bruce became "spark" to each other, after the infamous fermented juice Gebusi love to drink to have fun—and leading to yet again another genius streak of improbable gift-exchange names. One is left with so much more than a hangover in the morning. Celebrating and remembering the moment for years on end—that is a baptism in its most meaningful form. Plus, the whole village gets to know what potentially infamous story you share with whom.

One day, Dugam, who was around 20 years old and unmarried, came to chat with me. She was not an archetypal Gebusi woman; she strongly refused the future of a "sweet potato lady," as she put it, whose existence would range between garden clearing and child rearing. She wanted to study, leave this place, stay unmarried, and invent herself. More pragmatically for the moment, she had heard about tampons from a friend who had come back from town and wondered if I would give her a few. She confided in me that using pieces of sheet that had to be washed all the time was not terribly convenient. Since one of my anthropologist friends, who did her fieldwork in the far north, told me that emptying her cup was risky as she could attract wolves, I had always actively avoided complaining about my period in the field, even though it is neither comfortable nor easy to manage all the time. Dugam and I chatted the afternoon away and started drinking the Southern Comfort that Bruce had brought from Atlanta. This fruity liquor that tastes vaguely like scotch is little known in my native France but is often called "Soco" in the United States. Dugam shared with me her fears and hopes in life, her dreams, and her frustrations. I talked about myself, too, and introduced her to pieces of my universe via magazines I had brought from Europe. She saw pictures of French towns and said: "When I see this, these cities, all those places . . . my thoughts expand." We ended up rather tipsy, chatting like old girlfriends ("but . . . once you have it in your mouth, what do you do with it?"). Forever, Dugam and I will be "Soco" to each other.

Because everyone knows your gift-exchange names, they create surreal conversations in reference: "Good morning, my peanut, I was talking to your hook this morning. Your coconut went off to the bush for a few days. . . . Hey there my deck of cards, have you seen my

Anne-Sylvie with Gebusi women, 2016.

Milky Way?" I had on average to remember three names for every person: their vernacular name, their Christian name, and their gift-exchange name. "Ah I'm sorry, river lobster is already taken. But I've got fishing line for you if you want!"

Ethnographies of the Pacific do not talk about friendship much; everything seems to stem from kinship relations, blood, and alliance obligations, with no sense of feelings, no other trajectory between two individuals other than that going through a common ancestor. The actions of Gebusi undermined this perception.

Bruce: In the earliest colonial reports, Gebusi were described as "quiet tractable people," and they were left largely alone by the Australian patrol officers. This stood in stark contrast to their tribal neighbors, the Bedamini, who were much more warlike—and numerous—than the Gebusi. Before pacification, Bedamini formed war parties that burrowed deep into Gebusi territory; using brutally efficient tactics, they would surround a Gebusi longhouse at dawn, set it ablaze, and kill and then cannibalize the fleeing inhabitants. With just 450 people against the Bedamini's 3,000, Gebusi were no match for the Bedamini. Indeed, if Australian officers had not forcibly stopped Bedamini raiding, Gebusi would have become just a remnant people within a few years. By the time I first arrived, Gebusi's perception of white-skinned outsiders was sky high: after all, Australian intervention had literally saved them from extinction! Hence the irony, and the benefit to me as an anthropologist, that as Bedamini had in recent years been forcibly pacified by armed colonial patrols, the neighboring Gebusi had been left on their own to maintain and expand their indigenous traditions—without threat of being killed and eaten.

Though Gebusi appeared at first to be a pristine people, customs that I first took as traditional had in fact elaborated substantially during the colonial period—along with the use of steel tools to clear larger gardens and build bigger houses. Because Gebusi associate growth with spiritual support, these changes affirmed their religious values as well as their social life. Like streams converging in the forest, material production and spiritual vitality came increasingly together in major Gebusi rituals, especially the initiation of young people into adulthood (see chapter 6.) Ironically, colonial intrusion gave Gebusi more freedom to become yet more "Gebusi-like" than they had been before.

That Gebusi had both exuberant traditions and desire for contact with outsiders made them perfect for me. Little wonder that I was enamored of them or that they wanted me, wanted both Eileen and me, for themselves. At first, however, we weren't interested.

My first journey to the Gebusi began with a blank spot on a map. That was where my graduate advisor at the University of Michigan thought that I would find the most fascinating people to study. The largest-scale maps then available were produced by the US Army—in case even the remotest parts of the globe needed American military intervention. The map of Papua New Guinea's Western Province contained an unknown space that stretched across a swampy rainforest north of the Tomu River. Lacking a name for Tomu River people, I talked by phone to a missionary who had completed an aerial survey nearby. He said these people were probably the "Kramo." Armed with this information, I obtained funding from the US National Science Foundation and the US National Institutes of Health to study political consensus formation led by shamans among people called the Kramo in the remote rainforest of Papua New Guinea's Western Province.

As it turned out, there was a good reason for the blank spot on the map: no one lived there! I finally accepted this after trudging for what seemed like forever to the far distant village of Honabi. There, the inhabitants told us consistently, and in as many ways as sign language would allow, that nothing was farther ahead of us but swamp and mosquitoes, both of which we had already endured to our limit. Even if we had wanted to continue trekking ahead into uninhabited territory, our carriers would not go with us. Professionally speaking, I had traveled across the world to Papua New Guinea armed with doctoral research grants to study people who didn't exist.

Alert to my uncertainty and perhaps my fear, the people at that distant village of Honabi brightly insisted that we stay and live with them. They claimed to have a tradition of spirit séances, through their assertions betrayed ambivalence. When we probed about their lives, they admitted typically abandoning their settlements during the dry season, splitting into tiny groups, and foraging ever deeper in the rainforest. As the evening grew longer and the mosquitoes bit harder, the idea of adapting to their lifestyle—living for two years in tiny encampments that shifted idiosyncratically deep in the bush—seemed more dreadful than admitting failure.

Not knowing what else to do, we trudged back to the government station via the village that our carriers lived in, which was roughly on the way. The more we found out about this other village, the more interested we became. By this time, our carriers were becoming real people to us. Yuway was a wonderfully decent young man—tall, sensitive, and strong for a Gebusi. He had a spontaneous sense of concern, interest, and patience even though we couldn't yet speak with him. He waited to help us over slippery log bridges and often shouldered the heaviest load. Gono never said much, but he was as sinewy and dependable as a stout tree, and always alert. Hawi was our nominal interpreter, and though his translations finally proved more troublesome than helpful, he was socially and physically agile. Finally was Swamin, older than his unmarried companions but more muscled than they. He would flash a captivating smile under his impish hooked nose and pepper remarks with articulate outbursts that, given the reactions he got from the other three, convinced us he was both very funny and quite smart. Hawi told us that Swamin was also a shaman who regularly held communal séances.

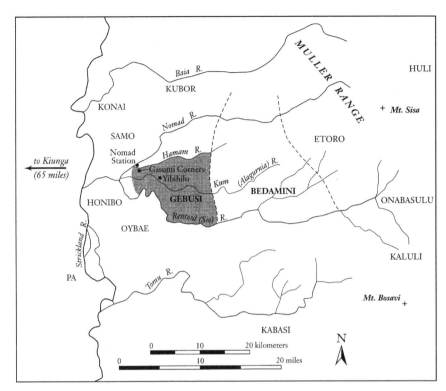

Gebusi and nearby groups.

When we finally reached their village of Yibihilu, the "place of the deep waters," we thought we had reached nirvana. Having stumbled for days through a sea of leaves, mud, and vines under a closed rainforest canopy, we felt like the miniature children in *Honey, I Shrunk the Kids!* who had navigated huge obstacles in a galactic backyard of foliage. I yearned to look up and out, to see more than the next hidden root that could send me sprawling.

By contrast, the "place of the deep waters" was perched on a 40-foot bluff overlooking a serpentine bend in the Kum River. The porch of the longhouse extended out over a canyon through which the river rushed before pooling in a serene basin some hundred yards wide and across which we could see a crocodile lazing in the sun. Farther downstream, the watercourse was calm enough to be traveled by canoe—which was far preferable to tromping through the muddy forest. At dusk, the sky above the river became a breath-taking sunset. The villagers stopped and stared. *Bubia maysum*—"The crimson is being laid down."

If the village seemed majestic, the people were yet better. Having learned more about us from our carriers in five minutes than the other villages had in five days, their kin and friends gave us the kind of warm welcome, especially in such a remote place, that made us feel on top of the world rather than at its end. As the traumas and troubles of our journey were discussed to the tiniest detail, the villagers laughed good-naturedly. That we were already trying to speak their language—however haltingly—was widely and enthusiastically noted. That we ate local food and that I had somehow carried my own backpack, which the men enjoyed trying on, were also taken as positive. It all seemed amazingly friendly.

Anne-Sylvie on arriving among the Gebusi

I feel the relentless grip of the tropical heat, bottled up during the day, with nowhere to escape and no way to evaporate, instead accumulating back into heavy drops and coming down to inhabit unsuspected bodily cavities. There is a tarp between the floor and my mattress, a mosquito net fixed on top and underneath to prevent cockroaches from playing rodeo on my nose—and not a whiff of air from the one window near my bedside. How can air both allow you to breathe and prevent you from doing so? Fieldwork is not the place for balance. It is woven with extremes, all the way to the core, from vital functions down to elements of the world we otherwise rarely stop to consider. Why is temperature queen in this realm?

Despite the heat, I already feel decidedly more at ease among the Gebusi than I did among the Baruya, a different group, from the highlands of Papua New Guinea, with whom I worked in 2013. Maybe it is a by-product of experience, of my familiarity with both uncomfortable situations and Tok Pisin, the lingua franca, the common language, of Papua New Guinea. Maybe I am helped by the sound of cicadas at night. Maybe my intestines have turned to iron— but Bruce brought water filters, and filtering local water, mind you, is the determining factor in preventing "piping issues."

Right away, given Bruce's long-standing familiarity with his Gebusi friends and informants, I have inscribed myself in a whole network of people who, by transfer, have given me the same level of trust and openness. What took weeks and months to establish among the Baruya has congealed immediately with Gebusi. The slow, maturing process of creating intimacy has been almost immediate here. Plus, the field and its associated habits have finally started to sink in. The least informed of anthropology's detractors tend to believe that we go to the field like others go to the zoo, that we "watch people live" as if they were on show. Let us remind them that the reverse is closer to the truth: the distraction offered by the whites to locals is endless. Plus, an ethics committee back home helps ensure we have people's approval before invading their daily lives. Among Gebusi, our arrival was celebrated.

Bruce per first fieldwork, 1980: In remarkably short stead during that first fieldwork, our physical presence, possessions, and desire to speak the vernacular painted us as paragons of beneficence, a gold mine of goods, and a three-ringed circus of entertainment. Our fingers were snapped (like shaking hands in America) and bellies gorged with countless gifts of food. Everyone seemed quite genuinely to want our friendship. If our reception was anything less than overwhelming, we were too euphoric to notice. As if we needed further encouragement, Swamin held an all-night spirit séance. Word of our presence drew villagers from surrounding hamlets, and given the convergence of many people in high spirits, a songfest was almost inevitable. The stars shone as they only do when there is no competing light for hundreds of miles. The songs of the men swelled as the moon rose from its silhouette in the forest canopy. Beneath its glow, their deep-throated harmony echoed as if in a wild cathedral. The music was nothing like, and more amazing than, anything I had heard before. I knew that Gebusi believed in a world of unseen spirits and in places that come alive through the shaman's songs. But as the sound washed over me, I knew almost nothing of its meaning. In the moment, however, this only added to the mystery and splendor of their cosmos—a world of wonder I had come to explore.

There was so much we didn't know about the Gebusi at first—including their name, which outsiders had told us was "Bibo." The people of Yibihilu found this terribly funny. They brought us a large starchy banana and indicated that this was their only "bibo"—one of their three-dozen varieties of plantains. They proudly proclaimed that their own identity, and also their language, was "Gebusi."

Discoveries of fieldwork had already brought us full circle. Having gone half-way around the world to study a people who didn't exist, we found ourselves living instead with a group that was unidentified by anthropologists and in that sense "unknown." In retrospect, though, our "discovery" of Gebusi revealed more about our own biases than anything else, that is, the tendency of Westerners to project onto other peoples our own sense of discovery. The same was true of the name of the government station, "Nomad." This had been based on the false colonial assumption that Gebusi and their neighboring peoples were nomadic, that they did not live in permanent settlements. As was quickly evident, this was far from the truth, another example of outside projection. But we each bring to a situation our own particular history and sentiments.

Anne-Sylvie

I was going to live among the Gebusi people, in an area appropriately called "Nomad." I felt I had always lived from my suitcase over the years, so even though this was a fixed point on a map, I appreciated the movement associated with its name.

Bruce: Beyond names, during my first fieldwork I quickly encountered one of Gebusi's central concepts, which took a while to figure out. With difficulty, we had been trying to explain why we had come to the rainforest in the first place. To Gebusi, we obviously didn't fit the mold of other whites they had known or heard about. Were we patrol officers, who ordered people around and then disappeared for another year? No. Were we Christian missionaries, who read from a big book and told villagers to give up their customs and believe in a new spirit? No. We tried to convey that we wanted to learn their language, understand their daily activities, enjoy their songs and dances, join in their feasts—to be with them and learn what they were like. In a flash, they seemed to get our meaning: we wanted to know their *kogwayay*. They appeared so certain of this that we had no choice but to agree with them. Though we had no idea what *kogwayay* actually meant! In truth, however, they were quite right.

Kogwayay is—or at least was, during that early period—the single word that best describes the heart of Gebusi culture. In a way, the term presents their concept of culture itself—the beliefs, practices, and styles of living special and unique to Gebusi. At one level, *kogwayay* refers to customs that make their culture different from others, especially their distinctive traditions of dancing, singing, and body decoration. But what is the term's deeper meaning? Gebusi were not much help here; for them, *kog-*

wayay was a catchall marker of cultural distinction and not a tool for dissecting it.

When you think about it, it's not surprising that people have a hard time explaining concepts central to their culture; such meanings are often "beyond words." How would the average American be able to quickly define and explain what "love" is to someone who had never known of this concept? In terms of *kogwayay*, we were fortunate that the word itself has three meaningful parts, what linguists call morphemes: *kog-*, *-wa-*, and *-yay*. *Kog* conveys "togetherness," "friendship," and "similarity." These meanings reflect the collective and communal nature of Gebusi life. Gebusi prefer to do things with as many other people as possible. They hate being alone; they are the opposite of loners. The *wa* component of the word is the Gebusi root of *wa-la*, "to talk." It refers to pleasant and casual conversations that are roundly shared. This is what the men did in the longhouse at night—they shared news and gossiped for hours—joking, fantasizing, and telling stories around the glow of a small resin lamp. Hour after hour, I realized how rare it was for Gebusi to get upset during these gabfests. Potential disagreements were covered with friendly smiles, embarrassments were soothed with jokes and shifts of conversation.

Yay supplied men's exuberant conclusion to *kogwayay*, its exclamation point. To *yay* or to *kay* is for a man to cheer, yell, joke, or cry out as loudly and happily as possible, preferably in union with other men. These yells have bodily meaning as well. When a man cheers with those around him, his "breath-heart" (*solof*) gushes out and mingles with that of others. To *yay* or *kay* is to send forth and unite male spiritual energy.

Two unrelated men of Yibihilu indicate their friendship by dressing in similar costume, 1981.

Taken together, what do *kog-*, *-wa-*, and *-yay* mean? And why should we care? No single English word captures their essence—and this fact is important. Anthropologists are charged to learn and convey concepts that are culturally important even and especially when these exceed our own background and understanding. *Kogwayay* was clearly important to Gebusi. The word was frequently used and talked about, evoked strong feelings, and was highly elaborated in rituals and ceremonies. In Gebusi culture, *kogwayay* was what anthropologist Sherry Ortner calls a "key symbol." Taken together, the three meanings of the word—togetherness, talk, and cheering—conveyed core male Gebusi values of happy social unity, of living in good company with one another. And *kogwayay* permeated Gebusi social life as well as being intensified at feasts, dances, spirit séances, and initiations.

Though *kogwayay* was a powerful and deeply held concept, it did not stand alone. It highlights the positive side of Gebusi culture, the bright side of their moon. Most peoples try to depict themselves in a good and favorable light, and Gebusi are no exception. If you asked what values are central in American society, you might get terms such as "freedom," "love," "money," "self-expression," "family values," or "tolerance." Of course, these are ideals as much or more than realities. Many American marriages end in divorce; many people are shackled by low incomes; and discrimination based on race or sex is arguably as deeply ingrained as it is illegal. A critic could argue that American society is cutthroat, egotistical, hedonistic, imperialistic, racist, sexist, and much less equal or free than we like to believe. If culture is an assertion of ideals and values, these easily hide problems or difficulties—and Gebusi are no exception. Yet where would we be without positive ideals to shoot for? In short, it seems good to appreciate the values of other peoples, including Gebusi, even as we don't neglect the underside of culture—realities neglected by positive ideals.

Where do we draw the line between an appreciative view of culture and a critical view of its inequalities? Do we emphasize the fight to free the slaves during the American Civil War? Or the history of slavery that caused that war? Do we emphasize the human benefit of toppling a dictator? Or the tens of thousands of lives lost in the process? These questions have few simple answers. But asking them makes us more aware of both the positive power of culture and the problems it can hide.

For Gebusi, *kogwayay* was a strong practice and a wonderful ideal—but it was controlled by men. Men rather than women collectively cheered and publicly yelled. It was men who gathered for public evening talk on the expansive men's porch that overlooked the river—while women were largely confined to whispered conversations in a tiny cramped female sleeping room on the other side of the longhouse. Men made major decisions: which settlement a family would live in, who would be accused of sorcery, when and how violence was called for, and when and how to stage ritual feasts—at which men themselves were the primary agents, performers, and gift-givers, including of food that women had themselves procured and cooked. At initiations, men were the principal focus and were elaborately decorated. As if to deny motherhood, as described in chapter 5, boys were nurtured to manhood by men themselves—through the transmission of male life force from one male generation to the next.

At spirit séances, men gathered in the dark longhouse around the shaman as he sat, smoked tobacco, and went into a controlled trance. As the words of the shaman's spirit became clearer, the men clustered around him—women were excluded—and formed a chorus that echoed and amplified his words, gradually singing louder and with greater confidence. The shaman's voice, however, was that of an ideal spirit *woman,* who flirted with the men and enticed them with salacious sexual innuendo. But Gebusi women in real life could easily be beaten and stigmatized by men if they exhibited any such behavior. In sum, spirit séances were in significant part a male fantasy that celebrated men's sexual desires while excluding, controlling, and then disparaging Gebusi women themselves.

Given male bias, what do we to make of Gebusi "good company"? For the most part, Gebusi women accepted and appreciated the culture they lived in. At spirit séances, they sometimes took offense at male joking, but more often they indulged and enjoyed it. Women were excited and galvanized by ritual feasts and initiations, and they actively played their own roles at these events. On these and other occasions, they enjoyed interacting with women visiting from other settlements. Gebusi women lived in the cultural shadow of Gebusi men, and occasionally they resisted their second-class status. But for the most part they appeared to accept and embrace

it. Women swelled with pride at their own and the men's accomplishments,
even when men presented the fruits of women's work. So, too, women
tended to accept and expect men's prerogative to take violent action against
sorcery suspects, and usually, as well, the right of a man to beat his wife.

Anne-Sylvie's reflections suggest that the first component of *kog-wayay*—*kog,* or collective togetherness, may be its strongest dimension for
Gebusi women.

Anne-Sylvie

Living with roughly 200 people in a Gebusi village is much simpler
than confronting a valley of some 2,000 tribal inhabitants, as I did
before among the Baruya. I quickly identified Gebusi families, memo-
rized their names, built special relationships, and came to understand
how they established friendship ties among themselves—and with me.
I came to understand that Gebusi like to keep each other company:
they stay by our side not as a means of control as I previously experienced, but because it strikes them as odd to want to be left alone. Soli-
tude has no purchase value, not individually or socially; such unusual
currency is only ever sought by potential "sorcerers," themselves loners, who attack those who imprudently venture out by themselves.
Invariably, on my way to the market or the toilet, I would find someone to either watch me or keep me company. When my female friends
knew Bruce had gone off somewhere, a whole line of them would
gravitate toward the house; they would not intrude, but they would
stay nearby, busily making a bilum (net bag) or chatting the afternoon
away, while I could be asleep or busy writing indoors. Theirs was an
attitude of protection and care. Our neighbors would always know
when we ate, what we ate, and probably when we did things they
didn't otherwise expect. Walls were too thin to allow for any pocket of
intimacy anywhere—and that worked both ways. I quickly understood
this, as Oymp's irritation with her crying baby and aging husband
would travel to us from the house beside our own, day and night.

Even beyond kinship and family relations, friendship is at the root of
Gebusi society—friendship is spurred by choice, freedom, and the
absence of structural determinism (being linked to another person by
birth). Everything is movement: individuals, with their own tastes and
inclinations, their random trajectories, and the relationships they weave
along the way. When this happens, as we are all friends, we all snap fingers (like shaking hands) and say hi. Our clicks resonate in the hot air,

Anne-Sylvie sharing pictures with a Gebusi woman and her children, 2016.

we laugh at the little music of fingernails and skin entwined, and we laugh when it fails because we're too sweaty (or incapable, like me).

Gebusi love being together. I might have failed to get Baruya's sense of fun, but among Gebusi, by contrast, I discovered that a party spirit can inhabit the bush. These are people who have always loved celebrating the night. Celebrating their friendship. Being with each other. Having a good time.

Bruce: In the beginning of my first fieldwork, decades ago, I didn't know what would happen next. I knew the people of Yibihilu were vibrant and welcoming and that their culture was alive with song and celebration. I had naiveté, energy, and trust in my purpose. These were indispensable for fieldwork that was both deeply difficult and ultimately limitless. After several weeks of visiting, it was time for us and for the people of Yibihilu to decide if a house should be built for us at "the place of the deep waters." The villagers continued to be friendly, and some of them were becoming our friends. But they were also very different from us, and I felt the force of this difference.

One night, the conversation finally turned—uncertainly, via Hawi—to how long Eileen and I would stay in Yibihilu. Dusk was turning into night, and the men and boys around me became silhouettes with bones in their noses and feathers in their hair. Trophy skulls of pigs and cassowaries swayed from the rafters. A chunk of resin sizzled on the stone lamp. I looked up and saw people and personalities I was beginning to know. But they also appeared alien. Some were covered head to foot with the scaly skin of ringworm. Others had streaks of soot or caked ulcers on their skin or large cracks in the thick calluses that lined their feet. Their toes splayed, as if they had been born to stride along mossy log bridges that I inched across timidly. Even when sitting down, I towered over them. My gawky six-foot white frame stood out against their dark bodies, which for men averaged just five feet four inches at full height.

Their skill and prowess in the forest dwarfed my own. How quickly and silently they could climb a tree, club a lizard, shoot a fish, or ford a stream. I knew that until recently they had eaten the flesh of persons killed as sorcerers. Their polished arrows were propped in the corner. Many layers of Gebusi culture remained obscure to me. The joy of our beginning made me question whether my giddiness would change to disillusionment when the novelty of their warm welcome wore off. But the dice had already been rolled. After years of scholarly training, traveling halfway round the world, and enduring all manner of physical hardships, and with personal and professional identity further on the line, what could be done but to stay? They asked, "How long you will stay?" I heard myself say, "Two years." My head swam as I heard the hubbub around me. But in the best Gebusi tradition of "everything is going to be fine," the discussion quickly turned to where our thatched house was to be built—on this side of the village, or on that one? The following morning, a string was laid on the ground to mark where the walls would be. Our house was built above it.

Update: See Gebusi video clips and commentary on the author's reentrance to Gebusi society in 2013 ("Anthro & Studying Culture") and on Gebusi language in the field ("Language in Practice") on Bruce Knauft's website or, on YouTube, search for "Gebusi videos" 2 & 3.

BROADER CONNECTIONS
Fieldwork and Culture

- Cultural anthropologists conduct **long-term ethnographic fieldwork** and study culture through **participant-observation**.

- **Gift exchange** and **reciprocity** are important ways that human social interactions are established and reinforced—including with anthropologists in the field. Gebusi employ exchange and reciprocity in food giving and in gift-exchange names between friends.

- Cultural anthropologists are often distinguished from government administrators, missionaries, or aid workers in that they typically try to participate in local means of **reciprocity** and **exchange**. Professionally, cultural anthropologists attempt to observe and learn about diverse peoples rather than actively trying to change their customs, behavior, or beliefs.

- Many peoples of the world have been influenced by external threat and pressure either from outside their country or nation (external colonialism or imperialism) or from inside it (nationalist domination or internal colonialism).

- The impact of external influence or **colonialism** is diverse; Gebusi largely appreciated Australian colonial presence, but the neighboring Bedamini people, who killed many Gebusi in raids, resisted and resented it.

- Among Gebusi and other peoples, **culture** is a shared public system of meanings, beliefs, and values.

- **Cultural change** not only alters practices and beliefs but can reinvent them in new ways over time (the **reinvention of culture** or the reinvention of tradition). Gebusi culture intensified in part because Australians pacified their tribal enemies while introducing them to modern goods such as steel knives and axes.

- Most peoples assert cultural values that they emphasize and share as a positive belief system (or as a cultural ideology). Among Gebusi and especially among men, deep cultural values are reflected in *kogwayay*—the "good company" of togetherness, friendly talking, and exuberant or playful cheering or yelling. Among Gebusi women, "collective togetherness" may be the primary feature of *kogwayay*.

- *Kogwayay* among Gebusi can be seen as a **key symbol** in Gebusi culture—a cultural concept or emphasis that is widely shared, prominent, emotionally powerful, and frequently demonstrated.

- In many societies, positive cultural values are complemented by troubling or challenging features of social domination, conflict, or disorder that are downplayed or papered over. Among Gebusi these include gender domination by men of women and the scapegoating of people through sorcery accusations.

- Cultural anthropologists often undertake **long-term ethnographic fieldwork** that is at turns both enjoyable and challenging or difficult. This is true both in remote areas, such as the Papua New Guinea rainforest, and also in highly developed areas, including modern cities in Western or non-Western countries.

Chapter 2

Rhythms of Survival

Boyl slung her load of leaves to the ground while other women staggered into the village and followed suit. The foliage had been stripped from sago palms, folded, and then loaded onto their backs in net bags supported by tumplines across their foreheads. These leaves would form the bulk of my very first home among Gebusi, as they do for all their dwellings. I hardly guessed that a house made mostly of leaves could provide shelter from up to 14 feet of annual rainfall along with temperatures that easily topped 100 degrees. But they could. The long leaves are carefully pinned with palm splinters to wooden strips about five feet long. Hundreds of these extensive leaf strips are lashed closely together, like shingles, to the beams of the house. For the roof of the village longhouse, which measured 74 by 34 feet, the many thousands of leaves easily weigh several tons. The large bulk of the dwelling is its massive roof, which peaks some 25 feet high and slopes over windowless walls till it almost touches the ground.

I was amazed to see my first Gebusi house take shape in 1980. Yuway and the other men scampered over its wooden frame like skilled acrobats, hoisting log supports and the heavy ridgepole. Without a measuring tape, a plumb line, or any materials other than wood, leaves, and vines, they built the roof and the entire house like a first-rate construction crew. Lack of formal training was overcome with practical ingenuity and intimate knowledge of forest materials. Their indigenous number system included

A Gebusi man, Bubiay, with leaves, 2013.

just three numbers: "one" (*hele*), "two" (*bena*), and "two plus one" (*bene bwar hele bwar*). Anything greater than that was simply "many" (*bihina*). Counting was as irrelevant to the Gebusi as their physical skills were finely honed. As ad hoc engineers, they were astounding.

This is not to say that arithmetic is unknown in other non-Western cultures. Like the ancient Babylonians, the Kapauku people of West New Guinea developed a base-60 number system, which they use to count items into the thousands for fun. But one group's chosen passion is another's apathy. Although the Gebusi short-changed their numerals, they had a rich vocabulary for a seemingly endless variety of plants, vines, and trees, each of which had special properties and uses.

If culture humanizes the physical environment, the Gebusi longhouse has been their biggest material culture accomplishment. Being the main gathering place for the 52 residents of Yibihilu, the "house long" (*masam sak*) was their tangible sign of village cooperation, physical prowess, and collective labor. Materially minded anthropologists describe culture as "adaptive" because human creativity and symbolic diversity have allowed us to survive in so many different physical environments—from the arctic to deserts to the tropics, and practically everywhere in between. Culture allows us to adapt to the world far beyond the constraints of our body and physiology.

Given the prominence of the Gebusi longhouse, it surprised me that it was so often empty. The longhouse was the permanent residence of just two extended families who, like all Gebusi, often left for treks in the forest. Others lived in smaller houses nearby. But as the longhouse was built by the community-at-large, it functioned as the evening gathering place and for community celebrations and ceremonies. Though humming with energy when the village was full of people, the central dwelling gave way to the surrounding forest as activity dispersed during the bulk of most days. Hawi goes off with a group of young men to spear fish. Boyl and her husband depart to collect bananas from a distant garden and to see if tubers are ready to harvest. Young girls leave with their adult sisters to forage for fresh bamboo shoots, rummage in the nest of a wild bush hen looking for eggs, or scoop under rocks in the stream for freshwater prawns. Along the way, they keep a keen eye out for a stray bush rat or snake that can be clubbed with a stick or sliced with a knife. Men carry bows and arrows and look for signs of a wild pig, a sleeping lizard, a possum on a low-lying branch, or a cassowary—a large, flightless bird that looks similar to an ostrich. Even a good-sized tarantula can be seized for the cooking fire. Gebusi eat practically everything that moves.

By late afternoon, those within reasonable distance return to the village for an evening meal and genial conversation. The atmosphere is languid and friendly as families congregate. Men sit together and share large bamboo pipes stoked with powerful home-grown tobacco. Women chat as they tend the fire and cook the bananas. Back in the forest, some families are too far away to return for the night; they make a temporary camp and sleep in a makeshift lean-to. Imba and his wife, Walab, walk for a day to distant clan land, accompanied by their siblings and children. The men in the group chop down and split open a stately sago palm; the women then pound its interior pith into flour. Deep in the forest, women may take two weeks or more to process the sago and leach its fiber into weighty bundles of caked flour. Meanwhile, the whole group lives in the forest. Imba and his male kin hunt and forage; the children play together or set off with adults to gather breadfruit or Tahitian chestnuts. Members of the small community sleep in a temporary shelter topped with sago leaf thatch. When the sago is completely processed, this fruit of women's labor is bundled in bark, wrapped in leaves, slung on the women's backs in big net bags, and hauled back to the village or loaded in canoes and paddled back upstream. For weeks on end, the heavy parcels supply starchy flour that is easily wrapped in leaves and cooked on the fire.

Beyond its food, the rainforest is ripe with meaning. Hogayo lingers by an old settlement where his father was born; Oyam stops to drink from a stream that belongs to her mother's family line. Memories are associated with each stand of trees, creek, small hillock, or patch of old garden land. As the Gebusi walk through the forest they relive past experiences and remember what the forest has provided their kin, their ancestors, and themselves. They rediscover how the trees have grown, when their fruits will be ripe, what animals have left traces nearby, and when the area should be revisited to reap one or another natural harvest. The forest is not simply "land"; it is a living cornucopia with meaning and nuance in each nook and wrinkle. Gebusi describe their lands with fondness and nostalgia. They name individual places and luxuriate in their tranquil distinctions. When Gebusi sing at dances and séances, many of their most haunting songs recall special places in the forest.

Between daily trips and more extended ones, the residents of Yibihilu spent almost half their nights in 1980–82—45%, to be precise—in the forest or at another settlement. In earlier days, they could easily scatter to the bush if they thought enemies or intruders were nearby. Partly out of frustration, colonial officers called the local population "nomads" and gave the name "Nomad" to the nearest patrol post. But anthropologists consider nomads to be people with no permanent residence. By contrast, sedentary peoples build durable houses and live in long-lasting settlements, as the Gebusi do and always appear to have done.

Though Gebusi flirt with being "semi" nomadic, they benefit greatly from growing food in regular gardens. Most of these are within an hour or two walk from the main settlement. Game animals aren't plentiful in the Gebusi's portion of the rainforest—mostly wild pigs and cassowaries—and though Gebusi eat and enjoy smaller forest creatures, these don't provide many calories day-to-day. Gebusi could not survive as foragers without plantains and other cultivated foods in their gardens.

The biggest task, at least for the men, is felling the trees. Though most families maintain small gardens, large ones are also cleared as a communal project. After several weeks at Yibihilu, we went to see how this was done. We left in high spirits, men whooping and children frolicking; it was going to be a big garden. Our 20-minute walk to the site felt more like a festive stroll than a work brigade.

With the rest of the men, I took turns chopping trees and resting by the makeshift cooking fires while chatting, munching bananas, and smoking Gebusi tobacco. To my surprise, Yuway told me not to chop any of the trees all the way; each time, I was stopped halfway through. The other men were doing the same. Perplexed, I asked why—but got only more confused when Yuway made dramatic pantomimes of noise and crashing. After two more hours of "half-work," hardly a single tree had been felled. Our work pace slacked until only a handful of men were left at one end of the large plot. There, they attacked a particularly large and majestic piece of timber—while the rest of us were waved off to the far margins of the area. Everyone said I should not, under any circumstances, wander back onto the garden site. Knowing that the Gebusi had strong spiritual ties to their land, including its tree spirits, I thought the area might now be under a sacred taboo until rites were made to supplicate the spirit of the tallest tree before it was felled.

I was wrong. The enormous tree began to creak and groan from the continuing blows of the senior men's axes. Though towering above its leafy rivals, a thick skein of vines and foliage knitted them all together. It tottered briefly, then thundered down in an amazing crash. Its force exploded in domino fashion across the entire acre of half-cut timber. Hefty trunks were toppled and flung in all directions, like telephone poles ripped up by a falling master pylon. It was frightful, wonderful, and aweful—an arboreal tornado. Then it was over, as quickly as it had started. All that remained were the whoops of the men, a blizzard of leaves fluttering to the ground, and a mass of fallen trunks and limbs. I was stunned and had to sit down.

Regaining my bearings, my confusion persisted. To be sure, the trees had been felled with little effort. But now their fallen bulk smothered the garden beneath. How could it be the planted, much less cultivated? Yuway and the others were unconcerned. They showed me that banana suckers and root crop seedlings had been stuck in the ground days before. When the trees had been standing, I hadn't noticed them. Though a few of these plantings were now crushed by fallen limbs, the vast majority were simply sheltered from the blaze of the day and the pelting of rains by the fallen branches now hovering just above them. Without this covering, the new garden would have wilted in the tropical sun or been washed away by torrential storms. As the foliage of the felled trees decomposed, the crops beneath sprouted through these fertilizing remains until strong enough to grow unshielded. Though the garden now looked like a chaos of fallen trees, it was actually a finely honed system of indigenous cultivation. Anthropologist Edward Schieffelin gave it a fitting name: "felling the trees on top of the crop."

As the Gebusi starch staple, plantains require almost no weeding, grow quickly, and don't bear fruit till the caloric pods have grown beyond the reach of hungry animals. As such, Gebusi avoid the hard work of having to fence their gardens. And by picking the fruit *before* it is ripe, they prevent marauding birds or bats from eating it. Instead, the bananas are softened by tossing them directly on the fire. Retrieved with wooden cooking tongs, they are scraped of their charred skin and eaten straightaway.

As their plantains suggest, Gebusi grow food without much work. Letting gardens lie fallow for years before recutting and replanting them qualifies Gebusi food-raising as "horticulture." By contrast, "agriculture" would require more labor per unit of land—irrigation, regular fertilizing, plowing, fencing, and/or terracing. Though these techniques increase the land's yield—and the number of people it can support—they exact a higher price in human work or mechanized intervention. Gebusi relax happily at the other end of this spectrum. Because they have plenty of land, they avoid the effort of repeatedly cultivating any plot. After a few years, the rainforest reclaims its terrain, first with tall grass, then shrubs, and finally trees, each providing nutrients that enrich the clay soil. Ideally, the grandson of the original gardener comes back to the plot and recultivates both its social and its nutritional essence. Gebusi cycles of regeneration and growth are hence spiritual and cultural as well as ecological and demographic: the rejuvenation of land, food, people, and spiritual connection. Because land is plentiful, it is easily lent to friends as well as kin, extending and intensifying social and spiritual networks.

Across generations, Gebusi have raised ample food, though their part of the rainforest is not bountiful. In the process, they don't seem to have strained themselves unduly. Certainly, Gebusi endure stints of intense labor. Women carry heavy loads through the rainforest, and they transport firewood, food, and even babies in net bags slung on their backs. Though men may also bear these burdens, women provide the ultimate "carrying capacity." Even for women, however, many hours on most days drift by in relaxation—conversing, eating, and playing with children. Men have even more time for social pursuits. Their palavers extend for hours into the evening. Every week and a half or so, they additionally convened an all-night spirit séance. After this extended songfest, they typically sleep for half of the following day. Added to these are all-night ritual feasts and dances that energize the entire settlement about once a month.

Marshall Sahlins called simple human cultures "original affluent societies." Though their technology and material culture

Sefomay, an adult Gebusi woman, carrying two net bags and her son, Moka, who wears his own net bag, 1980.

are often rudimentary, people spend hours each day socializing or lazing about. Though obtaining food and providing shelter require work, this ebbs and flows in harmony with the environment rather than as a struggle against nature. From the icy arctic to the parched deserts of Australia, simple human societies have survived with plenty of time to spare. By contrast, the advanced technology of modern societies has arguably reduced rather than increased our leisure time. On most nights, the Gebusi get a good nine hours or more of sleep. Here in the United States, I am often lucky to get seven. Each of our intended labor-saving devices brings new demands for productive work.

If Gebusi throw the frenzied pace of modern living into relief, they also have their own afflictions. Their deeper struggle has not been so much to acquire food as to fight off illness and, as discussed later, to endure human violence. Some of the Gebusi's biggest enemies have ultimately been small: mosquitoes bring the scourge of malaria and parasitic worms inflict chronic and draining illness. Tuberculosis and introduced influenza wreak havoc. In the hot, humid climate, cuts and scrapes easily fester into putrid skin ulcers. All these ailments sap energy and could be combatted by better nutrition. But Gebusi traditionally have been at pains to improve their diet. Staples of plantains and sago brim with starch but give little protein. Forest animals are hard to find and kill, and hunting more intensely in the forest would expose Gebusi to yet more mosquitoes and malaria—and greater risk of accident and injury. Malnutrition has been a significant problem, and young Gebusi often have had tiny limbs and the distended "sago belly" of a high-starch but low-protein diet. Ultimately, the "affluence" of Gebusi leisure has itself been an adaptation to their environment: it is better to conserve energy and relax than to work harder and only marginally improve nutrition.

This illustrates a larger point: Anthropologists often class societies according to their mode of livelihood or subsistence, their style of residence, and their type of economy and politics. But these categories are not rigid in practice—and people like the Gebusi often defy them. Gebusi subsist through gardening as well as foraging and hunting—they are "horticulturalists," but their practices also include "foraging." In residence, their lifestyle is mobile and almost "seminomadic," yet they build durable houses and are "sedentary." They efficiently raise pigs, but the animals are "semidomesticated." In terms of leadership, Gebusi have neither the aggression and status-competition of so-called big-men (often associated with the political form of "tribes") nor the completely decentralized leadership typically associated with "band" societies of foragers. Personally, I like the fact that Gebusi are "in-betweeners." Like many peoples when considered closely, they crosscut the concepts and classifications given in textbooks. Such terms remain important for general understanding and for allowing broad comparisons across cultures. But they don't reveal how a society or culture is put together in actual practice, much less in the modern present. It's in part for this reason that individual case studies, such as the present one, are a useful complement to textbook overviews.

However one slices it, the different ways that people pursue their livelihood is a testament to human creativity and the power of culture to collectivize this process. I am continually struck by how people not just survive but find meaning and purpose across different environments, including in the intense modernity of our digital 21st century, on the one hand, and in the most squalid refugee camps or slums—or on the streets, as in my home city of Atlanta—on the other. If the task for many of us is now to find balance between labor and leisure, between work and life, the examples of other peoples and cultures, including the Gebusi and people elsewhere, are useful to consider—a full arc of human possibilities to learn from. Particularly as we confront the ecological limits and climate change of our own shrinking world, we can positively benefit from reconsidering the great resilience and creativity of human adaptations elsewhere.

For their own part, and amid their other challenges, Gebusi have basked in their environment. A storm blows in and doesn't let up for hours. Rain pelts and pockmarks the village, carving gullies and minicanyons in the central clearing. Streams swell, rivers roil and flood, and clay banks become muddy slides to any who would traverse them. Plans are canceled. But Gebusi simply take the day off. Toasty in their houses, men light up their pipes and chat while women play with children, toss plantains on the fire, or thread more inches on the large net bag they are making. Someone tells a story or a myth. Plans unfold for a coming feast. Those returning from the downpour make fun of how wet and muddy they are. Sometimes they defy the rain, whooping loudly and marching through it proudly.

When a dry spell descends and the rivers shrink, men make plans for spearing or poisoning fish. The low, clear water exposes their prey, making them easier to catch. Gebusi's ability to use periods of draught to their advantage has continued to aid their survival. In 2015–2016, a huge El Niño drought dried up all but the biggest rivers in their rainforest. Gardens withered and died, sago could not be processed, and the scrawny remaining game animals retreated to the deep forest. The people of Gasumi Corners were on the verge of starvation. But at the height of the crisis, Sayu and a group of young men realized that the precariously low waters provided access to huge river turtles that were normally beyond reach at the bottom of the deepest rivers. Diving deep, they overcame and hoisted seven of these great clawing creatures, each several feet across, to

Sayu holding the shell of one of the turtles he captured and subdued, 2016. Given the extensive ring of hard cartilage that was originally around the shell, its full size was almost twice as big as shown.

the surface and onto a small boat, where they were splashed with water to keep them alive, and paddled upstream to Gasumi Corners. (If the turtles had been left out of water to die, their meat could not have been brought back to the village before rotting in the heat.) All the people of Gasumi were hence able to enjoy a huge communal feast of abundant protein at the very height of their food crisis, lifting their spirits and confidence, as well their nutrition. This was vintage Gebusi: thinking creatively, adapting energetically, sharing generously, and asserting collective well-being and effervescence in the bargain.

While the Gebusi seemed to luxuriate in their environment, it was hard for me to follow suit. Daily physical routines proved a major challenge. Ailments and illness became chronic over the course of two years: headaches and chills from malaria; digestive disorders; intestinal worms; skin lesions, boils, and rashes; and jungle rot that thrives in your body's most private places. Our lives were made bearable by the arsenal of medications we brought, both for ourselves and for Gebusi. But not being doctors, it was hard to know what to do or how we could help our Gebusi friends. However, the people of Yibihilu were wonderful role models. They accepted infirmity when it came and made the best of life while it lasted. Tabway was afflicted with a putrefying ulcer on her thigh. Her leg would shudder in torment but her face was calm and even showed a soft smile. Sefomay's leg was permanently and painfully swollen to twice its normal size. She would joke that her "leg was rotten"—but that her spirit was not.

During my first fieldwork, sickness and death visited Gebusi at every season of life. Malaria, pneumonia, filariasis or "elephantiasis," tuberculosis, influenza, and diarrhea were at once causes and contributing factors. Gebusi were distressed by microbes, parasites, clogged lungs, contaminated blood, and swollen spleens. By the time they reached what we would call middle age, most of them were physically wizened. Almost all adults had had at least one near-death illness. Sickness dovetailed with poor nutrition as weakened bodies struggled to fight infection. Of girls during that early period who lived to be five, only one in three survived to age 40. For boys of similar age, only on in about six lived into their fifth decade.

If Gebusi could not cheat death, they savored life while it lasted. They enjoyed simple pleasures, smiled often, laughed easily, and celebrated when they could. Notwithstanding their crusades against sorcery, there was little they could do to reduce their physical risk—either from disease or from each other. The deaths that we witnessed were met with quietude and acceptance, the warm hands of friends giving way to piercing wails only at the end. Gebusi ailments put our own in perspective. On a daily basis, my biggest challenges were heat, insects, and reptiles. Such "little" things are almost embarrassing to admit, but chronic discomforts loom as large in fieldwork as they are typically neglected in scholarly accounts. If heat and humidity turned our papers limp and our shoes green with mold, I easily felt the same way.

> Bruce (from field notes): When humidity and temperature both exceed 98.6, you can't be cool. Though I sit in the shade of my house, calming myself, my throbbing head fuels sweat. I stay absolutely still, motionless, eyes closed. Sweat beads then dribble from my brow, chest, and thighs. I splash with water from my basin, but sweat just replaces it. I lie down in my sleeping room, a bit darker, and take off all my clothes, every stitch. I kneel on the floor beside my sleeping net, since fractions of confinement make a difference. The three-point stance is my naked attempt to dispel the heat. My three points of contact are the tip of my big toes, kneecaps, and elbows, reducing my area of contact to a few scant inches. The sweat still collects across my cheeks and drips from my nose. It splats onto the floor, but softly, slowly. After ten minutes, I'm as serene as I can be. Relaxation is key,

since heat makes friends with anxiety and stress. Yesterday I misplaced my notebook—and my frustration quickly steamed my glasses! My three-point stance won't cure the heat, but it makes it easier to live with.

Anne-Sylvie

Darkness from 7:00 p.m. I am going to the bathroom in flip-flops. Until then, apart from a big spider and a family of rats, I have not disturbed too many inhabitants; I always have difficulty determining whether I am the one invading their home or the other way around. There is, however, one cohabitant that does not bear any questioning in terms of what I am allowed to exterminate: cockroaches. I am not a big threat to the pest that can survive a nuclear attack, and while the presence of that vermin does not concern me for my life, it suffices to dent my already compromised serenity. I had not, during my time in the Highlands, been used to their swarming presence, as cockroaches were rare and tiny up there. Here they are an infernal and daily battle. At night, as you come into the main room and shine your light on any surface, suddenly a thousand little shadows gallop in all directions, emerging from invisible nooks and crannies to rush into new cracks. This accelerated ballet seems to defy you. Sometimes it falters, and the seemingly coordinated dance loses a member, a big brown bug falling onto your naked shoulder as you come back from the bathroom, sneaking into your bedding to test your sheet. Coming nose to "nose" with one such creature when returning from the toilet at night is not the best recipe for falling back to sleep. And they reek of almond when we crush them. Bruce, a practicing Tibetan Buddhist, would always wish them a good reincarnation before I smacked them with a flip-flop, but in that system of values, I am not sure it can get any better for them.

One night, suddenly a dark premonition came to life, a thought that had always kept me company but that I envisioned only: a snake—springing from within the darkness and from within the outhouse as I sat. As often when faced with danger, my whole body froze. But my mind had enough time to imprint the terrifying vision. Long, thin, black. I vaguely remembered that the infamous "death adder," which can kill you within 10 minutes, is short and fat. But does the line between life and death really stretch there, in the quick estimate made by a pair of stunned eyes in the middle of the night? Note that said animal was probably more alarmed than I was; that I did not step on it; that I had time to see it coming, even. But what suddenly opened within me was the possibility, always latent, like a sorcery attack, that all questions could end in a matter of seconds. Once my paralyzing spasm was over, I ran back to the house. Screaming. The memory was sinking into my being. As if to validate my terror, I was buttressing it, persuading myself of its own legitimacy. It wasn't a grass-snake, right? Then I burst into tears, tears that turned into a multitude of tiny stones, blocking my eyelids, building up in my throat. I experienced sheer panic. Nothing could stop my suffocating. Not his reassuring arms, not the thought of shelter, not the wine, not even the Beatles. Never have I cried so much, screamed my despair, wished to be elsewhere, anywhere, wished for the whole universe to dissolve, only to adopt the dimensions of my anguish.

The neighbors came rushing; they had heard me from a distance and were at least as frightened as I was. "We thought a sorcerer got you!"

Bruce: I was bitten by a death adder back in 1998, but I survived the experience intact and have tried to forget it. Insects are harder for me to ignore, as they keep coming back. Oversized grasshoppers give a startle when they land on me suddenly. Five-inch spiders raise my adrenaline when I find them sharing the outhouse. Cockroaches are everywhere. Hundreds of the big ones live in our cardboard cartons and eat the labels off our precious tins of food. But the mosquitoes I hardly even count as insects because they are more insidious. Not just because there are so many of them, nor because they fly into our thatched house without pause or restriction. It's the malaria and elephantiasis they bring. They wait like cowards until dusk before taunting you with their mock fragility. They lilt in squadrons on low power while floating somehow just beyond your grasp, waiting like lunar modules to hit your pay dirt. Swatting hard only flits them away to a yet choicer landing place. "One small bite for one mosquito, one giant risk for mankind."

> Bruce (from field notes): There is a special insult to getting several bites. How many did you really receive in the dimness? Was it only two? Or six? Is that another new one now, just beside the others? Did you really take your antimalarial pill (none of which are completely effective)? The best thing is to go inside the mosquito net—and that very quickly, because nothing is worse than having mosquitoes *inside*

your net. But I can't live under a mosquito net from six at night till six in the morning; we have to eat and wash, write our notes, and of course, be with Gebusi. The evening should be the most enjoyable part of the day, but that's when "mossies" come out most. Going to the bathroom remains the worst. Mosquitoes love the bottom of the latrine—and fly up in droves whenever something goes down the hole. They attack our most vulnerable parts when we are most exposed. Talk about a bite in the butt!

For their part, the Gebusi hardly minded either the temperature or the humidity or the bugs or snakes or spiders. They often kept cooking fires smoldering in their houses, which have no chimneys. The heat and smoke dispersed mosquitoes and drove away vermin that would otherwise infest the house. But we couldn't tolerate the added heat of a continual fire in our main house. So we opted for less fire—and got more bugs. But if heat and insects were our daily scourge, Gebusi kept our irritations in perspective. Despite their much graver ailments, their vibrant lives pulled us outside the orbit of our own discomforts.

Call it cultural gravity—the ability of others' lives to sweep you up and draw you in against all odds and to your own surprise. This is the deepest part of fieldwork, the part that makes you grow. We joked with Gebusi, shared with them, took part in their activities, and became part of their world. Reciprocally, they seemed to enjoy us, accept our idiosyncrasies, and include us in their activities as much as they could. In professional terms, this is what is described as the primary method of fieldwork in cultural anthropology: participant-observation.

Professionally, the biggest challenge was learning the Gebusi language. There being no way to do this before my first fieldwork, I got training in how to learn an unknown and unwritten language—without help from translators. In the field, bit by slow painful bit, I recognized and spoke sounds that were meaningful in Gebusi, what linguists call "phonemes," that do not exist in English. I compiled lists of Gebusi words and phrases, and puzzled over their meanings. In all these tasks, Yuway was my patient, insightful, and pleasant helper. Over weeks and months and eventually years, he and I became special friends. He even helped me tackle the complexities of Gebusi tense and grammar, which were the worst. Gebusi pile meanings into verbs while omitting nouns and other phrases. For instance, the question "Would he have killed me?" is spoken in Gebusi as a single verb, "kill" (*golo*), which is then modified by a string of suffixes to indicate a presumed subject, a presumed object, conditional tense, causative action, and interrogative aspect. The whole sentence is one word: *golo-hi-lay-ba*.

Fortunately, I knew from the start that learning the language would be my most difficult task. After a few weeks, I could make simple communications in broken Gebusi. But only after many months could I meaningfully comprehend what Gebusi were saying to one another—not in the simple, slowed-down language they used with us, but in the idioms, quick pacing, and elisions they used with each other. My advisor had told us not to get too discouraged: if we focused on language learning for the first six months, we would be okay. He also said our language abilities would improve and that two-thirds or more of our understanding would emerge during the last third of our fieldwork. He was right: we had to be patient.

When returning with Anne-Sylvie in 2016–2017, however, the situation was different. From her time in the highlands of Papua New Guinea, she had become fluent in Tok Pisin, the national language, which I could speak and understand only partly. While my ability to converse in Gebusi was far greater than hers at first, I was amazed at how Anne-Sylvie's fluency in Tok Pisin enlarged rather than diminished our fieldwork. Concepts and ideas that had become socially, economically, and politically important to Gebusi—concerning government, development projects, money, health care, and all sorts of modern things—could be communicated about and discussed in only a circumspect or round-about way in the Gebusi vernacular, which lacked words for many of these things. Tok Pisin, by contrast, afforded a way to bridge the traditional and the modern of Gebusi culture in ways that I had not envisaged.

Fieldwork is ultimately its own brand of optimal foraging. As Gebusi shifted activities and forms of language to gain the most from their surroundings, we tried to do the same. But as professionals, our desire to participate, to observe, and to record our experiences became a continual dance between "living with" and "writing up." Days during fieldwork blended language learning, observation, note-taking, interviews, writing, and reflection—amid the ongoing intensity of public social scrutiny, stress, and physical discomfort. I was continually surprised at how long it took me to type up my notes and organize them into topical themes. Even when not much was going on, I seemed to be behind writing up my field notes. It became painfully obvious that fieldwork was not a process of quickly discovering "the truth."

My learning with Gebusi emerged gradually through a blur of confusing experiences and competing interpretations. I found repeatedly that my language skills were inadequate, my interpretations misleading, and my assumptions wrong. I remember during my first weeks pointing to various objects with my index finger and asking in simple Gebusi, "What is it?" (*ke-ka-ba*). But no matter what I pointed to—a stone, a tree, myself, the sky—the answer I got was the same, "*dob.*" What was going on?!? The mystery was explained when I learned the meaning of *dob. Dob* is finger. Gebusi don't point with their fingers the way we do. So, whenever I stuck out my finger and asked what it was, the answer was as obvious to them as it was opaque to me: It was my *dob,* the finger I was pointing with!

Understanding is always a process of learning from mistakes. We began at the lowest rung, including asking nonsensical questions like, "Is your son a girl?" But just as quickly, we learned to laugh at our foibles. It helped a lot that Gebusi laughed so good-naturedly along with us, just as they did at their own mistakes and problems.

As time went on and comprehension improved, I came to see cultural anthropology as a kind of dialogue—a conversation between Gebusi meanings and my own understanding. The process is always incomplete. Every time I go back to the Gebusi, I realize yet again how partial and inadequate my understanding of them has been—and how my previous understandings are surpassed by the passage of time. This balance of cultural give-and-take has become key in my field-life. And in this, Gebusi have been wonderful teachers. Reciprocity has always been at the heart of their social life and in their relationship with me. Apart from their gendered divisions, Gebusi are egalitarian to a fault, and they reinforce this norm by striving to give rather than just take.

> Bruce (from field notes, 1998): The big feast was yesterday, and today our friends are happily eating the remains of the celebration. Since I contributed fish and rice to the collective effort, people now want to repay me.
>
> A member of each major family came this morning and presented me with a bird egg. I was deeply touched. Most memorable was five-

year-old Kawe, who has become my "Biscuit" exchange-name friend.
I saw him coming from across the village. With the confident stride
and smile of a grown-up, he looked at me from twenty yards away
and walked over directly, never shifting his gaze. Stopping in front of
me, he flashed his cutest tooth-missing grin, extended his little hand
that held his egg, placed it in my palm, turned around, and walked
back proudly, neither uttering a word nor looking back. I will not forget it.

Update: What has happened to Gebusi livelihood and health over the
decades? Their subsistence has both persisted and "exploded" in the best
sense of this term. By the late 1990s, as discussed later, Gebusi were raising
a whole host of new and intensified crops to sell for money for the Nomad
market. But by the mid-2000s and dramatically since 2010, the bottom has
fallen out of this market—and Gebusi have been cast back upon their
means of traditional subsistence. In the bargain, however, the new foods
they have learned to raise—pineapple, pumpkins, squash, corn, peanuts,
and nutritious root crops like sweet potatoes, which are now themselves a
major starch staple—have stayed with them. As a result, Gebusi now have
a far more varied and nutritious diet than they did before. Though not
entirely a thing of the past, malnutrition is far less than it used to be.

A further big benefit is the continued absence of Bedamini raiding,
which allows Gebusi to be much more secure and stable in residence and
organization. Villages are now fewer but larger, and much more permanent than before, lasting decades. In ways I hadn't fully appreciated, the
shifting traditional residences of Gebusi life had been, at least in part, a
strategy to avoid being sitting targets for Bedamini attacks. With this
threat gone, Gebusi have settled down, become less anxious, and travel to
garden lands more freely and in smaller groups. This trend has intensified
over the years, allowing Gebusi to exploit their land yet more flexibly without fearing for their lives. At the same time, collective life in the village is
more populous than before, including in large meeting houses, built with
traditional materials, which function like the old residential longhouse.

Material investment in heavy-construction items like hand-hewn
canoes has also increased. This is significant since Gebusi now cultivate

large gardens along long stretches of riverbank, from which they can easily transport supplies, food, and themselves back and forth. Indeed, to make more use of navigable watercourses, including for fishing, Gebusi have gradually tended to move downstream and to live near rivers. In the bargain, they have increasingly become "canoe people," in contrast to their lives in 1980 and before.

In all, the remarkable pattern of Gebusi subsistence has not just persisted but intensified. This enables and supports a much larger Gebusi population than before—up from 450 to more than 1,200. And yet, happily, Gebusi continue to have plenty of land to sustain their livelihood; their subsistence regime is not only homegrown but really sustainable. In a modern world of ecological stress and environmental destruction, Gebusi provide a fine current example of how careful local management of land, resources, and people can provide "rhythms of survival" that draw deeply upon cultural traditions to chart a rich and sustainable future in the 21st century.

> *Note: See field video clips of Gebusi subsistence livelihood ("Livelihoods") in 2013 on Bruce Knauft's website or search "Gebusi videos" on YouTube.*

BROADER CONNECTIONS
Subsistence, Health, and Language

- Though they travel flexibly and might even be considered seminomads, Gebusi live in permanent villages and thus are **sedentary.**
- Gebusi are also partly **foragers**—they hunt and gather wild food—in addition to being **horticulturalists** who raise food in gardens. Their gardening shifts flexibly and does not require the intense labor that would be associated with **agriculture.**
- Gebusi illustrate how **human adaptation** is deeply cultural. This allows human groups to survive and to thrive in diverse and challenging environments.
- Simple human societies like the Gebusi have leisure that qualifies them for being what Marshall Sahlins has called "original affluent societies."
- Like many remote or poor peoples, Gebusi endure severe health challenges, including malaria, childhood malnutrition, elephantiasis (filariasis), tuberculosis, worm (helminthic) diseases, and influenza.

- Gebusi had **low life expectancy**, with death striking at any age. But with better nutrition from introduced crops, their health and longevity have increased.

- Gebusi have also benefitted from greater residential and social stability associated with absence of Bedamini raids.

- Ethnographers in the field often face special health challenges, risks, and physical discomfort or stress. But the richness and power of what they learn and their human experience help compensate for if not transcend such challenges.

- Like many anthropologists, Bruce's biggest cultural challenge in fieldwork was learning the Gebusi **language.**

- Gebusi language included culturally recognized sounds or **phonemes** that are not distinguished or "heard" as different sounds in English.

- **Morphemes** are the smallest units of meaning in language. In the Gebusi language, morphemes include the many prefixes, suffixes, and "infixes" of Gebusi verbs—including the four components of *golo-hi-lay-ba.*

- Bruce took many **field notes** as events were happening. Writing these up and configuring them supported his ethnographic write-up or **ethnography.**

- As in many or most societies, establishing **social reciprocity** was personally and professionally indispensable to **long-term fieldwork** among Gebusi.

- Drawing upon their cultural past, Gebusi have intensified and expanded their traditional subsistence regimes to develop **sustainable patterns of livelihood** and to effectively support a growing population in the 21st century.

Chapter 3

Lives of Death

It is hard to watch a baby die. Its scrawny shell cries until its wails lose force, leaving a ghostly little corpse. It was also hard on us that Gebusi men didn't seem to mind. During the first five weeks of my first fieldwork, we saw one baby die and then another. As the mother wailed, her women kin gathered in support. But the men continued joking and smoking in the longhouse, and boys played gaily in the village clearing. Only the baby's father stayed close by, and this with an air of detached waiting, until the small body could be quickly buried. Managing babies and managing death were women's work; if women bore the day-to-day challenge and joy of caring for new life, they also bore the sting of its death. I visited the mother in each case to lend support. But both times, being a man in women's space, I felt the most courteous thing I could do was to leave. The father of the second infant, Owaya, said the baby was dying "just because"—but then added that maybe a woman from Wasobi sent a sorcerer to kill it. Gebusi attributed all natural deaths to sorcery. But they only investigated the deaths of adults and older children.

Until infants are about seven months old, when their first teeth emerge, Gebusi didn't think of them as fully human. Before then, they're thought to lack a full human spirit and weren't even named. Many infants only flirt with life; by compiling information, we found that a whopping 38% of babies died in their first year. It was almost as if the community was protecting itself from identifying too closely with so many young lives lost so quickly. But this "protection" was not shared by the mother, red-eyed and weeping, nor by her closest female kin. I was confused at heart; it was my first real lesson in the cultural divergence between Gebusi emotions and my own.

Just three weeks after the second infant died, a third death hit the village: Dugawe killed himself. Unlike the infant deaths, which were "normal," this one shocked the community. No one could remember a man having killed himself. Dugawe's death drew me into a whirling cultural vortex. Confusing events and experiences flew by; I struggled to piece them together. People I knew and liked suddenly did things I could not believe. In retracing this path during 1981—its twists and turns, and my own confusions—I came to know much about Gebusi life and death, the importance of kinship in their society, and exactly how, during fieldwork, one tries to make sense of a very different culture.

Just before his suicide, Dugawe had fought with his wife, Sialim, about a generally acknowledged sexual affair between Sialim and a young man, Sagawa. Publicly cuckolded, Dugawe had wanted to kill his wayward wife, and probably her lover as well. But Silap, Yuway, and others had discouraged him from doing this. When Sialim had gone off to fetch water, the men said, Dugawe took tubes of poison he had previously made to kill fish in the stream and, in a fit of rage, drank them all. Empty tubes with the smell of the deadly toxin were found nearby. Dugawe had died a writhing death after poisoning himself in anger against his wife. But he was so much bigger and stronger than she. Why was his anger so self-directed?

It was all confusing. For the moment, all I could do was try to keep up with events as I rushed out to the garden settlement where Dugawe's body lay. The men lashed his body to a stretcher, and marched it briskly back to Yibihilu. En route, two women converged on us in the forest. They were extended "mothers" of Dugawe who had come to view his body. Seeing his corpse, and his wayward wife behind us, they virtually exploded. Screaming, they tore straight into Sialim. She turned to avoid them, but the lead woman walloped her on the back with a steel ax, blunt side forward. This was followed by another heavy blow. The woman then turned and threw herself on Dugawe's corpse, pawing it and crying in great screaming sobs,

Woman grieving
the death of her
husband, 1981.

as if her emotion would wake it up. The second woman then resumed the
first one's attack, screeching at full pitch and shoving Sialim with a pointed
stick as if she were going to drive it right through her. Silap and Yuway
rushed in to hold the attacker, while another man wrestled Dugawe's closest "mother" away from the corpse. The rest of the men quickly picked up
the body and raced with it down the trail and out of sight. Yuway, Silap,
and I followed closely, with the women coming more slowly behind.

When we arrived at Yibihilu, Dugawe's body was laid in state in his
family house, just 25 yards from our own. A crowd of women wailed
loudly while others arrived in short order. Many of them pummeled and
berated Sialim, who hunched and whimpered but could not run away
without neglecting the duty to mourn her dead husband. Our neighbor,
Owaya, emerged waving a firebrand in her face and shouted, "*Si-nay!*" I
later learned this meant, "We're going to cook and eat you!"—which is
what Gebusi traditionally did to persons executed as sorcerers. Sialim
gasped and whimpered, but could do little else.

The following morning, Dugawe's body was grossly bloated. His swollen limbs oozed corpse fluid, and his peeling skin exposed putrid green-
yellow flesh. His belly and even his genitals had swelled with decomposing
internal gases. The stench was unforgettable; it burned up my nose, down
my throat, and into my brain. Equally powerful were the actions of
Dugawe's female kin. With unearthly sobs, they draped themselves physically over the corpse, lovingly massaged its slime, and rubbed their arms
and legs with the ooze of the body. They made their bodies like his own

A very ill man,
Solwoy, in
Yibihilu, 1981.

corpse, a tangible sign of grief, of physical as well as emotional connection
to him.

The men of Yibihilu dug Dugawe's grave by his house, and the women
rolled his corpse onto Silap's back. As he strained and stood up under the
weight, the body's arms flung out dramatically to both sides. The women
shrieked. Men rushed to steady the corpse and help Silap place it in the
grave. Dugawe's possessions—his bamboo pipe, bow and arrows, and so
on—were broken and arranged in the grave by his female kin. Bark was
placed over the corpse, then the hole was filled in. Just as directly, the men
retired to the longhouse to rest. The closest female relatives threw themselves on the mounded grave and wailed.

Prior to fieldwork, the only dead body I had seen was the sedate face
of a friend of my parents at an open-casket funeral. Now I was shocked
and repulsed by the events surrounding Dugawe's death. It seemed hid-
eous that his corpse was allowed to decay and that our female friends wal-
lowed in its stench. But I also began to see that this raw transformation—
of a human being decomposing into a natural object—was an emotionally
and physically honest acceptance of death. Dugawe's disfigurement
showed me the fact of his death like nothing else could. His demise was
not hidden, not made pretty, not covered up in attempts to "spare grief."
Were Gebusi customs improper? Or, was it my own culture's crusade to
sanitize and downplay death that was off-kilter?

I was bewildered. Which details concerning Dugawe's death were rele-
vant, which were superficial? How did Gebusi funeral practices and sor-

cery beliefs influence their social relationships and their emotional lives? I tried to connect the dots, but as pieces of this blurry picture emerged, further questions came. What did Dugawe's sexual and marital problems with Sialim reflect about Gebusi gender relations? How typical, or anomalous, were the events of Dugawe's death in Gebusi society? As I struggled for answers, further events sharpened my queries. Gradually, the events following Dugawe's death unfolded into a sorcery investigation—an inquiry into who had "killed" him. Its twists and turns helped me address the questions I had, but not in ways I had expected. In retrospect, this trail of figuring things out reveals much about the practice of ethnography, as well as about Gebusi customs and beliefs.

With benefit of fieldwork, anthropologists are charged to make sense of different societies and culture. Fieldwork becomes experience; experience becomes ethnographic writing. But how does this occur? No Gebusi gave me a summary narrative of Dugawe's death, its aftermath, or the events that preceded it. Rather, the story emerged in disparate and fragmentary events and observations, pieced together after the fact.

Though the big funeral feast for Dugawe took place just two days after his burial, it ended up as a sideshow to events that occurred weeks later. And by the time this sorcery investigation resumed, my opinion of Sialim had changed. At first, I thought she had acted irresponsibly: she had carried on an adulterous sexual affair with Sagawa, and she had shamed her husband into killing himself. But additional facts painted a different picture. It turned out that Dugawe had previously killed not only his first wife but also his own small son. These murders were so awful that villagers informed the police, and Dugawe served a five-year term at the Western Province prison. As far as I know, no other Gebusi has been incarcerated there since.

With his prison term over, Dugawe returned to the Gebusi and married Sialim, who had recently been widowed by the death of Dugawe's "brother." But knowing Dugawe's history, Sialim did not want to marry him. As newlyweds, they fought, and he frequently beat her. On one occasion, she showed her bruises to the police in Nomad Station. Knowing his violent history, they put him in jail. It was while he was there that Sialim took up with Sagawa, her young lover. Perhaps she hoped her new relationship would become a de facto marriage. But Dugawe was released earlier than expected. Enraged, he wanted to kill Sialim and Sagawa. But Silap and others told him that this would only give him a longer prison term than he had already endured. Dugawe took up again with Sialim. But after their fight, he killed himself.

Five weeks after his funeral, the real inquiry into Dugawe's death began. In a nod to neutrality, the inquest séances were conducted by a shaman who had hardly known him. But when these turned out to be inconclusive, further investigation was led by our clever friend Swamin, the main shaman of Yibihilu. To make a long story short, Swamin's spirits suggested that the sorcerer who had driven Dugawe crazy and staged his suicide was in fact not Sialim, but an unnamed man from a distant village. The men of Yibihilu, with me in tow, actually tried to track this supposedly invisible or barely visible sorcery man back to his village, aided by otherworldly clues interpreted by Swamin, who led the way. But the ostensible trail of the sorcerer was lost in a distant uphill stream, and we returned empty-handed. Further investigation was deemed to be fruitless and the result ultimately inconclusive.

I thought this would be the end of the story, but in Gebusi society, as in our own, poignant events often cast longer shadows. The verdict of Swamin's spirits provided a reprieve for Sialim, who had not been implicated. During the next seven months, she spent more and more time with Swamin's household. Eventually, she willingly consented to marry him—over the entreaties and objections of her young lover, Sagawa. Strong and robust for a middle-aged man, Swamin had been a widower. During the final year of my first fieldwork, he and Sialim seemed happily married.

Though this would have been a good Hollywood ending, it was not the one I ultimately came away with. It turned out that three years previously, before our arrival, Swamin had killed Sialim's mother. The old woman, named Mokoyl, had been named as the sorcerer responsible for the death of Swamin's first wife. A few weeks afterward, Swamin cornered Mokoyl alone in the forest and split her skull with a bush knife. As the spiritual evidence confirmed Mokoyl's guilt, most in the community agreed she had been guilty and had deserved to die. Her body was summarily buried in the forest—though villagers from another settlement, knowing she had been killed as a sorceress, dug it up and cooked and ate parts of the body before it decomposed. In doing so, they indicated their own support for the killing. Government officers never discovered what happened. This was likely the last Gebusi cannibal feast, around 1979, a year before my own first arrival.

What is participant-observation in such a world? And, in the process, how can a fieldworker keep a sense of ethics and wits about him or her? For Dugawe's death, I observed and to some extent participated in the retrieval of his body, his funeral and burial, and the shamanic séances and sorcery investigations that followed. However, I did not want to participate in an attack on a suspected sorcerer. We tried to facilitate Sialim's departure to a safer place when sentiments against her were highest. This said, we worried that more severe violence might occur. Later in our fieldwork, when our understanding was better, an older woman in the village was accused of being a parcel sorcerer. In that case, we were able to act like kin supporters and side with the woman's family when she was forced to test her innocence by cooking a divination sago. Fortunately, no violent action was taken against her, but she nonetheless had to move out of the village with her closest kin. As this indicates, cultural anthropologists often court risk and uncertainty as they decide what to observe and how and when to engage the "participant-observation" of fieldwork. As discussed later, ethics in fieldwork are always important. This is true for the very reason that, amid fieldwork's surprises, it's not always clear how to handle situations that are difficult, delicate, or dangerous.

Between events observed and those that could be reliably reconstructed, and those we could participate in with good conscience, what larger patterns emerge concerning Dugawe's death, its history, and its legacy? What can we say about Gebusi culture generally by drawing out this story?

Concerning sorcery and gender relations, the events surrounding Dugawe's death illustrate—as I have elsewhere documented in greater detail:

1. Gebusi women take primary responsibility for mourning and for emotionally identifying with the person who has died. Men inves-

tigate the death and take action against those deemed responsible as sorcerers.

2. Gebusi visitors' burials and funeral feasts express antagonism, but this aggression is undercut by the hosts' hospitality. Deeper anger is usually not expressed until proper inquests and divinations have been arranged.

3. Gebusi have believed that all adult deaths from sickness, accident, or suicide are caused by male assault sorcerers (*ogowili*) or by male or female parcel sorcerers (*bogay*). Of the two, suspects for parcel sorcery (such as Sialim's mother) have been more likely to be executed.

4. There is very little evidence that the Gebusi actually practice sorcery, though they believe firmly in its existence. Gebusi sorcery is a form of scapegoating. The identity of sorcerers is "confirmed" by elaborate spiritual inquests and divinations.

5. Male spirit mediums play a key role in Gebusi sorcery accusations. The opinion of spirits during all-night séances has been especially influential for finding and interpreting the "evidence" of sorcery.

6. Though spirit mediums should be neutral parties, the outcome of the sorcery inquest may benefit the spirit medium who conducts them. In Dugawe's case, Swamin's spirits directed antagonism away from Sialim, who he later married.

7. After sorcery inquests are completed, social relations are often reestablished between the families involved, even if an accused sorcerer has been attacked or killed. After Sialim's mother was executed, her relatives made peace with the killers. Sialim herself continued to live in the Yibihilu community after both her mother's killing and her husband's suicide. Indeed, she ended up marrying her mother's killer! (We don't know how Sialim felt about this, but it was clear that Swamin was a stalwart protector and shielded her from antagonism or aggression by others in the community.)

8. Gebusi sickness, death, sorcery, and marriage—events that may seem spontaneous, idiosyncratic, or even bizarre—often link in a cycle of reciprocity and balance over time. In Dugawe's case, Sialim was attacked in reciprocity for his suicide. The earlier death of Swamin's wife was balanced by Swamin's killing of Mokoyl and then by

the "replacing" of his deceased wife by Swamin's marriage to her daughter, Sialim.

In ethnographic writing and in anthropology textbooks, one often finds statements to the effect that "people in society X do or believe Y." But in most if not all cases such statements collapse and compress a tangled web of ethnographic information. As generalizations, such statements can be useful and are not "wrong." But in lived experience, they admit many exceptions and provide only a glimpse of human experience and diversity.

Anne-Sylvie

Chris Thomas is about the only Gebusi who was well enough educated to be paid as an administrator by the Papua New Guinea government; he enjoyed a regular salary and lived in relatively modern comfort in the town of Kiunga. In 2016, as we passed through Kiunga en route to the Gebusi, Chris opened our field season by sharing stories of recent deaths in his home village of Sirigubi. According to his account, these deaths led to sorcery accusations and homicides, including the beheadings of three suspected sorcerers. The chilling stories of multiple beheadings questioned the validity of our fieldwork data. Based on what Bruce had previously collected and published, we were to study how and why the rate of Gebusi homicide had declined so greatly to zero for over three decades since the late 1980s. Now the question became: are Gebusi still murdering "sorcerers"?

Until the late 1980s the Gebusi had one of the highest rates of adult homicide documented in history. A third of all adult Gebusi were violently killed, sometimes beheaded, largely on suspicion and accusation that they were sorcerers who caused the deaths of others. In the West, our own inclination for medical causality leads us to ask: "*what*—an illness, a disease, a bad fall?—caused this death?" But for the Gebusi, in the old days, people always wondered: "*who* caused this *murder*?" Death was always the result of a social act, not a natural one. A pain, a fall, an ailment—all these resulted from an attack. An unexplained death was calculated, directed, and inflicted by someone with agency, by a "sorcerer." Nothing was random, everything had a motive. So, too, each adult death could trigger the murder of the person publicly accused of causing the death, and that "sorcerer" had to be amputated from the social body—and eaten by its members.

Sorcerers were believed to send lethal sickness for a reason. Selfish interest and pent-up resentment were motivations behind any spiritual attack. The community would retrace the various interactions and stories linking victim and assailant, finding in retrospect what had fueled the sorcerer's need for aggression. Almost any older person could be accused and made the next victim, the victim of a sanctioned murder—an action seen and represented as fair and necessary for and by the community. A death for a death. The "sorcerer," who was denounced by his or her own guilt and revealed by an ostensible sign, would sometimes be executed immediately. And life would go on in the village. Ironically, this twist on "an eye for an eye" was not seen as multiplying the killing but rather as limiting its multiplication. When the agent of death had been killed, the community could sigh in relief and get on with their lives. Until the next attack.

But since 1989, as Bruce meticulously documented, not a single homicide had occurred, and in 2016 he and I came to investigate the mechanisms that had allowed retributive violence to settle down. What had changed? Did people stop believing in sorcery? If so, was it the work of newly established institutions (such as the church or the state)? Was it pressure by external authorities that modified behaviors and representations to such a great extent? Or was it a local transformation of previously deeply anchored traditions—a seismic shift in cultural values?

Various theories of homicide and its reduction had been proposed in the general scholarship, and we had a few hunches ourselves. Judging from other parts of the country, it was likely that the increasing use of money had changed at least some dynamics. When a promise of money is made to settle an old debt, especially in a remote place like Gebusi-land, where money is so hard to come by but has quickly become indispensable, the possibilities for nonviolent compensation widen. Payments in cash—and sometimes their mere promise— could either launch sorcery attempts or appease them, at least as efficiently as or more so than the presence of churches or government officials. Attacking a "sorcerer" was still a latent option, as belief in sorcery had not at all left the Gebusi cultural realm. But retaliation attempts were more and more defused. At least most of the time.

So how did these more contemporary ways of alleviating sadness and mitigating retributive violence square with the story Chris had told us at the very start of our fieldwork? Our arrival in the village was heavily marked by the tale of this triple execution, as people openly discussed it, allowing us to quickly cross-check information. It was not a flat-out lie, it seemed. But the more we tried to clarify the specifics, the more the whole story crumbled. It was confusing no matter the language through which we approached the tale.

The horrendous scene Chris related to us was so rich in details and fortified by statements like "seen with my own eyes," on what grounds could we question it? Yet this very story came in so many versions over time that we were led to ask whose eyes had actually seen it. As it turns out, Gebusi think of the "mind's" eyes, not the "body's" eyes, when they assert seeing something with their own eyes. Seeing is a social or spiritual construction, which for them is tangible.

There were facts: three old men died, rather suddenly it seems, but from what we in the West would call "natural causes." One condition or another got the best of them, some disease/s whose manifestations were spectacular, even, but a condition just the same. They were not killed by a human hand, but to many Gebusi, these were homicides. Many people thought that aggrieved relatives had secretly contracted a shaman to bewitch and kill the three men, beheading them by spiritual means, and then making it "look like" a natural death.

Following sickness deaths in an outlying Gebusi community, the accuser [right] makes an accusation against the sorcery suspect [left] for allegedly sending illness out of anger over land encroachment, 2016.

As anthropologists who intended to test facts to answer a non-negotiable question, we encountered the question: At what point should we dismiss our own concepts, deconstruct our assumptions, and "decenter" all that we know, including about "sorcery," "death," and "killing"? To some extent, anthropology asks for that shift from concepts we have taken for granted for so long to local notions of reality: when viewed otherwise, are a death by beheading and a death by imagined beheading not one and the same?

I have struggled during all my fieldwork experiences to abandon my own concepts and adopt Papua New Guinea visions of the world: to open myself up to the possibility of seeing and doing things according to other logics, to bring about that ultimate shift in perspective that sees things differently. With Gebusi sorcery I have been compelled to consider the ontological difference between deaths that were homicides and others that were not. I found this forced reversal in perspective ironic, to say the least. Until the day Powa was executed (see chapter 4).

BROADER CONNECTIONS
Life Stories, Death from Sorcery, and "Doing Ethnography"

- Like many cultural anthropologists, Bruce's **fieldwork methods** among Gebusi included **participant-observation**, structured **interviews**, informal conversations, unstructured interviews, **oral histories** (including life histories, event histories, residence histories, and dispute histories), **genealogies**, census and residential surveys, and **verbatim text transcriptions and translations** from recordings, including of Gebusi speeches, music, and spirit séances.

- Anthropological **ethics** and the **protection of human subjects** are important to cultural anthropologists. These include the principle of "do no harm" and, especially under conditions of danger or uncertainty, reduce risk and increase benefit to local people.

- Anthropologists need to be self-aware and **reflexive**, especially under conditions of danger or threat, to minimize the risk of their actions to others.

- The **cultural construction** of the Gebusi **life cycle** included pronounced beliefs about infant identity and becoming human, maturation and adulthood (see chapter 6), the cultural construction of disease and death as caused by sorcery, and dramatic practices concerning death and the treatment of corpses.

- Gebusi **gender relations** include male dominance and sometimes gender violence—including by Dugawe and other members of the community against Sialim.

- Gebusi have believed in **sorcery** of two major types: *bogay*, or parcel sorcery, based on belief in imitative magic, and *ogowili*, or assault sorcery, based on magical attack by warriors against the victim.

- Gebusi sorcery inquests rely on spiritual guidance through **shamanism** (or spirit mediumship) and various kinds of divination.

- Gebusi sorcery accusations illustrate the cultural projection of **stigma** and social control through **scapegoating**.

- The **anthropology of violence** and conflict provides a complement to emphasized cultural values, such as Gebusi's emphasis on good company.

- **Ethnography** proceeds by piecing together and analyzing disparate information, a process that continues for Bruce to the present.

- Gebusi patterns of death and dying have changed since the 1980s: fewer babies die, corpses are buried without divination, sorcery accusations have declined, violence is less, and the population has grown. However, general patterns of balance and reciprocity across death, marriage, and exchange continue to the present.

Chapter 4

Getting Along with Killers

by Anne-Sylvie Malbrancke

Eternal law of the field: between extreme moments comes a whole lot of nothing. Long hours go by and lead nowhere. Boredom is an interesting creature. I find people are always amazed to hear about it when they look at pictures from the field and let their Indiana Jones–infused imagination unfold. How can you get bored there? And how can you get bored when such extreme things happen? Boredom is not a black hole; it is simply another way for time to pass. There will always be specific logics guiding some actions that do not fully make sense to us. We cannot fully get it. We do not feel the weight of carrying sweet potatoes on our back. We do not feel terror at the thought of a sorcery attack. No matter how interested we are in a story, some of that focus, some of that sympathy, will always dissolve into our incapacity to fully grasp it. I believe boredom is a by-product of that.

Stamina is something we learn in the field. Mine had the unpleasant tendency to dilute itself into the heat, dripping down between two work sessions, falling at the bottom of a canoe after my own bottom had stayed there for over six hours, and finally steaming out of the longhouse where

Gebusi would hold interminable chats to discuss community matters. In French, instead of "grin and bear it" we say, "Take your pain with patience." I did that, literally. I absorbed the cramps that were sneaking up my back and butt cheeks, ignoring the pins and needles that colonized each part of my body as we sat here or there—or worse, stood, for hours on end—all the while trying to put this away in a little pocket labeled "fieldwork."

I was constantly oscillating between vertigo and nausea, caught up in the complexity of the thousand tales of infamous beheadings, faced with the constant threat of all sorts of creepy-crawlies, and always haunted by the idea that being here to work meant making the most of each waking hour. Yet while I would palpitate upon hearing about the extremes of humanity that I was given on a platter, I could also yawn.

Then, in late May 2016, during a casual conversation, we got new news: "a sorcerer has just been executed."

We were told an old Bedamini man died and that this event had been enacted like an execution. Such accounts were frequent and numerous enough so as not to surprise us anymore. We listened to the diverging versions of the story and learned that this man, Powa, who had been accused of killing many people through sorcery, had been tied to a coconut tree, after which he allegedly confessed to his crimes before his rib cage was crushed by the tight rope that lashed him to the tree. A large crowd was reported to have gathered for the execution in the small village of Tigar Miaym, located some 12 miles south of the Gebusi village where we lived. This hamlet was populated mostly by Bedamini, a neighboring tribe of fierce warriors who had massacred Gebusi prior to Australian intervention (see chapter 1). Gradually, all strands of conversation converged toward this story, with details swelling up as whispers fell victim to local inflation. Various details included: the old man's penis was cut open while he was still alive; he was placed in a toilet hole; and a thorny branch was stuffed inside his anus. One massive clarification was recurrent: Bedamini had committed this execution, not Gebusi, whose cultural beliefs and practices are, on the whole, otherwise pretty similar.

Bruce has had his share of gory stories over the years: since the start of his investigations in the early 1980s, a staggering number of actual homicides have been confessed to him, the details of which were shared with no restraint. I am more of a novice in that area, even though in the first few weeks among Gebusi, a skinny old man, very calm and always smiley, now working for the Catholic mission to pick up their papayas, told me during an interview how he killed a "sorcerer" back in the 1970s and, to be safe from the news spreading, killed his whole family, too. He was particularly generous when sharing the details of how he drowned the youngest child. That same man also asserted that human meat tastes more like pig than chicken. Bruce confirmed that the details of this execution were exactly the same as he had obtained from the same man, and others, during his first fieldwork.

With regard to Powa's execution, we spoke to Brother Greg, an out-sider priest-in-the-making who currently served at the local Gasumi Cath-olic Church, who confirmed the story and said another man was being hunted down. The execution had been represented and justified as revenge: three months earlier, in that same village, Powa's son-in-law had died brutally, in his sleep. He had been in his 40s and in good health, a fact that made people suspicious about his death. Needless to say, in small and close-knit communities, where having a row and patching things up are daily affairs, it is virtually impossible not to find a bone of contention between two people. But sometimes anger festers and builds up. Lack of adequate compensation for a woman given in marriage or a dispute over land could be major reasons for releasing pent-up anger, and they were often sufficient to justify a sorcery attack.

In Powa's case, the violent events may have been linked to the desire for land. For a few years the region has become a playground of sorts for ExxonMobil, the world's largest energy company. ExxonMobil has been extracting natural gas in the Highlands. The gas is then transported via huge pipes that run across local land. Although billions of dollars are at stake and huge amounts of money flow in, most people have received no compensation for the use of their land.

In the Nomad area, people have very few sources of money. They do not cultivate cash crops, nor do they do receive remittances from family members employed outside the country. Thus when the locals thought they could receive compensation from ExxonMobil for their land, individ-uals competed with each other for this fantastic if unlikely possibility—hence the emergence of a new terrain for sorcery accusations.

People said that Powa coveted his son-in-law's land and that he and his son killed him by sorcery—so they could later lay claim to, and pocket, the projected (and completely imaginary) land compensation money. Suddenly, Bruce and I understood that the prospect of wealth, which at times had the power to defuse anger, could conversely fuel it, giving old practices new vigor. At least the desire for money was locally understood as a strong motivation for sorcery attacks—while presenting itself as the remedy to the very need for revenge that it inspired.

I was not sure what to think, in the great indigestion of the moment. Something like a crevasse opened within me, a pit whose depth I could not quite gauge. My mind was coming to terms with a reality it had only ever conceived on paper: the actual murder of a man. And while this notion had remained a faraway concept for so long, it suddenly crept up on me as the specter of its repetition got ever closer.

Imagine that a healthy 40-year-old man probably died of an aneurism in his sleep and that an old man (Powa) was murdered for this (and his son was being hunted down). In our own value system, this action would be completely misguided, even apart from the ethics of killing. But we had to remember that our value system is not that of the Gebusi; we are the ones who came to live with them, not the other way around. On what grounds can we defend and save a "sorcerer"? But on what grounds can we not? I had the sense that, possibly like the early-days' colonizers when faced with beliefs alien to them, I had to be right, indisputably right. But, contrary to those colonizers, I felt I could not impose my own views on people. That being said, murder is a crime in Papua New Guinea, so it is not only my law but also theirs, and that law would have to be respected and Powa's hunted son spared. This even though local people, and even police in the nearest town of Kiunga, think such executions can in fact be justified as quite appropriate.

The next day, the locally elected government representative or *consol* of Gasumi Corners, Bayi, asked the whole village to gather in the long-house for a highly important talk, a *ta kala*. Usually this type of announce-ment would make my heart sink, as I quickly understood in my flesh the soporific power of such endless confabs where absolutely every adult in the village takes turns to speak out and voice their thoughts, under all pos-sible angles and in all shades of feelings. This time though, Bayi stands up and speaks, his voice is swelling up and creating vibrations through the heavy breeze. His gestures do not leave much to interpret as he is describes Powa's execution. But he is overdoing it. I look around at the faces of the adults and young people gathered here, all frozen in expressions of terror—and then bursting into macabre laughter. Fascination breaks here and there to give way to mockery of the Bedamini, as the pantomime taps into a whole range of contrasting emotions. Bayi's gesticulations are now mimicking the victims'; the father, then the son. I can guess the various torments he is depicting as I try to match up what I know of the story so far with what I am seeing. I can identify all the elements that were flying around in the rumor's wind a few days ago: the details of the severed penis, even that of the thorny branch going through Powa's anus, all minutiae now ratified by the account given by Bayi, this figure people listen to, not so much because he is a *consol*, but because he is asserting that he knows it all, having just visited the village.

Then, one after another, all the adults in Gasumi Corners addressed the community. Individually they developed a collective story, a variation on a theme. Each one systematically renounced sorcery and expressed how much they rejected the practice of sorcery. They all professed to know nothing about it—and yet they assured everyone around them that they had nonetheless forgone it. Even and especially the oldest lady in the village, whose skin had turned green from being so worn and ancient, and who could so easily become the victim of an accusation, could not be assumed to be innocent.

Nobody got upset. Bayi even explained that his own

Bayi, the Gasumi village *consol*, portrays how Powa's hands were allegedly tied up to enable brutal torture before he was executed, 2016.

father had been convicted of sorcery but his whole family had now rejected the practice. No residual knowledge, no latent tendency, no possible temptation remained. As a result, there was no shame among Gebusi in admitting to having a "sorcerer" in one's genealogical tree. Given the frequency of homicides in the old days, this was almost inevitable. There was no sadness in seeing them get executed either, as it was a good thing for the community.

Bayi thought, like everyone else, that "sorcerers" had to be killed; he could not shame or blame Powa's torturers. If an individual was "proven" to be guilty of sorcery, then it continued to be his own role, as *consol*, to encourage people to get rid of that individual, that is, to protect others. Bayi himself privately asserted on another occasion that he had in fact recently killed a woman who was a sorcerer—though we carefully and fully confirmed that this was not an actual reality as opposed to a mental projection. In short, rejecting the practice of sorcery does not mean rejecting the belief in it or even the killing of a sorcerer. But to avoid reaching such extremes, to nip in the bud any such suspicion before it could form in a bereaved or angered mind, it was important to drill into everyone's heads that nobody in Gasumi did sorcery anymore. Though none of them believed this.

Bayi's performance in front of the assembled village, in the local language, gesticulating as people felt both terrified and amused, was very different from the sober account he later gave me in Tok Pisin when we were alone. This dual representation of reality led me once more to doubt his word and wonder which eyes exactly had "seen" all this. No, there was no torture, he said; not a drop of blood was shed; nothing was cut off. Powa? Ah, yes, now he was dead; they killed him for real. And the Bedamini had threatened to kill *him*, Bayi, if he further advertised the fact of the killing to the police in Kiunga, who had no desire to take further action. Bedamini were said to be different from Gebusi: "We have changed, you know, we have the church now, and no longer have sorcery." At least, that is where Bayi closed the cultural gap in order to divorce his community from that of his Bedamini neighbors. Like us, Bayi must have felt how tenuous this local renouncement of sorcery was; all the declarations that saturated the air in the longhouse that day seemed to dance on a very precarious thread, this repulsion of sorcery immediately followed by the irresistible terror and excitement of its seduction. Either way, murderous practices associated with sorcery were still part of the daily landscape: Bayi's performance only reinforced this reality.

We went back to the village to talk it over with our friends. We concluded there was no doubt: we had to approach things culturally. We could get killed if we ourselves forced our way into Powa's village to investigate and ferret out the facts. There would be fear that we would further advertise the killing to the police in Kiunga and force them to take action, fear of some official reckoning about what had happened—or even just an angry knee-jerk reflex from an arm holding a bow and arrow. Bayi forbade us from going to Powa's village, and, anyway, a taboo had been put into place, he said, to prevent anyone from leaving or entering the place before the "wanted" man—Powa's son, the remaining male sorcery suspect—had been caught. Basically, they were in lockdown.

But other close kin of Powa in his village remained in danger of being killed, it was said, including not just his son on the loose but three women who were still staying there in fear. How could we go, and how could we help them? (The priest-in-the-making at the local Catholic Church also wanted to get involved. That is a separate story: see chapter 7.)

To our good fortune, a woman, Kwabum, who Bruce knew well from his early days, had just come back to visit Gasumi with Somlom, her husband—from the very village in which the execution had taken place. Given his deep family ties there, Somlom easily agreed to guide a small group of neutral men, including Bruce, to the supposedly tabooed village. In the mix, it was decided I would stay in Gasumi; it was not useful for me to be in this male-dominated situation, including where Gebusi vernacular would be the best way of communicating. I was also in the middle of my period, which would be quickly known in a place where it would be virtually impossible for me to change and wash discreetly and where women's menstrual blood was still associated with pollution and the potential for transmitting sorcery.

After several long days away, Bruce finally came home. At the village, he had visited with an assembly of very anxious Bedamini men who felt threatened by the "sorcerers" around—and by the fear that someone from the outside might criticize or bring action against them. With utmost solemnity and pride, they showed Bruce the evidence that firmly and unequivocally justified their actions. This is what they had recovered from Powa's net bag before

Sorcery paraphernalia allegedly found in Powa's net bag following his execution, 2016.

his execution: two small bottles, a small piece of "glass," a banknote, and two batteries belonging to his victim. In the first vial, there was a rectangle of black fabric that Powa had allegedly taken from the trousers of his son-in-law to bewitch him. In the second bottle was an unidentified piece of material, a small slice of some dark organic material that Bruce was told was the skin of the victim. Next to it was an equally unidentifiable piece of something, perhaps an inch long. He was told this came from the penis of the victim. Finally and most importantly and powerfully was an odd piece of partly translucent resin or glass. This most awesome item was said to be the sorcerer's glass or telescope that allegedly allowed Powa to "see" his victims and act on them remotely. Collectively, these objects found in his net bag were taken as absolute and irrefutable proof of his explicit practices to get rid of his son-in-law.

The men encouraged Bruce to take photos of the objects to document their veracity. They were proud to have killed Powa, proud of the lives thus saved. They gladly posed for Bruce's camera, choosing to hold up their bows and arrows to bravely take credit for executing a confirmed sorcerer in their midst. Bruce was amazed: it was his first, at least apparent, "evidence" of a sorcerer's actual doings—and his first exposure to Bedamini sorcery. Bruce then got further details of Powa's actual execution. He was shown the palm tree at which he was crucified—hoisted and tied to its trunk so tightly around his chest that his ribs broke as his feet dangled above the ground. After Powa finally died, they stuffed his body down the hole of the village outhouse.

As we drew the contours of this story again and again, some conclusions formed in the hot air of our house that afternoon. Of course they believe in sorcery, and of course they did what they thought best. Bruce met them,

Men of Tigar Miaym in proud warrior display concerning their having killed Powa as an alleged sorcerer, 2016.

The tree on which Powa was crucified, 2016.

talked to them, looked them in the eye. And he saw the same humanity as elsewhere. They did not consider themselves to be murderers in this case, but victims. Victims of a potential attack. Victims of their fear. Nothing we could do or say could change this: "To them it is as clear as finding fingerprints on a gun." A court of justice in the United States would not have acted differently if they found "evidence" that was "real" and beyond doubt. We could neither condemn nor absolve them. But by translating the story into concepts that were culturally closer to ours, we could at least understand them.

In the process, we were "taken." Taken on this journey where we oscillated between a world of horror and one of quasi fiction. We encountered an intricate pattern of overlapping elements—real or made-up, seen or retold, witnessed or fantasised—ultimately drowning our own concepts and expectations. Finally, this canvas that had occupied us for a few weeks—centuries, in emotional life—was presenting us with a finale, for there is always one, whatever our culture and our way of telling stories.

All this was a great reminder that not being involved in what was unfolding before my eyes, not being "taken," would have meant not seeing anything, not understanding anything. At all.

BROADER CONNECTIONS
Violence, Scapegoating, and the Ethics of Response

- **Stigma and scapegoating** are evident if not prominent in almost all human societies. Among Bedamini (and Gebusi) this takes the form of suspicions about, if not executions of, persons suspected or accused of practicing **sorcery.**
- The ethnographic process of understanding other peoples' values—as expressed in their own perceptions and projections—can cause us to reconsider and reevaluate our own.
- Despite and amid the confusions and ambiguities of fieldwork, it is all the more important for ethnographers, as best as they can, to document behavioral facts from a **Western perspective.**
- Especially for key and important information, **ethnographers** need to verify and double-check their information for truth and accuracy.
- Fieldwork often highlights the fact that ethnography almost invariably harbors the possibility of uncertainty or ambiguity concerning sensitive information. This is not a cause for limiting or stopping ethnographic work; rather, ethnographic work should be conducted in an increasingly refined, diplomatic, and sensitively dedicated manner.

Chapter 5

Spirits, Sex, and Celebration

Gender, sex, and spirituality are wildly different among Gebusi from that in Western cultures; they stretch our envelope of understanding. In the bargain, we reflect on our own vantage point, whatever we may presently think about gender bending, cross-dressing, same-sex sexuality, as well as patriarchy and the domination of women. These facets have all been connected in Gebusi society in ways that reposition the kaleidoscope of our own admissions, expectations, and tolerances—and their lack—in sexuality and gender. Though Gebusi have embraced alternative sexuality for men, this doesn't mean their practices have been a model of tolerance, much less of gender equality. But neither is it to say they have nothing to teach us. Amid tensions and challenges, exposure to Gebusi sexual culture was a rich part of my fieldwork. Though I thought I was tolerant to begin with, I came away with a greater respect for sexual diversity than I could have imagined. I also became more aware of gender discrimination than I had been before. If sex is often a delicate topic, it is also an important one, and one that needs to be studied sensitively.

Since long-standing Gebusi sexual customs were most prominent during my first early fieldwork, this chapter privileges that frame of reference. My first confrontation with Gebusi sexual culture was at ritual feasts, dances, storytellings, and spirit séances. Here is an example of sexual joking among three Gebusi men:

> YABA [TO DOGON]:   *Go over there and sleep with the women. Build your "fire" over there.* [Go over and have sex with them.]
>
> SWAMIN [TO YABA]:   *If he goes over there and lies down, where are you* [Yaba] *going to put your "forehead"* [phallus] *to sleep?! You'll just have to go over and lay your "forehead" on* his [Dogon's] *grass skirt!!*
>
> YABA [TO DOGON]:   *You're wearing a big grass skirt* [for me to lie on].
>
> DOGON [TO YABA]:   [You do and] *I'll pull off your loincloth!!*
>
> YABA [TO DOGON]:   *And you'll sleep there* [in my crotch]*!!*
>
> [Whooping and laughter from the other men.]
>
> DOGON [TO YABA]:   *No! I'll give your loincloth to the women and take off their clothes for you!!*
>
> [More laughter from the men.]
>
> SWAMIN: *The younger men must be getting tired from ladling out all their "kava"* [semen]*! I'll ladle out mine with a thrust!!* [Kicks out his foot.]
>
> [General laughter.]
>
> DOGON [TO YABA]:   *Can you give some to me??*
>
> YABA [TO DOGON]:   *We'll have to lay down "forehead"* [phallus] *as a gift-exchange name!*
>
> YABA AND DOGON [LEANING THEIR HEADS TOGETHER]:   *YAY!!*
>
> [Laughter and yelling.]

Simmering in everyday life, male joking found its greatest outlet in traditional Gebusi feasts and celebrations. At the time, all three of the men above were widowers in their early 30s. Were Yaba and Dogon really apt to have sex together or to use "phallus" as their gift-exchange name? No; their joking reflected nonsexual friendship. Most Gebusi sexual joking, some of it quite physical, flirts with possibilities that aren't consummated. Thinking back, the same was true of the locker-room pranks played by members of my high school soccer team in Connecticut. In a similar way, much Gebusi horseplay is what we might call "homosocial" rather than "homosexual" per se.

At first, I wasn't really sure if Gebusi guys engaged each other sexually at all. A young man might shout, "Friend, your phallus was stroked, and it came up!" But beneath the surface, how much was orgasmic fire and how much was playful smoke? I suspected that male trysts took place near the outhouse at night during séances and festive dances. To find out, I sat near the appropriate longhouse exit so I could see who went out and if they hooked up. But I felt uncomfortable doing so, as if I was being a voyeur. Yet, I didn't want to project male–male sex onto Gebusi if it wasn't the case. And other anthropologists would want to know one way or the other. My Gebusi friends seemed unable to talk about sex in a serious way; any sober query just became another joke—perhaps like today in many college fraternities. At ritual feasts, I ultimately did see pairs of guys slip outside in the dark, cavort with each other in the night shadows, and return visibly relaxed a few minutes later. But these pairings were not between principal joking partners. Rather, they tended to occur, quite consensually, between an initiated man and an uninitiated teenage boy.

Hawi later verified that the main sexual connection between men was fellatio—a "blow job"—in which a teenager manipulates the phallus of his elder counterpart and orally consumes the semen. Beyond sexual release, it turned out that such insemination had an important cultural function: it supplied male life force to the uninitiated bachelor for his masculine development. Unlike girls, who were believed to mature without intervention, Gebusi boys were "grown" in part by the masculine life force of semen from adult men. Hawi verified that, as a rule, men who had been married for a significant time— like Swamin, Yaba, and Dogon—do not tryst with each other, however mightily they may joke about it. In effect, they relived their youthful virility through sexual banter without being seen as what we might call gay or homosexual. Though the analogy isn't exact, it's a bit like, in our own society, middle-age men joking sexually

Men's sexual joking while making a canoe, 2008.

with each other during a drunken 25-year reunion at their college fraternity. I was told at one point early on that stably married men wouldn't have
sex with boys, since they already had their wives as sexual partners.

Armed with this knowledge, and being married at the time, I felt comfortable accepting and participating in male jests. Then one day, I went to a
séance held by Swamin at a distant bush hamlet. The singing warmed up
and exceeded even its normal heated pitch. In song, a "playmate" spirit
woman hovered atop the house, showed her private parts, and cried to screw
the men present. Pandemonium broke out as men screamed their own sexual desire. Doliay straddled a house post and yanked it back and forth
between his legs until the whole house shook. Hawi bellowed that he had to
"let go" and shot an arrow through the roof thatch "up into" the spirit
woman. Egged on by the bravado, the younger men and teenage boys paired
up and started leaving for trysts in the darkness to "relieve their frustration."

It was then that Mora stroked my arm and leaned his head close to
me, "Let's the two of us go off together!" He rubbed his fist up and down
over the index finger of his other hand, motioning that I would be the one
satisfied. I shouldn't have been surprised; Gebusi men had been open with
me about their sexuality. After my shock, I thought I recovered rather well.
I smiled back at Mora: "I'm really sorry, but, well, I'm already married. So
I can't go off with you; it would be taboo for me." But I was as unprepared
for his reply as I had been for his overture: "Don't worry. Didn't anyone
tell you? We break those rules all the time! Let's go!!"

I broke out in a sweat. I was not about to join Mora for a sexual tryst.
But what would happen to men's trust in me—their willingness to include
me in their ritual world? Would Mora be insulted or slighted? Would my
status as a welcome observer be compromised? The men were already gear-
ing up for the elaborate rituals and secret practices of the male initiation.
Would I be excluded from learning key customs of private male culture? I
already knew that insemination had cosmic and spiritual significance. The
Gebusi word for initiation, *wa kawala*, means literally, "boy become big"—
and this "bigness" was enhanced by ingesting male semen.

In answering Mora, I tried to suppress my anxiety. I said that having
sex with a young man just wasn't my custom, my personal *kogwayay*. I said
that back where I came from, some men had sex with young men like him,
but others didn't—and I was in the latter group. So, I apologized, I
couldn't go off with him.

Anthropologists are sometimes chided for generalizing about the people they study—for instance, that "Gebusi men have sex with each other." Such generalizations cover up much variation. When Mora replied to me, he seemed to underscore this point. "That's okay," he said. "Some of us have sex with each other a lot, but others not so much." And with that, the séance went on as before. Relieved, I continued my role as observer and shadow participant—trying to sing, ask questions, record the proceedings, and joke, if anything, more good-naturedly than before.

It turned out that Mora's reply was truer than I first realized. Though Gebusi teenagers did, in principle, increase their growth by consuming men's semen, their own growing sexuality is not so easily bottled up. Sometimes, the initiates-to-be found sexual release with each other. This was especially true of Hawi and Doliay. We have encountered Hawi before—my initial helper and uncertain translator, accomplished fisherman, and energetic young bachelor. Among the soon-to-be-initiated young men, Doliay was his closest comrade. Though he was the shortest of the initiates, topping out at just four feet ten inches, Doliay was a vacuum-packed firecracker. Intense, funny, industrious, smart, and completely undaunted, he was also a little Atlas, as if his lost stature had congealed into muscle.

During the months prior to the initiation, Hawi and Doliay were a hilarious pair. At séances they would rush out together and saunter back a few minutes later, happily spent. Reclaiming their energy, they would stand together and jive, as everyone laughed, reaching for each other's crotches while guarding against a similar riposte. Like other men, they never indulged in public nudity or open sexuality. But they swelled with bravado and boasted that they would never get married because they had each other as sexual partners.

According to academic views of insemination or "ritual homosexuality" in Papua New Guinea, boys who receive semen are said to be discouraged or prohibited from themselves having sexual release prior to initiation, lest they deplete the male essence they have been accumulating. Rituals of manhood were assumed to be trials of self-discipline, with boys being sexually as well as socially subservient to older initiated men. But Gebusi defied these assumptions.

What is more, Hawi and especially Doliay were drawn to Gebusi women as well as to each other. Before the initiation, Doliay was caught having sex with Nelep. When her husband entered the house from a nighttime gathering, Doliay's shadowy figure bolted from Nelep's sleeping quarters, leapt out a side door, and fled into the night. The implications were scandalous. A teenager and not yet initiated, Doliay was some 15 years younger than Nelep. Their encounter had probably been as brief as it had been illicit. But clan genealogies were dotted with cases in which an unguarded widow or middle-aged woman had become pregnant by a younger man. Nelep's husband, Wasep, beat her, but not as severely as most men would have. Saddled with skin bruises and a scalp laceration, Nelep cried and whimpered in the public clearing. She recovered and reentered village life without further incident, apparently having paid the price for her indiscretion.

For his part, Doliay fled to another settlement until tempers cooled. Upon his return, he was not beaten—the Gebusi double standard remained in effect—but was chastised to the point that it appeared he might not be initiated. Denying initiation is a severe sanction for young men who flout the rules against having illicit sex with women. Sagawa had

Woman in costume, 1998.   Mosomiay in costume, 1998.

already been precluded from initiation because of his affair with Sialim and her husband's subsequent suicide. However, even those teenage boys who had to forego initiation still became full adult men.

Some cultures, including our own, can fuel the same desires they forbid. So it was ultimately not surprising that Gebusi men's fantasies of illicit sex with women sometimes became reality. This tension was indeed the central theme of Gebusi folktales recounted by senior men to other men and boys. In these, a lone handsome bachelor was typically enticed by an equally solitary, and gorgeous, young woman. Brought together by forces beyond their control, such as the death of their parents, the couple typically lived on their own together though they were neither married nor related as kin. The strong attraction of the couple with no one to prohibit them from having sex formed the dramatic centerpiece of the tales. Though on the surface the couple exercised restraint—despite titillating opportunities to the contrary—for the males present the tales were anything but heroic or restraining. Rather, they served as a foil for them to joke with gusto. "If it had been me, I couldn't have waited; I would have had sex with her again and again!" The tension between the self-disciplined hero in the story and the unbridled desires of the male audience was itself the centerpiece of the stories' emotional charge and intrigue, a forum for openly expressing male fantasies.

What of Gebusi women? Wives cared little if their husbands had sex with teenage boys or with young initiated men. But they were furious if their husbands seemed attracted to other women. At spirit séances and storytellings, women listened to men's antics from their side of the sago leaf wall that separated them from the men's area. Sometimes, they responded with their own smiles and suppressed joking. As Eileen wrote on the basis of our first fieldwork, "Gebusi women regard sexuality as a positive force in the formation of marriage—as long as such relationships are based on reciprocal sexual longing." But women at that time were severely berated and easily beaten if they flirted with a man in fact, especially if he was married.

Given the general Gebusi emphasis on sexual desire—both heterosexual and homosexual among men—did Gebusi women have their own lesbian relations? Though older and younger women are known to have had sexual relations among the Kamula, a group to the Gebusi's southeast, there is little good evidence of lesbianism from other groups in Papua New Guinea. Has sex between women been rare in the region—or has it merely been unreported by male anthropologists, from whom it has been hidden? With tactful diplomacy and in private, Eileen asked women whom she knew and trusted if Gebusi women had sex with one another. Their responses were uniformly negative, ranging from incredulity to disgust: "No." "Certainly not." "How could one even do that?" "Is that really something that women do where you come from?"

In fantasy, Gebusi men were clearly enticed by women's sexuality. Yet as much as they wanted to, they couldn't have sex with spirit women—since these women lived in the world of the spirits! The big exception here was the Gebusi shaman. In his dreams and at séances, his own spirit experienced the spirit world "for real." Over time, he came to have a spirit world wife, spirit children, and a whole set of spirit world friends and relatives. Among these, the beautiful unmarried spirit women sang through the his body during séances and joked salaciously with Gebusi men. The male spirit child of the shaman was also important; his voice at the end of the séance, at dawn, provided key information about the deeper reason for holding the séance: whether a sick person would recover, the identity of a sorcerer, whether a lost pig would be found, or if an anticipated hunting or fishing expedition would be successful. During the bulk of night, however, the shaman's songs were sassy tales sung by spirit women. Their unbridled libido was pure grist for the mill of men's sexual fantasies.

Having traversed a full circle—from men's sex with each other back to their attraction for women—we can understand Gebusi men's bisexuality more fully. Gebusi dances are rife with sexual allure, and men are the dominant focus of performance, beauty, and attraction. Gebusi strongly associate the dominant costume features of the male dancer—his red body paint, feathers, black eye-banding, and hopping dance steps—with the red bird of paradise (*sagrab*). And *this*, for Gebusi, is the beautiful form taken by young spirit *women*. In essence, a Gebusi man dancing in resplendent costume is cross-dressing as a very beautiful and seductive young spirit woman. Male audience members voice great attraction to this male-cum-female presence, and Gebusi women also accentuate this cross-gender imagery; they accompany the man's dance by sitting offstage and singing haunting songs of women's loneliness and sexual desire. As the men in the audience look at the dancer, hear the women's singing, and pine for the beautiful spirit woman, they joke about having sex with *women*—at the same time that they redirect their arousal as homoerotic horseplay to other *men*. It seemed to be a classic case of "bait and switch": male sexual desire for women was heightened and then redirected onto men and teenage boys. In parallel fashion, in séances, the male shaman's impersonation of the female spirit woman made her both the object of men's heterosexual arousal and the reason for redirecting this arousal onto other men.

When a man cries out *"Ay fafadagim-da!"* he proclaims, "I'm frustrated!" "I'm sexually pent up for release!" and also "I'm aggressive and angry enough to act!" That erotic arousal conveys aggression and even anger, which seems politically incorrect from a Western perspective but makes perfect sense to Gebusi. That men can't attain their object of erotic desire makes them angry as well as playful. During the dance itself, the more humorous side of this aggressiveness is emphasized. But in spirit séances for sorcery, the sharp edge of aroused anger, fueled by the spirit women's allure, has a more sinister side: the enraged desire to take revenge against the loneliness and loss provoked by sickness and death in the community. This is also *fafadagim-da*. Though strange to us as Westerners, it was no contradiction to Gebusi men that their spirit séances aroused *both* sexual desire *and* the possibility of homicidal revenge against sorcery suspects. Gebusi connections between sex and violence that at first seemed bizarre ultimately made cultural sense. This crystallized in the Gebusi word *gawf*, which means hard, angry, muscular, aggressive—and, also, having a hard erect penis.

What does the kaleidoscope of Gebusi eroticism tell us about human sexuality more generally? First, it underscores the variability of sex and gender across cultures. Gebusi men's sexual customs made mincemeat of our own categories of "homosexual" as an enduring life identity, of "bisexuality," and also of "tolerance" of sexual diversity. Young Gebusi men having sex with each other was highly tolerated by both men and women. But men's double standard against women's sexual expression was doubly pernicious in the bargain. And the idea that women might have sex with each other was so weird to Gebusi as to be unthinkable. In many parts of highland Papua New Guinea, anthropologists considered gender relations to be shot through with "sexual antagonism" by men against women—at the same time that gender polarization fueled elaborate male-dominated costuming, display, myth, and ritual. In some of these societies, men had sex with boys as a key if not indispensable feature of male initiation.

This is just one example of historical Papua New Guinea's remarkable sexual diversity. Among the few million inhabitants of indigenous Melanesia, sexual customs ranged from prolonged male chastity and beliefs in women's depleting impact on men, to fervent love magic and serial sexual intercourse—heterosexual as well as homosexual—including to collect or ingest semen and/or vaginal fluid for a variety of ritual and magical purposes. Yet in most of these societies, monogamous marriage remained the norm for most adults. In many if not most of these cases, adult women were active not just in accepting but in enforcing male-dominant beliefs and practices.

Bringing this back home, we can briefly consider current sexual culture in many American colleges, especially during the first and second year of life in dorms on campus. Just how do we square our strong emphasis on sexual equality and tolerance of sexual expression among men and women with a drunken hook-up culture, a sexual culture in which women are so often shamed by guys and often by girls for being either "sluts" or "prudes"?

There is no simple answer here. And if you tried to provide one, it would certainly be argued against by one or another competing view, either on grounds of judgmental morality or on those of sexual irrepressibility. How do we square our deeper values of morality and sexuality with our actions, on the one hand, and respect for others who we try to understand even if we may disagree with them? Drawing the line between "anything goes" and "taking a stand" may be as hard on college campuses as it was for me among Gebusi. Yet we do make decisions, as I did, concerning what we do with our bodies—even as we may try as mightily as possible to understand the decisions and actions of others. I don't want to condone what I think is wrong, but I don't want to be closed-minded either, much less sexist or homophobic—or reflexively male-bashing. Amid complexities and uncertainties, the first thing may be to drill down and get in touch with what we ourselves actually feel good and comfortable with. Knowing that more clearly can help us understand the difference or distance between ourselves and others—and what we want to do or not do about this. Such questions have few easy answers, but among ourselves as well as among Gebusi, I think it is important to ask and reflect on them.

A final point here concerns one's personal point of view and identity, what anthropologists call one's subject position. I am a man, and a senior straight white man to boot. This chapter has been written by a man, largely about Gebusi men, but for a readership that is certainly mixed if not, speaking statistically, dominantly female. Though I have tried in the field and otherwise (see chapter 8), I have not been able to provide an adequate female point of view. For that, we turn to Anne-Sylvie and her fieldwork.

Anne-Sylvie

Over weeks and months, the various stories Gebusi women shared helped me better understand what shaped and wove the fabric of their lives. One of them was laughing over having been locked up for hours in a small hut because she refused to get married; another one casually talked about being kicked out of her home after she "went to the bush" with a boy, with no intention of marrying him; another gloated about hiding from her husband her share of money gained at the market. Jokes and lightness of tone punctuated such accounts, all actually converging toward a bleak state of affairs behind the cheerfulness adopted to face the heavy and systematic grip of men.

Women were managed by men; they were moved from one house to another or from one village to another; they were taken away, repudiated, or taken back. They would travel along the various geographic and emotional maps of their social universe, rarely in control of decisions that impacted their lives. Forced to marry into other tribes, sometimes sent to live far from their parents at an early age, prevented from going to school in order to get married, they were like pawns in the infinite array of male strategies, and their opinion was seldom asked or listened to. A husband might decide to take another wife without regard for the feelings of his first one.

What I describe above is not as spectacular as what I witnessed in my other fieldwork in New Guinea, among the Baruya of the Papua New Guinea Highlands. On my second day of that fieldwork, I saw a woman get crushed with a log wielded by her husband, who accused her of stealing his money. In the end, this act was condemned by the community as "violence for no reason," since there was no evidence of theft. But this itself indicated, beneath the surface, that there was a whole universe of "legitimate violence"—including if a woman took something her husband thought was his—that could be directed against women at any point.

Bullied, beaten, used by men in their matrimonial strategies, Baruya women nonetheless showed a great capacity to resist and fight back—whether it was "legit" or not. They would strike back with their own blows and even place stones in their net bags, which they swung to hit lazy husbands. They were allowed to divorce and could develop their own businesses; their school attendance was in equal proportion to that of boys. They even told me about a committee they established to handle their problems and present their complaints to the provincial authorities. Compared to the "male domination" that existed in the past, one could only conclude that things had gotten better for Baruya women.

How do we measure and compare levels of gender violence? How do we decide on degrees of betterment when we are starting from a point unknown to us and the scale recognizes a set of values different from our own? This challenge is thrown into relief by trying to compare gender relations even across two cultures in different nooks of the bush from the same country. The whole array of possibilities cannot easily be put into words.

Because they would laugh casually, because some couple dynamics seemed more tender, and because some sexual relations were

Men of Gasumi Corners yelling orders to women at a village feast, 2017.

Man in costume for the Yibihilu initia-   Gebusi man in aggressive, costumed
tion, 1981.   pose, 2017.

more relaxed—in other words, because their way of life seemed
closer to mine—I had at first concluded that Gebusi women were not
so "dominated."

I had not understood anything.

Update: Over the years, a number of things have influenced Gebusi
sexuality and gender, including the impact of Christianity, the decline of
male initiation, coed schooling, the prominent role of women at the
Nomad market, the virtual if not complete absence of contemporary sexual relations between Gebusi men, and a marked softening of divisions,
pollution beliefs, and social distance between men and women—amid
continuing male prerogatives, domination, and male joking. Gebusi men
and women interact more easily and casually than they used to, including
not only husbands and wives and boys and girls but unrelated men and

women in the village. But this does not mean that patriarchy and male dominance have been dethroned. Patriarchies have a frequent tendency to reemerge in new guises, including in our own society.

Note: See Gebusi video clips and commentary on Gebusi male–male sexual and social relations ("Sexuality") on Bruce Knauft's website or on YouTube (video #6) by searching "Gebusi videos."

BROADER CONNECTIONS
Sexuality and Gender

- As Gebusi illustrate, **sexuality and gender** are highly variable across cultures.
- Sexuality studies are an important but delicate area of anthropological investigation that needs to be considered carefully and respectfully.
- Gebusi practices of **male–male sexuality** and of male transmission of life force as semen from one generation to the next illustrate the cultural construction of life-cycle reproduction.
- That Gebusi men to joke energetically about activities they might not actually practice highlights the importance for anthropologists to distinguish between verbal statement and actual sexual behavior.
- Bruce's response to Mora's sexual advances illustrates that, for their own personal reasons, cultural anthropologists may choose to not engage with some cultural practices even as they attempt to understand or appreciate them.
- Gebusi illustrate that some societies are more accepting of alternative forms of sexual expression than others. In the country of Papua New Guinea as a whole, as is also the case in selected countries of Africa and elsewhere, sexual relations between persons of the same sex are formally illegal, even when these relations are based on mutual consent.
- In societies such as the Gebusi and in Melanesia as a world region, alternative practices of sexuality easily coexist with heterosexual marriage.
- Sexuality is strongly and importantly linked to other features of culture, including, among Gebusi, ritual and religious symbolism, sorcery accusation, and both camaraderie and violence within the community.
- Gender and sexuality can be highly variable by personal preference within cultures as well as between them.
- Understanding sexuality and gender in other cultures, including Gebusi, can help us better understand patterns of **individual and collective diversity** in our own society.

Chapter 6

Ultimate Splendor?

T he Gebusi celebration of life, spirituality, and sexuality—among men, and apparently among women and children as well—came together most fully and completely in the climactic events of the male initiation, the biggest and most elaborate spectacle in Gebusi society. Even in Gebusi's deeper past, this typically occurred just once in the lifetime of each major settlement. The cycle began with the building of the village's central longhouse: the communal dwelling provided enough space to house relatives, friends, and visitors from all surrounding settlements at the initiation itself. At Yibihilu, the longhouse was built by six extended families from four different clans whose six young men, ranging from 16 to 20 years of age, lived in the village and were initiated there in the early 1980s.

For more than half a year at the time, much and then almost all activity in the village focused on the upcoming celebration, a celebration that would bring together a large portion of the Gebusi "tribe" as a whole. For such a small and isolated forest people, the scale, effort, and energy of these preparations were amazing. In October and November, villagers spent several weeks amassing huge piles of firewood to be used for cooking immense quantities of feast food—with men doing much of the chopping but women undertaking the more laborious work of carrying the wood to the village. In December, January, and part of February, families went deep into the forest to cut and process sago palms—with men cutting and splitting the tree and the women laboriously pounding the sago pith into starch, putting the heavy loads into net bags, and carrying them in human caravans back to the village. In late February and early March, the men of Yibihilu dispersed into the forest to hunt game, especially wild pigs and cassowaries. At the same time, women went off to process yet more sago.

Finally, it was time for villagers to reassemble. The large pigs of the settlement—one for each of the initiates—were tracked down, lured back to the village, penned in wooden cages, and fed to fatten them further. By late March, the village was again a beehive of activity. Enormous piles of leaves and cooking stones were stacked next to the firewood. Food piles grew larger, including coconuts, greens, nuts, bamboo shoots, kava roots, and dried tobacco. By the end of March, everything was finally ready. During this time, they had amassed enough food to feed most of the more than 400 Gebusi—with plenty of extra for visitors to carry home and share with those who didn't come.

If food represented the initiation's material foundation, the costumes of the initiates were its artistic centerpiece. As previously mentioned, the Gebusi term for initiation is *wa kawala*, "boy/child become big." This refers simultaneously to the growth of the initiates and their donning of elaborate costumes at the initiation itself. The costume parts came from far-flung networks that spanned the entire tribe. From diverse settlements, people were mobilized to obtain materials and construct the score of elements needed for each male initiate's final outfit. Leading up to the initiation, men painstakingly crafted armbands, leg bands, waistbands, chest bands, feathered headdresses, shell necklaces, and looped earrings; they carved and strung long hardwood bows; and they shaved and ornamented elaborate decorative arrows. Rounding out the initiates' gifts were household items newly made by women, such as large, beautifully woven net bags and sago-carrying sacks. But none of the items were displayed, much less given, until the final celebration.

Eventually, the effort of the community, indeed, practically the entire tribe, grew to a final climax. But how? Gebusi have no central leadership to orchestrate such large undertakings. Part of the answer lay simply in tradition. Based on past experience, households knew the sequence of preparations and the time needed for each. They also knew how those in other settlements would respond to the delays and complications that invariably arose during months of preparations. Collective discussion bubbled when people returned from the forest and met in the village.

Though each extended family was ultimately autonomous, men were eager to trade information, strategize plans and contingencies, and keep track of each other's progress. The people of Yibihilu had already worked together to build their big longhouse. Now they were charged to bring together their grandest features of Gebusi society and culture.

To this end, the spirits of the Gebusi world were enormously helpful. At each stage, a lively séance was held whereby hurdles to the preparations were addressed and positive resolutions charted. As Swamin described it, the spirits were planning to hold their own initiation at the same time that villagers would be holding theirs. Predictably, then, spirits were generous with advice and support.

Armed with otherworldly confidence, our friends at Yibihilu planned with excitement and worked with keen anticipation, women as well as men. During months of preparations, they overcame periods of poor hunting, cured persons who were sick, endured two additional deaths and associated sorcery inquests, found and retrieved their pigs that had wandered deep into the forest, and arranged for a full complement of sponsors across settlements for each of the six initiates. Their enthusiasm stoked a rising tide of good company among everyone in the village. I had never experienced such a frenzy of collective friendship, laughter, and enjoyment along with plain old hard work. Everyone—women, children, men, and, of course, the initiates themselves—were swept up in the happy maelstrom. Just when I thought the level of camaraderie was about to level off, it would ratchet up yet higher.

As I gradually realized, the festivities leading up to the initiation mirrored the basic structure of Gebusi ritual feats, with which I was already familiar. Elaborately decorated visitors would descend on the village in a show of force and aggression. They would then be appeased by gifts from the hosts—the smoking of tobacco, the drinking of water and kava, and eating piles of food. Hosts and visitors would then celebrate through the night while eating, talking, and generally having a good time—men in the center of the longhouse, women along the sides. One or more of the visiting men would often dance in costume as women sang and men joked lustily. Or an entertaining spirit séance would be arranged. At dawn, when everyone seemed happily tired, outstanding issues of political contention or dispute would finally be addressed. With so many people from so many kin groups feeling so good, amicable resolutions were all but assured. The visitors would then return home, weary but happy, while the hosts retired for a daytime sleep. During months prior to the initiation, this same basic pattern of hosting and feasting—and amicably discussing any issues of tension—was used to dedicate the longhouse, commemorate the ear piercing of younger boys, and celebrate other milestones.

Eventually all was ready for the climactic festivities. These began with what anthropologists call a transitional or "liminal" period for the initiates—a bit like the hazing of new fraternity members before their admission to the club. For Gebusi initiates, their in-between status was signified by bold stripes of yellow ocher, painted on them from head to toe. The Gebusi word for yellow, *bebagum*, literally means "to be in the middle of" or "wedged in between." As a finishing touch to the elaborate costume, a broad white leaf was attached to the front of the initiate's waistband so it hung down almost to his knees, like a giant penis. A topic of lewd joking and teasing by the men, this phallic leaf was a very public symbol of the initiates' pent-up sexuality. Each of the male initiates was costumed identically, down to the smallest detail. As they lined up and stood with proper humility, their individual identities fused into a beautiful and yet humble collective whole. Selected women danced alongside them and sang, though in costumes nowhere near as ornate as those of the initiates themselves.

The initiates' biggest trial was to wear the new wigs that their sponsors from other villages then came to give them. Wig-wearing may not sound traumatic, but the adornment was made from large wads of sodden yellow bark that were tied in bulky bundles to narrow strands of each initiate's hair. The wet bark was so heavy—I estimated 80 pounds for each initiate—that after it was tied to the initiates' hair, it had to be supported with a pole held by two helpers, who strained to raise it as each of the young victims, in turn, was ordered to stand up. All the while, the surrounding men crowded around, whooping and joking with abandon. The prime sponsor of each young man then trimmed off the wig's long streamers, reducing its weight on the scalp of the initiate to perhaps "only" 25 pounds.

Fighting back tears of pain and discomfort, the silent initiates were then ordered to line up and listen to their elders. The senior sponsors of each initiate came forward and lectured him on Gebusi values of generosity and virtue: "Always be generous with your kinsmen and in-laws, however long they live." "Don't be stingy with your food. Always give yourself the least." "When you come across your uncle's garden and see he has some nice food, never just take it." "If you ever steal, you will be rotten and no one will like you." "Whenever guests come, you must snap their fingers firmly and warmly." "Never hide your tobacco away, always share it with anyone who visits." Predictably, the greatest admonitions concerned sex: "You can never, ever, chase after another man's wife." "Never flirt with your uncle's woman." "When you see a female 'bird' alone in the forest, you can't just go and 'shoot' it because you think you are 'hungry.'" "Don't you ever pry open the 'cooking tongs' [legs] of a village woman."

Yibihilu initiate, Momiay, wearing a heavy bark wig, 1981.

Although the sponsors started out seriously, their diatribes quickly lost steam; after a few minutes, their speeches labored to sustain their invective. When the sponsors finally got to their warnings about sex, the men and even the uninitiated boys could barely suppress their chuckles and smiles. Then, with loud cries of "*SUI-SUI-SUI,*" the sponsors shooed the initiates outside to fetch water from the spring, 10 minutes away. Amid whoops and hollers, men and boys accompanied the initiates, who carried water tubes and strained to walk while wearing their wigs.

This trip to the watering hole turned out to be the prime occasion for revealing male secrets. In many Papua New Guinea cultures, elaborate restrictions surrounded the transmission of sacred male knowledge. In some cases, this information was doled out piecemeal over many years. Measured against such standards, the Gebusi were amazingly carefree.

While approaching the spring, men spoke in only slightly lowered tones about the various foods that the new men, once initiated, would not be allowed to eat. Red pandanus could not be eaten because it formed red paste, like menstrual blood. Slimy forest greens could not be eaten because, when they were cooked, they oozed like a woman's genitalia. River lobsters could not be eaten because they once pinched a woman in her upper thigh, which made them turn red. The list went on and on until I tallied 23 food items that would now be taboo to the initiates. In each case, the reason for the prohibition was the same: the food had some association, however circuitous, with women's genitalia. As I later found out, initiated men were not supposed to eat these foods until fathering their first or second child. But most of the taboos were observed only loosely in practice. I was told that a hungry man might easily break them when out in the forest, especially if experience had taught him there was little harm in doing so. And though the list of dietary proscriptions seemed long, almost none of the items were frequent sources of protein.

As for additional male knowledge, there seemed to be none. At first I thought Gebusi must have had deeper male mysteries for me to discover. But I gradually came to recognize that the best-kept secret was the one I had overlooked: Gebusi men simply had few initiation secrets. Male sexual encounters with other men had not been hidden from women, and the initiates had taken no pains to hide their trysts. As for the telling of food taboos at the watering hole, the reactions of the younger boys were revealing. Though men urged the boys to stay away and to cover their ears—lest premature knowledge stunt their growth—most of them edged closer. Some boys even cupped their hands *behind* their ears rather than over them, to better hear the secrets. No one seemed concerned. In fact, the telling of "secrets" was mostly an occasion of male laughter and bravado. Some men proclaimed they would gladly die from breaking food taboos and by having illicit sex with women. Like in their myths and séances, Gebusi male secrets were more a source of ribaldry than of sobriety. Ultimately, the same was also true of the initiates' biggest trauma—the wearing of their bark wigs. Though the wigs were painful, the initiates quickly learned to manage them by hunching their weight onto their shoulders. By 2:00 p.m., Hawi had cut off his wig entirely. When I asked him why, he claimed it prevented him from preparing sago for the upcoming feast. By evening, only Yuway and Doliay still wore their wigs, and both of these were gone the following morning.

In some Melanesian societies, traditional rites of manhood were genuinely brutal. And they sometimes began when boys were only six or seven years of age. Ordeals might include nose bleeding, penis bleeding, tongue bleeding, cane swallowing and vomiting, body scarification, and being beaten, berated, rubbed with stinging nettles, and forced to live in seclusion, in their own excrement, without food or water. Men in male-dominated societies were typically far from pampered as children. In some societies, new initiates were threatened by senior men with violent punishment, including death, if they violated taboos or revealed male secrets to women. Against these extremes, the Gebusi initiation seemed thankfully mild. Older men said rites of manhood had always been this way—more a celebration than a trial of suffering. The same was true of some other groups in Papua New Guinea, including the Purari, who, as it also happened, were vigilant headhunters. Once again, cultural diversity was surprising and remarkable.

After wearing their bark wigs, our young friends enjoyed one last night of sleep—as much as they could get, amid their excitement—for several days to come. The following morning, after being repainted in yellow stripes (but without their bark wigs), they left to revisit their main sponsors. I went with Hawi to Swamin's little hamlet. There we were crammed into a mini-longhouse with 50 other people who had come from settlements farther afield. A similar gathering was held simultaneously at the settlement of each initiate's main sponsor, coalescing most of the tribe at staging points the night before finally coming together at Yibihilu.

After a festive midnight hike back to the main village, lit by the moon, I awoke to find smoke from a score of blazing cook fires fingering up to shred the fog and greet the morning. The whoops of those stoking the fires soon mingled with the squeals of dying pigs that had been shot full of arrows by gleeful men. Singed and splayed to cook on top of the sago, the six large pigs—one for each initiate—would provide the most lavish meal since the last initiation had taken place in a neighboring community several years before. By midafternoon, the six initiates were finally ready to become truly "big"—to don their crowning costumes. We thronged around and escorted them out to the nearby forest, where they could be dressed. The atmosphere was too festive to be exclusive, and in addition to the young boys, some of the women who had woven parts of the initiates' costumes also came along.

Each initiate was painstakingly dressed as an electrifying red bird of paradise. The sponsors and helpers of each initiate took primary charge, painting them with meticulous precision. Then they scrupulously dressed the initiates with the ever so carefully made gifts of feathered headdresses, waistbands, shells, armbands, leg bands, woven chest bands, nose plugs, looped earrings, and more. The closest parallel, it seemed to me (although I had never actually witnessed it!), was the careful dressing of a traditional American bride prior to her wedding. The analogy wasn't completely far-fetched in that the initiation served, in its own way, as a kind of male wedding. Each young man would now be suddenly and imminently marriageable. All but one of the initiates would, in fact, be married within a few months. The additional gifts that the initiates received were a virtual trousseau to begin married life. In contrast to the initiation itself, the marriages that would follow—to women whose identities were not yet known—were starkly unceremonial. As we later discovered, marriage itself was a tense affair characterized by worried courtship and adult irritation. Marriage was generally devoid of festive gift giving, costumed dancing, and public celebration. It was initiation, not marriage, that involved the cooking and distribution of the village pigs and the public celebration of transition to virile adulthood.

If Gebusi initiation was like a marriage without women, the initiates themselves were tantamount to brides. The bright red paint that graced them from head to toe was the ultimate feminine color. Its association with crimson menstrual blood grew deeper as the various food taboos were retold to the initiates during their decoration. In the process, a large new phallic leaf was attached to hang down between their legs. Even more than the standard dance outfit, the initiation costume was the purest expression of the beauty, allure, and sexuality of the red bird of paradise—a spirit woman. But before they could be formally displayed and celebrated, the initiates had to be completely costumed and publicly paraded back to the village. Given this importance, the initiates' sponsors refused to hurry despite an afternoon drizzle. Huddled under trees and with bystanders holding palm fronds to protect them, the initiates gradually emerged in final splendor. Each painted stripe, leg band, armband, and headdress feather was perfectly aligned and exactly identical on each of the initiates. I was deeply moved to see my young friends—Yuway, Hawi, Doliay, and the rest, whom I had come to know well—so beautifully transformed.

Against this aura, the rain fell harder. The costuming was now complete, but a grand procession back to the village had become impossible. So we retired with the initiates to their family houses on the periphery of the village, waiting for the storm to pass. Unfortunately, it did not. Instead, the rain grew stronger and stronger. We sat and sat as minutes became hours, from late afternoon into evening, from evening into night. It was an incredible, pelting rain, and it was completely unpredicted. Even as dawn broke, the water continued to thunder down. The smooth village clearing had become a torrent of mud.

There were plenty of ironies. If the storm had held off for just another 15 minutes (or if the sponsors had been a touch quicker with their decorations), the triumphal procession could have quickly taken place. We would all then have been happily together under the sheltering roof of the main longhouse. The visitors would have descended with great whoops to "confront" the initiates and have had their "anger" dispelled by the silent beauty of their immovable presence. Food would then have been served and eaten, and dances by the visiting men would have continued until morning. In short, everything would have gone according to plan. Now, however, the initiates, their sponsors, and the rest of us had stayed sitting up all night waiting for the rain to stop. Things were worse for the throngs of visitors. Festooned for their own grand entrances, they had retreated to the forest and huddled in makeshift lean-tos in a futile attempt to keep dry. Neither they nor we had had anything to eat. Everyone was very tired, wet, and hungry.

Why couldn't the initiates simply be led under cover to the longhouse, so visitors could enter and their food be served? The answer was consistent: "Because the initiates' red paint would run down their bodies." Beyond the importance of the triumphal procession, it was unthinkable to Gebusi that the beautiful red of the initiates, the congealed symbol of femininity that framed their masculinity, could be allowed to dissolve and drip down their skin. The specter of red liquid oozing down their carefully appointed bodies seemed tantamount to male menstruation—the destruction of masculinity rather than its crowning achievement. So we waited and waited for the rain to end.

To my amazement, almost no one got visibly upset. The main exception was Silap, who cursed angrily and chastised whatever nasty spirit was raining so literally on his parade. Everyone else eased into a kind of meditative doze, neither anxious nor despondent, but serene and trusting that all would work out. Despite the months of preparation and the sheer scale of the event—its social, spiritual, and material significance—the response to the storm was vintage Gebusi: quiet acceptance in the face of a reality that couldn't be changed. When the rain finally broke, by midmorning, my compatriots managed a few whoops of relief and anticipation. Cooking fires were now restoked and foods reheated. I checked our rain gauge. It was filled to 93 millimeters—just shy of four inches. This ended up being the fourth-biggest single rainfall during our entire two-year stay—and the biggest within a month on either side of the initiation. Villagers shrugged it off as part of their unpredictable weather: "That's just the way it is."

The six initiates were finally lined up in front of the central longhouse. Shoulder to shoulder, they were individually brilliant but most stunning as a collective whole. Uniting the visual and the physical, they literally embodied the full power of Gebusi male society—Gebusi society as a whole?—including its material culture, its networks of kinship and friendship across space, its symbolism and beauty, and its deep identification with spirituality and sexuality.

Yibihilu initiates lined up in full costume, 1981.

Into this electrifying vista, visiting men now rushed with abandon—a human stampede of celebratory aggression. Painted warriors bellowed and screamed. They sprinted through the mud and plucked their bows, spiraling in tightening circles around the initiates in happy displays of mock antagonism, wave after wave, group after group. One man was carried in, covered head to foot in mud. His tongue hung out, and a huge fake phallus was tied to his waist. At least for the moment, he was a bloated corpse covered in cadaveric fluid—indicting everyone around him as a sorcerer. As might have been guessed, even this gruesome display did not unsettle the initiates, who stood their ground with serenity even as children scattered from the "corpse" with ambivalent screams. Excited adults just smiled.

Eventually the "attacks" subsided and the feasting and celebration began in earnest. Festivities started with seemingly endless rounds of finger snapping, smoke sharing, kava drinking, and, especially, food giving—primarily by and among men, but also among women. With thunderous whoops and hollers, the identity of an initiate's sponsor or other recipient was shouted. Representatives from each of the six initiates' families then rushed to press a mound of food upon the besieged but pleased recipient. Special pleasure was taken to "force feed" key visitors great globs of dripping pig fat—pushing it to their faces until they had taken at least one or two gooey bites.

By midafternoon, it was the visitors' turn to reciprocate by giving gifts to the initiates—especially hardwood bows and sheaves of elaborate arrows that men had carved. Many of the male sponsors dramatically plucked the bow they had carved before handing it to their initiate, showing him how strong it was. Previously allowed to use only unpainted arrows for hunting, the initiates could now use painted and people-killing arrows in ritual display and, if needed, in warfare. Exhausted as they were, however, the initiates could hardly do more than stand. Even that became difficult, and by evening, they resorted to propping themselves up while sitting lest they topple over in sleep and smear their costumes. As part of their proud ordeal, they had not talked, eaten, or slept for two days.

Seemingly oblivious to their plight, everyone else was now revved up for a night of partying—eating, smoking, and drinking numerous bowls of kava root intoxicant. Jokes flew as thick and fast as the rain of the previous night. By now, the whole longhouse was packed wall to wall with men in the middle and women on the periphery, with just a small space in the middle for the dancers. The yellow light of bamboo torches cast a golden glow across the faces and costumes. The outfits of the male visitors were as spectacular and creative as they were plentiful—bird of paradise and cassowary headdresses, face and body painting in innumerable patterns and combinations, bone and bamboo nose plugs and beads, leaf wreathes, and woven chest bands and armbands. Women were also festooned, wide-eyed, and excited. Almost all of them donned fresh grass skirts, bead or seed necklaces, and woven chest bands and armbands. Many also wore headdresses of fringed fiber strips and long egret feathers.

Beyond the usual male dancing, a special dance involved several young women wearing their own red body paint, black eye banding, and red bird of paradise headdresses, echoing those of the initiates. During the plaintive songs of the women's chorus, the female dancers lilted up and down as they faced their male counterparts. Each held a long, thin rattle that she thrust up and down in front while pulsing to his pounding drum. The sexual charge of these pairings was impossible to miss. The men in the audience went wild, while the women joked and laughed from their own sitting places. A few women could be seen joking and flirting directly with men. It was as if, for a single night, the erotic mirth of the spirit woman had become acceptable for real Gebusi women as well as for men to enact. The night was swept up in festive abandon. I will always remember its joyful intensity.

The morning after was just that. As the visitors left, those from the host village crashed and slept, and so did we. While Gebusi had been busy partying, we had undergone our own initiation. Pumped by adrenalin and coffee, we had primed ourselves to observe and record what we had waited months to see—and what we knew we might not see again. Unlike the Gebusi, we didn't know what was going to happen next or when or how it would unfold. We worried that we would miss important events. I remembered the story of a well-known anthropologist who, working alone, fell asleep from fatigue at the height of a male initiation rite and missed a key sequence of color-coded costumes that he could never reconstruct. But in our case, we were cajoled good-naturedly by Gebusi not only to be present but to participate as fellow residents of Yibihilu. This included our happily accepted offer to give rice and tinned fish as food, to help host visitors, and to serve as secondary sponsors for the initiates. When men gave the initiates bows and arrows, I gave them each several prized shotgun cartridges—"Western arrows"—for the hunting shotgun we had given to Yibihilu and which they cherished for providing them extra meat. We also gave each initiate a pair of blue satin gym trunks that we had bought during a field break. These gifts were wildly popular and widely talked about, as it was (and remains) difficult for the Gebusi to obtain such items in the rainforest. In return, the families of the initiates gave us pork and sago. To each of the initiates, we became *tor,* sponsor.

That morning, however, all we could think of was sleep. But just when we thought the initiation was over, an additional climax erupted. In the early afternoon, we were awakened by loud noises and stumbled out of bed to see what they were. The initiates were herded out of the village, their costumes retouched, and then paraded back in. This time, though, they were joined by two unmarried young women who stood alongside them in costumes that were, in body paint and feathers, virtually identical to their own. Together, the six young men and two young women linked fingers and stood in a single line. They bobbed up and down in unison as Tosi, the senior woman of the community, came forth to address them. Going down their line, she gently hit each of them with a sheaf of special leaves and chanted that they would henceforth be strong in heart, in breath, and in spirit. She said to each that he or she would have the inner

Women lined up with male initiates at the concluding initiation ceremony, 1981.

energy of a buzzing hornet. Then she told them to be kind to and protective of others in the village. Finally, she declared for each the name of a young child to whom they were unrelated but whom they were charged to help and protect. With that, she turned and walked away. The initiation was over.

Thinking we had seen everything the night before, we wrestled anew to make sense of this wonderful ending. Although women had been off-stage for many of the initiation's formal events, a senior woman had now conducted its final ceremony. Young women had dressed up and danced the previous night, but now two women dressed up like the initiates and linked with them physically. The beautiful red bird of paradise had finally enveloped real Gebusi women. If this had been implicit in the previous night's dancing and joking, it was now formally proclaimed. What had seemed like—and in many ways was—a rite of male initiation was now a ritual celebration of male *and* female adulthood. The boundless imagery of spirit women, so dominantly appropriated by men, was finally accorded and publicly acclaimed for Gebusi women as well. It was almost as if, in its final moment of ritual celebration, Gebusi culture transcended its own deepest gender division.

This theme grew stronger that same night. Though the initiation was over, the young men and women were now adults—and free to dance on their own. Still dressed in their red initiation costumes, the male initiates added the feathered halo of the standard dance costume and danced for the first time with drums. Moreover, they danced in pairs with the young women who had stood alongside them at the initiation's benediction. Like their linkage earlier in the day, their ritual union encompassed the male–female beauty of Gebusi as a whole.

Given these final events, I wondered how much I should rethink my understanding of the initiation. Was it a *male* initiation—or not? As before, the intricacies of Gebusi made my simple questions deliciously difficult. On the one hand, young Gebusi women were painted similarly to the young men, lined up with them, danced with them, and were charged along with them during the final ceremony to protect a young child. Their maturity and sexuality were on obvious display alongside the young men. In social terms, their costume elements, though not as elaborate or copious as the young men's, linked them to kin networks that had given or loaned them these items.

On the other hand, unlike their male counterparts, the young women were not inseminated or otherwise sexually initiated. They were not subject to painful trials testing their stamina, and they did not receive bows and arrows or major stocks of ritual or domestic items. They did not have pigs killed for them, did not have important gifts of food given in their name, and were not enjoined to observe special food taboos. They did not establish lifelong relations of initiation-mate and initiate-sponsor with others in the community. Unlike the young men, whether a given young woman would get dressed up in a red bird of paradise costume was decided only at the last minute by the young women themselves. In contrast, the costumes, buildup rituals, and gift giving for the young men had been orchestrated and carried out months ahead of time.

In a way, the inclusion of women as important but secondary actors paralleled other aspects of Gebusi life. If the initiation symbolized the height of Gebusi male culture, it ultimately seemed to extol women and the Gebusi as a whole. Spirituality, sexuality, materiality, kinship, friendship, and gender came together with apparent joy and happiness. Against all odds and impediments, against all sicknesses, deaths, and frustrations—and even gender domination—Gebusi somehow came together to celebrate a larger sense of collective good company. I had never seen or felt such social unity.

Anne-Sylvie

Gebusi's constant and conscious effort at proclaiming and exalting their camaraderie is an essential aspect of their sociopolitical system. This companionship spirit has been established and regularly fueled beyond what genealogical ties impose, and it finds its full and dizzying illustration in nocturnal feasts. Back when Bruce started his fieldwork, Gebusi men would gather for a feast or spirit séance once every 11 nights on average. Nowadays women are involved, too, and they all congregate to eat pork and sago and then drink "spark" (a mixture of yeast and sugar, probably deriving its name from the sparks created in the brain of the drinkers) by the quart. Sometimes a booming battery-powered sound system is thrown into the mix, injecting heavy doses of heavy metal or Bob Marley into the jungle.

Though initiations are no longer held, one major feast, a funeral commemoration or *ebeb buala*, was held in May 2016—a bit like an Irish wake or a New Orleans "second line" funeral, in which sadness and grieving can mix with humor and commemorative celebration. Early that morning, preparations started: a pig was killed, and tubers and sago were cut up and cooked; it was all hustle and bustle under heavy clouds. Luckily, we were spared from the rain; around midafternoon the skies cleared up, and people gathered to swell the ranks around the fire and peeling stations, chatting near the big open houses as bananas were slowly roasting. When the food was ready, dozens of bowls were lined up—anything people could eat out of was used, from dried palm leaves to cracked plastic plates and tin pots of all sizes. Each container would eventually receive an equal amount of rice, instant noodles, greens, tubers, sago, and pig meat, all the sacrosanct elements of any good feast, no matter the size of the family that would dip into it.

Then came the moment to cut up the pig—a moment both hoped for and dreaded, as the organizers of the feast force a few chosen individuals to ingest pure pork fat. The morsel is pushed into your throat but should be gracefully refused while being half accepted but not swallowed too fully, lest you fall ill. I conveniently hid behind my camera: "Hold off, my friend, I might damage my equipment!"

Swarms of kids played around, happily screaming at wild birds and climbing big trees as the sun gradually set and the golden light of the late afternoon hour gently caressed the tall grass. At dusk, the women and children were ousted by the men and went home to sleep. Around 3:00 a.m. I could still hear the men's laughter, which seemed to emanate from a nook in this remote pocket of the world, both so far removed yet and so close to everything I knew.

A pale dawn finally emerged from the clouds, and so did we; all the women of the village gathered around the site of the nocturnal festiv-

Food apportioned for giving it away at a Gasumi village feast, 2016.

ities, only to discover the pitiful drunken spectacle of their brothers, fathers, sons, and husbands. Half-asleep older men rested on the laps of younger ones, all haphazardly piled up—a sleepy head here, a half-naked torso there, slumping into each other, like dislocated puppets whose only signs of life were gushing out from their guts and spilling into the cracks of the floorboards. Some were awake enough to gently comfort the most intoxicated of the lot; others were futilely trying to stand up, slowly piecing their minds back together, trying to yell, pointing their fingers at fate. I took pictures to show the women, and in our shared laughter we regained a sense of female superiority that had been lost when we had been banned from the nightlong party. But seeing now that its participants had drowned in a coma, we were relieved as women to have been spared from it.

Men passed out from drinking at funeral feast (*ebeb buala*) in Gasumi Corners, May 2016.

Women from
Gasumi Cor-
ners observing
drunken men
in the after-
math of the
ebeb buala
funeral feast,
May 2016.

BROADER CONNECTIONS
Ritual Initiation and Life-Cycle Transitions

- As is in the case in many other societies, **initiation** among Gebusi is a rite of
  adulthood, a rite of status elevation, and a so-called life-crisis ritual by which
  young men and/or young women, become full adult members of society.

- In most societies, major celebrations express and integrate **core cultural values.**
  Rich with religious symbolism and cultural expression, Gebusi initiation brings
  together sexual, social, economic, and political dimensions of their society
  while affirming their cultural value of "good company" (*kogwayay*).

- Consistent with the transition stages of **rites of passage**, Gebusi initiation
  involves (1) preparatory rites and ceremonies that separate initiates as a group;
  (2) an "in-between" or **liminal** period of category transition, and (3) climactic
  rites that celebrate **social reaggregation and reintegration.**

- Ritual initiation into adulthood can be severe or brutal in some societies, but
  among Gebusi it is mild to moderate, with the temporary wearing of heavy
  bark wigs being the most difficult custom endured by male initiates.

- The red bird of paradise emerges as a core symbol or key symbol in Gebusi cere-
  monial life. As a **polysemic symbol**—a symbol with many meanings—the red
  bird of paradise is literally embodied on the men, and, ultimately, on the women.

- Gebusi initiation is consistent with the classic perspective of social scientist
  Émile Durkheim, who suggested that **religion** reflects and projects the social
  features of society into a spiritual realm. Among Gebusi, the spirits are believed

to have their own dances and their own initiation at the same time that Gebusi do. The symbolism of the spirit world, and especially the red bird of paradise spirit woman, is embodied on the initiates in their costuming.

- As well as being observers, Bruce and his then-wife were participants in the initiation through **gift giving**, and they became a kind of sponsor (*tor*) to the initiates.

- The final rite of the initiation revealed that the Gebusi celebration of fertility and adulthood encompassed women as well as men. Though women's gift giving and rites were not as elaborate as men's, the initiation symbolized and socially enacted the unity and integrity of Gebusi as a whole.

- In recent years, Gebusi continue to enjoy and orient to festive celebrations. These increasingly include alcoholic drinking by men, which continues and reinforces the previous polarization of ritual participation and experience between men and women.

Young people in Gasumi Corners, 1998. →

Part Two

Radical Change

Chapter 7

Time for Change
Sacred Decisions

I feel like a neophyte all over again. Though at best not humiliating, fieldwork is always a humbling experience, and in a good sort of way. Arrows barbed at anthropology cast its knowledge as imperialist, gained at the expense rather than for the benefit of other people. But the gawky interloper is usually cut well down to size by the time he or she gets beyond the confines of the hotels, the taxis, and the urban elite to the place in question. Human leveling is ethnography's strength.

— Field Notes, June 1998

Anne-Sylvie

Our body leaves its sensations behind as it leaves a place. It has the capacity to abandon a whole world to the land of residual memories—forgetting sounds, smells, and even the daily discomfort of heavy legs swelling in the hot hours. This same body is also the first to recollect and relive the past as all its dimensions reemerge. The "far-away," which for a while seemed impossible to reach, now comes close and overcomes me; the overload of the past becomes present again. Not only is there no escaping these sensations and emotions, they are doubled up by the past version of themselves. "Oh, I remember." I remember how I felt, and I feel it again. Proust's *Remembrance of Things Past* on steroids.

Bruce, 1998: Sixteen years is a long time for the Gebusi. So, too, it was for me and for cultural anthropology, between my first and second periods of Gebusi fieldwork. While a whole generation of Gebusi was getting older and producing children, I went from young adulthood to middle age in Atlanta. My son went from conception to high school. The world also changed: market economies, modern ideas, and nationalist development spread to the farthest nooks of the globe. Cultural anthropology changed as well. If my first fieldwork reflected anthropology's long-standing interest in distant societies, Gebusi now engaged my newer interest in change and transformation. Ethnography is as real and important as the lives it encounters, regardless of their context. For Gebusi, traditional interests in kinship, social organization, ritual, and exchange now broadened to include a full range of contemporary practices and institutions—markets, churches, schools, governments, nongovernmental organizations, and the mosaic of social and cultural influences that tie people to their nation, their region, and the larger world. To engage such developments, cultural anthropology confronts the full ambit of contemporary human culture, from the most remote to the most urban, cosmopolitan, and digital.

External changes had already come to the Gebusi during my first fieldwork: steel tools; trade goods such as cloth, salt, soap, and matches; pacification of the neighboring Bedamini; yearly government patrols; and the potential presence the Nomad police. Subtler changes also sprouted. Most Gebusi cut their hair short rather than tying it in dreadlocks. Some men had even sported carefully trimmed sideburns, reminiscent of Australian patrol officers. Yet there remained a dearth of major intrusions, and there was no missionization, wage labor, cash cropping, out-migration, mining, logging, or connection by road to other parts of the country.

For millennia, armed traders, state empires, and other wielders of power have crisscrossed the world; commerce has been global for five centuries. From the 19th through the 20th centuries, parts of New Guinea were variously owned and colonized by Germans, British, Dutch, Australians, and Indonesians. Though outside influences seemed minor among Gebusi when I first worked with them, by the time the 2000 millennium approached, I strongly suspected that these had intensified. And new intrusions typically bring troubling new inequities as well as opportunities, including unequal possession of money and goods, and domination by outsiders.

The author in a welcoming line of Gebusi men snapping fingers, 1980.

A Gebusi woman and man "welcome" uce and Anne-Sylvie to Gasumi Corners their arrival, 2017.

3. Yuway as a young man in festive dress, 1980.

4. Young boy with flowered headband at an initiation feast, 1998.

5. Young woman, Toym, dressed for a Gebusi feast, 1981.

6. Costumed man at Independence Day display, 1998.

raditional dancer at a curing ritual, 2008.

8. Bayi, Yokwa, and Hawi welcome Bruce and Anne-Sylvie to Gasumi Corners, 2016.

9. Sayu as a bachelor, 1998.

10. Didiga as a bachelor, 1998.

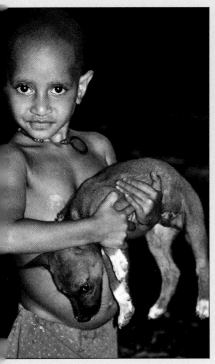

Dugam with her dog, 2008.

12. Dugam and Anne-Sylvie in festive costume, 2016.

Yamdaw (Luke) preaching at the Gasumi Catholic Church, 2008.

14. Halowa taking wrapped sago bundles for feast cooking, 2013.

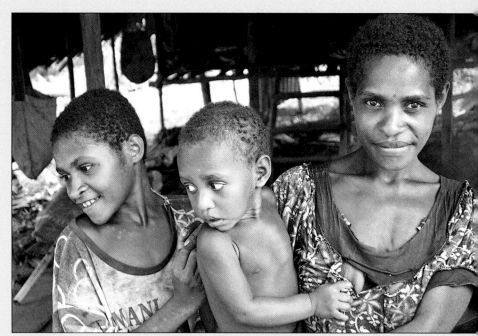

15. Delaw with children, 2013.

Mus, about 60 years old, carrying heavy net bags, 2013.

Gasumi villagers carrying Bruce's and Latham's trunk boxes from the Honinabi rip, 2013.

18. Rainforest morning at Gasumi Corners, 2013.

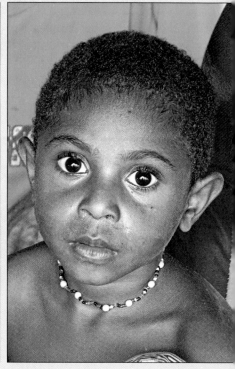

19. Gwabi, a Gebusi man, with only rags to wear, 2016.

20. A young girl of Gasumi Corners, 2016.

As almost no information had reached me from or about Gebusi, I remained in the dark. Among other things, had the gradual decline in homicide continued? Or had the continuing absence of Australian officers encouraged more killing, as had happened in other parts of Papua New Guinea?

Added to these uncertainties were those about myself. Before I had been a green mid-20s researcher, anthropologist on a shoestring, with little to lose and everything to prove. Youthful ignorance had given me blind faith in cultural understanding—crucial against the difficulties if not the impossibility of doing ethnography well in fact.

A decade and half later, the realism of hindsight made me more anxious. I was going back to people I knew and liked, but I knew how tough it was to live in the rainforest—and that my body was not as young as it had been before. Now a professor and author of several books, I was an established academic. Against this, new fieldwork would be humbling. Would my sense of being a successful anthropologist crumble like a house of cards? I was concerned as well about leaving my family, and how they would fare if something happened to me. I also had intellectual uncertainties. A middle-aged outlook can lack the openness of a younger mind. How would I square anticipated changes among Gebusi with my appreciation of their traditional culture? Anthropology crackles with debates between those who focus on global change and those who stress cultural continuity. Are societies more strongly influenced by long-standing values, or by new transformations?

Amid my doubts, I deeply needed to see what had happened to my Gebusi friends; this desire trumped other concerns. So I committed to go back to Gebusi after an absence of 16 years, just by myself. I told myself to take whatever I found at its own face value—to wipe my slate clean of expectations. After months of securing funds, navigating bureaucracy, obtaining visas, buying supplies, reviewing old field notes, and shedding tears of good-bye, I left for Papua New Guinea. After negotiating the national capital of Port Moresby and the provincial town of Kiunga, I finally chartered a single-engine Cessna to Nomad and landed with my supplies for a half-year of fieldwork with Gebusi on June 25, 1998. That night, I wrote the following:

> Tonight, this first evening back, I sit here with Sayu and Howe, who smile brightly as I type on this keyboard. We have just looked at the

screen saver, which has amazed them totally. I am caught in a time warp between the pidgin English called Tok Pisin, Gebusi language, heat, fatigue, and amazement.

First touchdown was a rush. Hawi was the airline agent who met me at the airstrip! He had a gaunt face and a receding hairline but was still strong and energetic. We hugged, shook hands, and snapped fingers about a dozen times. He told me he lives right at Nomad Station—and that he has three sons and a baby daughter! Then he had to attend to the paperwork of the flight. Turning around, I had the wonder of seeing age jump right before my eyes. One after another Gebusi whom I had known came up to greet me. The grown children were the most incredible. There was Sayu, our tiny little friend about whom we joked that we would adopt and bring back to the States. Now he is an adult, strong, handsome, and smart! He has already become my closest companion and helper among the younger men. He combines his father's quickness and his mother's intelligence, perceptiveness, and friendship—or at least so it seems on my first impression.

Most striking among my adult friends are their hollow faces, withered bodies, and wrinkled skin that I remember as smooth. But happiness in human connection transcends space and time. We embraced and snapped fingers mightily, including the women. Gazing into the eyes of those whom you know with fond memories from 16 years ago, and who suddenly live again in the present, is totally thrilling and completely unforgettable. In Gebusi legends, reunions and welcomes are so warm and numerous that people's hands are worn bare by snapping fingers heartily and repeatedly. Today, I allowed myself the hubris of feeling the same way. My middle fingers are really sore from the finger snapping that I could not keep myself from continuing even if I had wanted to stop. It is like on my wedding day, when the joy of the event caused an actual soreness of smile muscles that were so irrepressibly stretched as to turn anything in the world to their overpowering good feeling.

Amid the constant stream of visitors whom I did not want to stop, I somehow greeted everyone and found that virtually the entire generation of surviving Gebusi from Yibihilu now live in a "corner" of Nomad just 20 or 25 minutes' walk from Nomad Station. This is absolutely perfect, my ideal residential scenario! I should have easy access to the Nomad Station and its nationalizing influence while also being able to go with Gebusi back to the forest. Having stowed my things in the government house by 1:00 p.m., I couldn't resist the temptation to walk with my friends to their corner settlement and see for myself the lovely place where I will likely be living. It is all simply wonderful.

Good feelings notwithstanding, the day has been hot, and I have a mountain of decisions to make quickly. How many nights will I stay in this unpleasant little house at Nomad Station? Where will I live after that? How can I build on today's rush of positive feeling? How should I reestablish reciprocity with my Gebusi friends? How will I cook? How many boxes should I unpack? Where are the specific parcels of utensils, sleeping equipment, clothes, toiletries, and so on that I need for this first night? (As expected, there are no real stores at Nomad, so I am glad that I brought everything with me.) And yet, I simply must take time tonight to write the events of this astonishing day.

Within minutes, the Gebusi had again astounded me. And the descendants of Yibihilu now boasted a new flock of youngsters as well as children-become-adults. Within a few days, however, I found that few men my own age or older were still alive. Most of those whom I had known as adults had died, including Silap, Boyl, Swamin, Sialim, Sagawa, Tosi, Wasep, and Imba. Of the six young men we helped initiate, only three—Hawi, Doliay, and Yuway—were still living. I mourned the passing of friends even as I saw their personalities, amazingly, in their children, now pushing toward their own adulthood. In demographic terms, Gebusi were a new people and more numerous than before—up from 450 persons to about 615.

Change and turnover notwithstanding, and despite the heat and mosquitoes, it felt wonderful to be back. I was remembered fondly and welcomed joyously. Two children had been named after me in my absence. Once worn, the glove of friendship always seems to fit. Within a day of my arrival, Gwabi, who had been 12 years old but now had his own family, insisted that I live in the big thatched house he had just finished building beside his older home in Gasumi Corners. With this as my base of operations, I became quickly immersed in village life, going both to Nomad and to the forest, and rediscovering the joys and trials of fieldwork. I had worried about my ability to speak Gebusi after many years, but this came back faster than expected.

In short order, I found that the 122 descendants of Yibihilu and its sur-rounding hamlets had fashioned not just a new settlement but a new way of life. Now living on the outskirts of Nomad Station, they were just a short walk from its airstrip, school, churches, market, ball field, and government offices. No longer nestled in the full rainforest, their settlement was sand-wiched between cleared areas around Nomad Station and the primary tim-berland that Gebusi inhabited before. From Gasumi Corners, my friends could still hunt and forage deep in the forest, but their lives revolved increasingly around the activities and institutions of Nomad Station. This produced what might be called a new structure of feeling in Gebusi cul-ture. Against this new world, the social life of the rainforest, including our previous settlement at Yibihilu, was a fading horizon of the past.

Internally, the new community still retained its kinship connections, including via marriage and maternal ties as well as through clanship. But extended families and even nuclear families now lived separately in small individual houses scattered like islands in an archipelago across three hill-ocks and a stream. Strikingly, there was no longhouse—no central dwell-ing place where people gathered. More broadly, the traditional sense of good company—the togetherness, talk, and whooping/joking of Gebusi *kogwayay*—was reduced, especially among the men. But the lot of women, as we shall see, had significantly improved, at least in relative terms.

Materially, life was much as it had been before. Families had a few additional commodities—perhaps an extra knife, a larger metal pot, or a shovel. But the biggest visible change was clothing. Before, women were unashamed to walk about bare-breasted; now, they always covered them-selves, if only with a ripped blouse. Men invariably wore a shirt and shorts when they went to Nomad. Used clothes were intermittently flown in and sold at low prices at the station, and everyone wore them.

Along with new interests and activities, Gasumi Corners also had a new sense of time. In the relaxed world of the rainforest, rhythms of life had been languid and people could simply not be hurried. There had been little attempt to mark times of day, and there were no words for days of the week, months, or even seasons. We had easily lost track of days if we forgot to check mark them on our calendar. The Gebusi word for "tomorrow," *oil*, is the same as the word for "yesterday." The word for "the day after tomorrow," *bihar*, is the same as the one for "the day before yesterday," and "three days after today," *ehwar*, is the same as "three days before today."

Gebusi use the same word *owa* for both their grandparents and their grandchildren, and an adult man often called his own son "father" (*mam*). In the cycling of gardens and fallow land, a boy would ideally grow up to cultivate the lands and the trees of his father or grandfather. In short, time and life had rolled in a cultural circle. Even the male life force was physically recycled from one generation to the next. Things were ordained to repeat themselves rather than to change.

Now, however, days and even minutes were marked and measured. Everyone seemed to work by deadline to accomplish something that was different from, and hopefully better than, the past. I got a taste of this during my first Sunday. Sayu had said that church would begin when the sun rose above the trees. Such timing had always been as vague as the morning mist, and events invariably began late. I left early and thought I'd arrive before most others. But along the way, houses were curiously empty. When I got close by and heard hymn singing, I realized I was late. Late! The idea had been foreign to Gebusi. But the clock-watching pastor had rung the metal chime and I had missed its signal in the distance—while everyone else was on time!

Beyond Sunday church services, the new weekly schedule included classes for children at the Nomad school on weekdays, beginning promptly at 8:00 a.m. and lasting until 3:30 p.m. Mindful of time, children from Gasumi Corners left for school by 7:00 a.m.—and got home after 4:00 in the afternoon. Classes were divided into 16 timed periods, some as short as 15 minutes, with transitions marked by the ringing of the school bell.

For adults and especially women, Tuesdays and Fridays at 8:00–10:00 a.m. were market days. Weekend afternoons were carefully scheduled for rugby and soccer matches on the government ball field, particularly for men and boys, who arrived early so as not to miss their starting time. Games were refereed by timekeepers, who sounded a large horn to mark the end of the half and the end of the game. Though most Gebusi could not tell time, all the men seemed to want wristwatches—so they could appear to be acting based on knowledge of the hour.

If time for the Gebusi was increasingly marked and measured, its passage now reflected Gebusi hopes for—and failures of—progress and improvement. For schoolchildren, tests on Friday gauged what they had learned and accomplished that week. Unfortunately, few Gebusi children could finish elementary school, and none seemed slated for high school in

Kiunga. At the Nomad farmer's market, if food wasn't sold by noon, it had to be taken home or given away. In sports, Gebusi now kept score and played aggressively to win by the final horn. In short, the strivings and shortcomings of new activities were measured against a time line of hoped-for success and progress. Perhaps nowhere was this more evident, surprisingly, than in spirituality and religion.

Yuway's eyes simply sparkled. *"Koya, koya!"*—"Friend, friend!" We must have gazed at each other, snapped fingers, and joked heartily a dozen times. I had come to his house, just five-minute's walk from my own. Yuway had been my most helpful friend in 1980–1982, an all-around good person, and the tallest of the young men we had helped initiate. Shortly afterward, he had become a moon-eyed romantic with his fetching wife-to-be, Warbwi, and we had given him gifts for his marriage. That had been 17 years ago. Here he was again, in the flesh! It was so good to see him. Every few sentences, we smiled and clasped each other again, reassuring ourselves that our reunion was real. We quickly brought each other up to date. He was touched to hear that I now had a son who was full-grown and even taller than I. With subdued pride, he told me that he and Warbwi now had four children: an adolescent boy and girl plus two younger sons. I joked with him that he had been "busier" than I; we both laughed out loud.

As the minutes passed, word spread that we two senior men were having a good jokefest, and this attracted a score of spectators from surrounding houses. Good-natured as he was, I saw that Yuway was getting increasingly embarrassed by our traditional joking. Though I had taken our jests for granted, he started to suppress his grins. From the reactions of others, I sensed that old-time joking, though tolerated from me as a middle-aged man who knew the tradition, was both a spectacle and anachronistic, a bit out of place.

As if to punctuate this perception, Yuway finally told me with a smile that he was an SDA—a member of the Seventh Day Adventist Church. This was Nomad's most stringent Christian denomination. I was naturally intrigued, which led to a thoughtful discussion of Gebusi religious change. Yuway said that when he had arrived Gasumi Corners from Yibihilu, some 10 years before, he had, like most, joined the Catholic Church. The pastor had been welcoming of Gebusi and had even visited their settlements in the bush. When they moved their settlement, villagers relocated it close to the Catholic Church, thinking this would be a strong focus for establishing their new lives. As they got used to singing in church, Yuway said, they sang less with their own spirit mediums. Swamin, their village shaman, started going to church himself and then stopped singing traditional séances altogether. So, too, the other spirit mediums found themselves part of a community that was now singing to a new spirit, to a new God, and stopped their traditional spirit singing. When the Gebusi go to church, they literally, "go to sing" (*gio dula*). Within a few years, the spirit séances that had galvanized Gebusi social life had become history, a thing of the past.

Without spirit mediums, as Yuway explained, people in Gasumi Corners had no real way to contact their traditional spirits; this path of connection had been "cut" (*gisaym-da*). No longer could they joke with the spirits, ask their advice about sickness or sorcery, or enlist their opinions or support for fish poisoning, hunting, or the planning of feasts and rituals. Incredibly, the traditional world of Gebusi spirits had withered away. And with their departure, Gebusi social life also changed. No longer was male camaraderie and its sexual joking central. Those in Gasumi Corners sang to their new God not in the dead of night but in the brightness of morning, not with humor but with solemnity, not in lively spiritual conversation but in subservient listening. Apparently, the preacher and his God had simply become more powerful and important than the traditional spirits. Christianity had the prestige and wonder of coming from afar, of promising wealth, success, and accomplishment in a wider world. The Catholic lay pastor who lived near Gasumi Corners was literate and well educated. He wore nice clothes, had a house fully stocked with supplies and a radio, and flew back and forth to Kiunga. He seemed bent on presenting his way of life and his God as models for Gebusi to follow. They willingly obliged.

Yuway told me that he himself had been one of Gasumi's lay Catholic leaders from 1992 to 1995. (I pinched myself to note how Gebusi now kept track of years.) But after that, he felt more distant from the church.

"Why did you join the Seventh Day Adventists?" I asked.

"Well, the Catholic Church is kind of 'soft'; I wanted a church that was 'hard.'"

"How's that?" By this point, I was remembering that the Gebusi word for "hard" (*gawf*) also means "strong," "righteous," "angry," and "potentially violent"—as well as "difficult," "masculine," and "virile."

"If you are really worshipping God, it shouldn't be a small thing. It should be a big thing. You should really work hard to please God. And you have to be ready by Judgment Day. The Catholics make you work only a little hard. They let people keep lots of customs that God doesn't like—like dancing and smoking tobacco. The SDA Church knows that God doesn't like these and that they are wrong. They make their religion really hard by telling us we can't eat certain things that we like. They make us work a lot in the churchyard, and they make us come for Bible learning as well as their long service on Saturday morning. They have pictures that show just what will happen if you sin—you will burn in hell. With SDA, I know I am really a Christian and that I can go to heaven."

I paused to collect my thoughts. Yuway and my other friends had been so spiritually "Gebusi" before. But his answer revealed the attraction as well as the onus of a fundamental Christian faith. His remarks also underscored the distinction between local churches. Catholicism was taken as the "easiest" faith because it had the fewest restrictions. As long as Catholics attended church, worshipped God, avoided fighting, and didn't drink too much kava—their lightly intoxicating root drink (alcohol was not yet generally available), they could be baptized as full Christians by a visiting priest or bishop.

In many world religions—including Islam, Hinduism, and Judaism, as well as various forms of Christianity—fundamentalism has been on the rise in recent years. In Nomad Sub-District, including at Gasumi Corners, Christian churches were developed and run by fundamentalist Papua New Guineans who came to proselytize the area from other parts of the country. To me, all the sects had a fundamentalist air, though, as Yuway noted, some were perceived as "harder" than others.

In Gasumi Corners, 59% attended the Catholic Church and 22% the Evangelical Church of Papua New Guinea. Beyond the Catholics' strictures, Evangelicals placed a strong taboo against smoking tobacco and restricted participation in traditional rituals. SDA rules were even stricter. In fact, Yuway's family was the only one in Gasumi Corners that joined the SDA Church. Adding to bans on smoking, drinking, dancing, and observing traditional rituals, SDAs prohibited the eating of pork as well as smooth-skinned

Nomad Evangelical Church posters, 1998. [left] Enlightened Heart of Man. Inside a golden heart, the fire of the Lord is burning bright; the Bible is open to the "Good News"; the eye and mouth are open to God and the forces of tradition—such as the red bird-of-paradise and the devil—are extruded outside. [right] Death of a Sinner. The beer bottle, betel nut gourd, cards, and chest of traditional wealth indicate the dying man has been a heathen. Tortured by devils, his soul descends to the burning fires of hell.

fish. This was significant since eating pigs and fish remained prime features of major feasts. SDAs also prohibited any work or gardening on Saturday—their Sabbath, during which church services and Bible study filled most of the day. In principle, "frivolous" entertainment like playing ball, going to the disco, or attending traditional feasts was condemned as irreligious.

Because I knew Yuway to be a caring person, I wondered how his personal beliefs meshed with SDAs' reputation for intolerance. He said with all earnestness that he had no anger against those who went to other churches or even those who went to none at all—which included a few in Gasumi Corners. I decided to push him a little: "If someone who is a good person is Catholic or Evangelical, do you think he or she can still go to heaven?"

Yuway thought for a minute, but not too long: "I don't know. Only God knows these things. But for me, I think that someone who is good inside can go to heaven, and it shouldn't matter if they go to one church or another."

"What if they don't go to any church at all?"

"Well, if they are given the chance to believe in Father God but still don't do it, it might be hard for God to see them as a good person and let them into heaven. But it's not for me to say."

I was impressed with his answer. It was then that I remembered the arrows that Yuway had been fashioning when I had come up to greet him. Now they were lying next to him, elaborately carved and ready for painting with bright-red ochre.

"Those are really nice arrows. Aren't they the kind used to sponsor a young man at an initiation?"

"Yes, I'm sponsoring my clan nephew at Taylmi a month or two from now."

"Can you still do that and be an SDA?"

"Well, I myself won't get baptized into SDA until after the initiation. It will be the last time for me to eat pork. And if I go just to see the initiation and not because I believe in its spirits, it's okay."

As I mulled over this last response, the sky opened up as if by divine intervention; suddenly, rain came pelting down. Realizing that it was almost dark—and that the supper fire at my house had yet to be started—I smiled and snapped fingers with Yuway quickly before whooping loudly as I raced up the trail. I was thoroughly drenched by the time I reached home.

Reflecting that evening on the day's events, I was struck how Yuway's remarks resonated with what I was finding from Gebusi who were Catholics or Evangelicals. All three local churches featured a fierce God of fire and brimstone, threatening hell and demanding compliance. All held that Judgment Day could come any time—and that repenting now was key to salvation. All three churches were "hard," though some were "harder" than others. How was it that my friends belonged to these different churches, each of which drew additional members from other diverse communities? While visiting with Yuway that afternoon, his two married brothers, Keda and Halowa, had shown up. It turned out that Keda was a lay leader in the Catholic Church. Halowa, by contrast, was an Evangelical. Each of the three brothers thus belonged to a different church. I found increasingly that Yuway had been right: Gebusi accepted each other's right to choose the sect that suited him best. "Him" is significant here, because wives generally attended the church chosen by their husbands. If Christianity saved the soul of the individual rather than the group, so, too, each individual man, at least, could choose his church—and whether to believe in God at all. The Gebusi world of spiritual choices and consequences was no longer governed so strongly by kinship or clanship, but increasingly by a man's choice.

The second thing that struck me was Yuway's plan to give his nephew initiation arrows while himself completing the arduous requirements for SDA baptism. How was this possible? Was Yuway hypocritical? Or was this a classic case of "syncretism," in which two religions blend together? Neither possibility seemed likely to me; I suspected that something else was at issue. It turned out that Gebusi distinguish between witnessing a traditional ritual and actually hosting or performing in one. At a remote settlement like Taylmi—the last big Gebusi village that had not yet gone Christian—one could attend an initiation the same way that one might watch an action video without being a violent or dangerous person; it is viewed as an entertaining drama rather than reflecting one's own lifestyle. Indeed, not succumbing to "pagan ways" while witnessing them could itself be a kind of Christian commitment.

It has often been noted that redemption in Christianity is punctuated by trials and temptations. Preachers in Nomad repeatedly emphasized the dangers of "backsliding" into traditional sin and vice. Though Gebusi willingly submitted themselves to the harangues of the pastor, it was their deviation from Christian thoughts or interests that spurred their desire for atonement—the pang of conscience that begs for moral cleansing. Exposure to and ambivalence about traditional customs was integral to the jawboning process of Gebusi conversion to Christianity. Hopes of salvation seemed directly linked to threats of sin, as if neither could do without the other.

My field entry concerning Yuway's conversion concluded as follows:

> Now I can see, at least dimly, Yuway's attraction to this church. It is severe; it stresses the need to be hard and disciplined for God. This is the modern path of dignified compliance in and around Nomad Station as well as a path for everlasting life. It measures the present not against a happy standard of current success but against trials, and rewards, that were infinitely greater for Jesus. These give reward only later, in the future.

Yuway's choice foregrounds the path that Gebusi were increasingly taking not only in church but also at school, in the market, and even on the ball field: to meet deadlines in the present, wait patiently, and hope for deferred success. All these contexts encouraged an ethic of disciplined action, of being on time and meeting deadlines, and of accepting the authority of outsiders.

The most dramatic case of religious transformation involved Doliay, the youngest and smallest of the six young men whom we had helped initiate. Several years after my first fieldwork, Doliay married Boyl, Sayu's widowed mother. However, Boyl died shortly thereafter. At the death inquest, Doliay confronted the person accused of causing her death through sorcery—a man named Basowey. Doliay told me that his anger toward Basowey had completely taken over his thoughts and actions. In the days and weeks after the funeral, his revenge took on a surgical and almost Zen-like focus. Though Basowey was almost a foot taller than he, Doliay sought him out and confronted him alone in the forest. He dodged Basowey's arrows and split his head with a bush knife. Then he cut off Basowey's head and left it next to his body in the forest. He then went straight to the Catholic compound, told the pastor what he had done, handed over his beheading bush knife, and turned himself in to the Nomad police.

Doliay's killing of Basowey was a watershed. He was sentenced to six years in prison in the national capital city of Port Moresby. No Gebusi had ever traveled so far, but Doliay never saw the city. While in prison, he became exceptionally self-disciplined. He learned to speak Tok Pisin, converted to Christianity, became a model prisoner, and even became head cook for the warden, who entrusted him with the key to the prison's entire storehouse of food. Doliay proudly kept the letter of reference that the warden gave him upon his release. He recalled his jailers with great affection, still wore the shirt that one of them gave him, and named his first son, Willy, after his prison guard friend.

Returning to Gasumi Corners, Doliay became something of an ideal Christian. Unlike those who hung around the pastor's compound in hopes of wheedling a favor or gaining a benefit, Doliay worked for the church with

Doliay as an initiate in yellow-striped costume, 1981.

Doliay, a stalwart member of the Catholic Church, 1998.

personal commitment. He told me he waited for baptism until returning to Nomad because he wanted to be sure—really sure—that his bad ways were gone, that he felt no more hate in his heart. He felt grateful that God could forgive even as great a sin as his killing of Basowey. He said he would wait with a Christian heart until Judgment Day. I asked Doliay if he wouldn't be tempted to kill another person for sorcery, especially if his beloved son Willy were to die of sickness. His answer was immediate: "No. No way."

"Why not?"

"It's not for me to take revenge. That's something for the 'Big Fellow' [God] to decide. Besides, the people of Gasumi Corners don't practice sorcery anymore. Even if they wanted to, they would be too scared of what I did to Basowey to send sorcery again. If my son died, it wouldn't be from sorcery!"

Against traditional beliefs, Doliay's view was revolutionary. Before, Gebusi had attributed all fatal illnesses to sorcery. And a man's demand for revenge was greatest when a member of his own family died from sickness.

While Doliay had been in prison, his community had also changed. Incited by the pastors, villagers redoubled their rejection of violence against suspected sorcerers. The penalty Doliay had been forced to pay—years in prison, away from all kin—intensified others' reluctance of to follow in his footsteps. Basowey's killing became famous as the last sorcery execution, the end of an era. And in its wake, conversion to Christianity swelled rather than diminished. Since then, as far as I know, no Gebusi has ever been killed as a sorcerer—or for any other reason. This is quite amazing: a society with one of the highest rates of homicide ever known has seen it drop to nothing and stay at zero. I confirmed this by cross-checking the circumstances of each death in the extended community. To me, this underscores the degree to which human violence is not ingrained or inevitable, but strongly influenced by attitudes and beliefs. And yet, the Gebusi belief in sorcery had been so firm, and their desire to seek vengeance so strong, that I remained skeptical of this good-news story.

I had conflicting views about Gebusi Christianity. On one hand, much of value in Gebusi culture had been lost. The vibrant wonder of traditional beliefs had faded. The poetry, symbolism, and musical awe of their spirit world were almost dead. In their place was a demanding new religion, trumpeted from elsewhere. In the history of colonialism and postcolonialism, including in the global spread of Christianity, pressured or forced conversion has worked hand in hand with powerful forms of social, economic, and political domination. Though Gebusi were thankfully spared coercive intimidation, they nonetheless became passive recipients of outsiders' spiritual as well as political supervision.

On the other hand, Gebusi's Christian way of life had helped reduce their extraordinary rate of violence, indeed, dropping it to zero. Social life was more peaceful than before. Men, women, and even children could walk to Nomad or the nearby forest without fear of attack. Though the great camaraderie of earlier days was gone, so, too, was the threat of lethal violence. Life was tamer in many ways.

What about the experiences of Gebusi women? Previously, they had enjoyed the energy and splendor of the spirit world, but from the sidelines. Now, however, women were Christian along with men. The responsibility and the reward of being Christian—of repenting sins and gaining salvation—was individual for both sexes. In the church itself, pews were divided evenly, with women on the left side and men on the right. At the

Catholic services, men and women attended in roughly equal numbers, but at SDA and Evangelical services, a decided majority were women. Yet the church pastors and primary lay leaders in the community were invariably men. And the authority of "Papa God," as he was called, was both stronger and more patriarchal than that of traditional Gebusi male or female spirits. Sporadically, but notably, men in Gasumi Corners would sometimes echo the tone of the preachers or government officials, adopting a lecturing and authoritative tone in their own community.

Adding to my conflicted feelings about Christianity was another uncertainty: to what extent were the Gebusi's previous beliefs really dead? If only vestigially, the Gebusi still worried about sorcery. In many parts of Melanesia—and in parts of Africa, Asia, Latin America, and even Western countries—belief in sorcery or magic has persisted or reasserted itself over time. Such beliefs have sometimes melded with Christianity or world religions such as Islam, Buddhism, and Hinduism. In significant areas of Melanesia and Africa, sorcery beliefs play a major role in contemporary disputes and rivalries, including between political leaders. If these customs can continue in modern forms, couldn't Gebusi beliefs come back in new ways?

No matter what happens, however, and even if Christianity is later rejected or disavowed, its influence will have a significant legacy. The hands of time cannot be turned back.

How does the lingering legacy of sorcery beliefs and practices in the Nomad area look to the Catholic Church? And what can they do about it?

Anne-Sylvie

It was Brother Greg who confirmed that the story of Powa's execution was true: a Bedamini man was tortured and killed by other Bedamini, and another executioner was being hunted down but had escaped. The pastor had come in person to Gasumi to confirm this. Brother Greg comes from Port Moresby; he got around a lot in the country before entering the seminary a few years ago, and he found himself assigned to the Catholic mission in Nomad about a year before our own arrival.

In the story of Gebusi settlement, the arrival of the church federated formerly dispersed hamlets and brought them closer to this new center, and closer maybe to this God. Since the mid-1980s, this mission has been the one reliable source of work and income for the locals. More than saving souls, the place is efficient in saving stomachs, as few people regularly go to church, but they never miss a big parish feast. The Catholic mission is made up of various permanent structures, all nicely equipped (there is even a fridge—my absolute dream when the rainforest drips down my back). Electricity is supplied by a diesel generator. It has other nice oddities in the middle of the jungle, like a water tank, a rice miller, an outboard motor for a dingy (much quicker and more convenient than our slow canoes), as well as a tractor, not so much to mow the lawn (there is no blade) but to transport heavy cargo to and back from the airstrip.

Father Andrew, the head pastor who serves the Catholic missions in this area, is nominally present at the Gasumi mission. He has always maintained an appropriate distance from his parishioners— his impressive size, perfectly clear Tok Pisin, and impeccable white priestly frock command respect, at least as much as the infrequency with which he is seen. When he does appear, he is freshly shaven. Brother Greg, on the other hand, has a big Christlike beard, walks around the jungle in flip-flops, knows everyone by their names, and quickly acquired a few gift-exchange names. He goes fishing with the men, never says no to a patrol to a faraway village or to a hunting expedition, caught malaria several times, and always comes out smiling. He has never believed that Gebusi have in fact stopped killing each other. He just thinks they are not telling the anthropologist.

Beyond his own assertions of evil and sin, Brother Greg grasped the importance of approaching things from the local perspective and in locals' own terms, always believing in the mix that Christianity made its way through people's representations and practices. (God asked people to renounce practicing sorcery but not to renounce believing in it or fighting against it.) When Powa was executed (see chapter 4), Brother Greg thought that not intervening and not taking an official stance would be tacitly condoning this killing. He also wanted to protect Powa's three female kin who were thought to be at risk of attack and, potentially, execution as well.

After talking matters over with our friends and deciding that intervention was too risky, we went to check in with Brother Greg for the latest news. He did not beat about the bush. "I'm going, that's all. I came here ready to die." His round face looked serene under the flicker-

Brother Greg at the Gasumi
St. Paul Catholic Church, May 2016.

ing neon light of the veranda; thousands of tiny bugs were falling into
my hair as it got darker outside. I had difficulty stringing two thoughts
together, especially as the stakes suddenly got so huge. Of course, we
ourselves wanted to go to Powa's village to investigate as well. But what
was the strategy? Brother Greg pictured himself storming in, the mirac-
ulous saviour, sure of himself and of his right to descend on people in
the village. He would rescue the women also suspected of sorcery and
take them with him. But did he think people there would let him do
that? And how could three weakened, scared ladies, follow him?

It dawned on us that he had not thought it through one bit, probably assuming the waters, or the rainforest, would open up in front of
him. We tried to reason with him: let's say you get there; you will at
least have to negotiate—listen to their version of the story, show understanding. You'll need to "speak their language," abide by their social
rules—share bananas and tobacco first—to ensure they will not attack
you. Diplomacy 101. He systematically refused what he saw as bowing
and scraping. Which it was, admittedly, but like anywhere else, various
forms of "further ado" exist for a reason. But he thought those tactics
would only give the aggressors more time to get rid of their prisoners.

At first I thought his staunch determination was beautiful; from
his stature emanated the admirable nobility of sacrifice. Then I felt
irritated by his blind stubbornness, by this obsession to see his goal
without crafting a clever way of reaching it. This was not a movie, not
a parable; the situation would undoubtedly be chaotic and confusing.
Getting there without a semblance of a plan was very risky.

"This is suicide!" Bruce nailed it. Brother Greg was representing himself as a martyr and possibly already relished the thought of dying as such. He was not trying to convince us to come with him but would not budge from his trajectory. He was no longer listening to us, already gone as he was on his cloud of salvation, sustained by his stainless faith. I was thinking that his vainglory would quickly dissolve under the Papuan sun, as blood would gush out of his open skull, coloring the clayey soil of a remote hamlet. And then what? The death of a Catholic priest linked to a sorcery case would create a bit of a stir in town. As for the two whites involved in the affair, better not to think about that impact. I would just like to still be alive to tell the story.

Within three days, Brother Greg had gone and come back from the village where the execution had taken place. Nothing was resolved, but at least he had not died. Bruce, on his way to the village with a small group of men, and Brother Greg, on his way from the village, crossed paths, but different ones, and did not bump into each other (did I mention the jungle is not a one-way street?). Thus when Brother Greg came back, Bruce was long gone (see chapter 4).

Brother Greg delivered a very unsettling sermon that Sunday, inviting the locals to let go of their anger, to abandon their desire for revenge, and to trust the Papuan justice system for the rest. There was no appeal to Christian values in his exhortation to not kill, but, rather, an evocation of the very real risks people would face by murdering or attempting to murder a "sorcerer" on the loose. He anchored his peroration in the indefinite cycle of violence and revenge that this second crime would perpetuate. He mentioned the children of Gasumi Corners who would be turned into orphans if their parents were spirited off to prison for murdering a suspected sorcerer.

That afternoon, during the usual ball games where lots of people were gathered, Brother Greg and I sat under a large tree by the soccer field. He confided in me: he had thought he was going to die there. When he got to the village, an armed man pointed an arrow at him. They looked at each other, in the infinite seconds that populate such an intense couple of minutes. Then by virtue of one of those miracles we sometimes witness in Papua New Guinea, the most acute aggressiveness turned into the most intense demonstration of brotherhood: the two men hugged, and no doubt they would now be for each other *brata long laif,* "brothers forever."

Brother Greg had been able to assure himself that the three women were alive and well, and even asked them if they wished to leave with him. They told him that they were happy and wished to stay where they were—as they had also told Bruce, who was encouraged by them to take photos of their contented state. Brother Greg was then led into the longhouse to share bananas (not such a daft idea after all, it seems!). His hosts served him a story that largely deviated from everything that preceded it: it was a tragic accident, really; we only wanted to interrogate old Powa and his son Suwop, but the former was fragile and suffocated on his tree while were gone having a smoke. No, we were not accusing him of sorcery at all, but of direct homicide—armed with a machete—on his son-in-law whose land he wanted to appropriate. Suwop, who escaped, was his accomplice. We just wanted them to face a court of justice, nothing else, but we were suspicious of the authorities in the region. Apparently the villagers in Powa's village were now furious at Bayi for enacting this terrifying scene and spreading the idea in Gasumi Corners that they were a bunch of barbarians. "If he comes back, we'll do to him exactly what he described!"

This amused Brother Greg a lot.

Then Bruce came home. Brother Greg asserted that people no longer confided in the anthropologist. Given all the Bruce discovered and carefully documented, we could have quipped that, evidently, they confided even less so in the clergyman.

Woman—visited separately by Bruce and Brother Greg—thought by Christian outsiders to be fearing retribution as a sorcery suspect, Tigar Miaym, 2016.

Update: If the arrow of change has not been entirely reversed for Gebusi, its path of "modern" development has surely not been as direct as it appeared in the late 1990s. Since then, the dominant strength of Christian presence among Gebusi, though far from gone, has been greatly tempered by the weathering of time. The Catholic Church at Gasumi Corners still functions, but with much less energy and enthusiasm than before. Some of the other churches are moribund or struggling, and the Seventh Day Adventists attract no one from Gasumi Corners. Even Yuway gave up his connection with them within a few years.

More generally, the hopes and expectations of Gebusi progress—spiritually, economically, and in education and national development—have been greatly reduced if not dashed since the late 1990s. These changes are described in part three of this book, but the larger point here is that change in a modern world is not a one-way street much less an arrow of consistent progress. Twists, detours, and U-turns are invariable, as we know full well from the economic retrenchments in our own and other Western countries. This does not mean desire and aspiration for progress are extinguished, including among Gebusi. Rather it means that their intended path is checkered, convoluted, and sometimes reversed. So, too, this does not indicate that "development" is irrelevant or that changes, such as those embraced by Gebusi in the late 1990s, are without impact. The patterns of the deeper past can never be fully brought back. But neither are they supplanted as completely as it often seems during periods flush with dynamic change. This is indicated dramatically by Anne-Sylvie's recounting of the story of Brother Greg's involvement following the Bedamini execution of Powa as a sorcerer in 2016.

Gebusi did change remarkably during the 1990s, moving their village, associating with Nomad Station, and embracing locally modern ways of life as much as they possibly could. Among other things, shamanism, traditional spiritualism, and sorcery violence have never come back among Gebusi—and their homicide rate remains wonderfully at zero, notwithstanding developments to the contrary on their border. In the mix, they have been changed and influenced by Christianity. But they are to a much greater extent now ambivalent in relation to the external Christian church. The lay church leaders are still men, but from Gasumi Corners itself, women continue to benefit from greater spiritual participation and inclusion. In the mix, no Gebusi now seems to want, or to care about, having a wristwatch or keeping track of the hours of the day. In all, Gebusi's awareness and ability to manage outside influences and values, and their ability to combine these with the legacy of their own orientations, is now much greater, and more nuanced, than it was in the late 1990s.

BROADER CONNECTIONS
Sociocultural and Religious Change

- **Cultural change** is as old as humanity but it has intensified with globalization during the past 500 years and especially since the latter part of the 20th century.

- Like many people in remote areas, Gebusi's cultural change has often included armed **colonial intrusion** against local peoples (such as the Bedamini), the introduction of Western goods and clothing, and Christianity.

- Like many peoples globally, the move of Gebusi from Yibihilu to Nomad Station led them to experience modern changes such as schooling, a cash market, and adopting a national or world religion such as Christianity.

- **Cultural loss** is common among many peoples. For Gebusi, this has included a decline of longhouse living and the loss of shamanism, of major sorcery inquests or accusations, and of intense emphasis on *kogwayay* or "good company."

- Becoming modern often brings heightened desire for **material progress**. A concern with temporal progress was also evident among Gebusi, especially those who believed strongly in Christianity.

- Modern developments are often associated with increasing intrusion by external authority figures. Among Gebusi, these included church leaders, government officials, police, and, in some ways, the ultimate power of "Papa God."

- Modern development can also induce selected positive changes. Among Gebusi at Gasumi Corners, this has included a striking reduction of the rate of killing to zero since 1989.

- Many peoples develop resilient or resistant forms of local **expressive culture**. Among Gebusi, these include the continuation of feasts and celebrations, including sometimes in relation to the local Catholic Church.

- When a cultural anthropologist returns to the field, as happened to Bruce and also Anne-Sylvie, his or her connections to local people often expand and become enriched.

- **Sociocultural change** is not a consistent process or a one-way street. Among Gebusi, recent changes have reduced the impact of Christianity and external authorities, though their earlier impact continues to have some lasting influence.

Chapter 8

Pennies and Peanuts, Hopes of Success

Bosap was not happy. It was 1998. The market was winding down, but her piles of bananas and sweet potatoes still lay primped for sale, like wall-flowers that everyone saw but nobody wanted. The other women were also peeved; their produce was still competing with Bosap's. Trying to make light of things—and collect more information—I tried to view her glass as half full: "You sold at least a little, right? Maybe two or three sales at 10 cents each?" Bad questions, bad timing. Bosap's normally congenial fea-tures, already sober, flashed to a scowl. "Not interested," she said, turning away. She had sold nothing.

So, too, in her life, Bosap had been passed over, though she usually took it all in stride. She had laughingly said when I talked to her before, "No man wanted to marry me. But then, I didn't want to marry any of them, either!" Among Gebusi, Bosap had the rare distinction of becoming an older woman, now in her mid-50s, without ever having married. When she had been in her 30s, this hadn't stopped her from having a sexual affair with a young initiate. Her pregnancy had created a scandal, but she had carried on with determination. She didn't marry her young lover or any of his older clan-mates (who could have claimed the child and taken Bosap as a second wife). Instead, she raised Kuma herself with the help of her own kin. The pride of her life, Kuma became a strong and decent young man who was now himself almost ready to be married. Over the years I had known her, Bosap had maintained her pleasant disposition as well as the conviction to go her own way. Her good-spiritedness was confirmed by the fact that, even as an "old woman," she had never been suspected of sorcery.

Given this, I was caught off guard by her response to me at the market. Bad sales were a touchy personal issue, and there were few buyers—mostly government officers and their wives from Nomad Station. Nevertheless, women from Gasumi Corners and elsewhere continued to haul their best produce to market in hopes of selling it. At dawn on Tuesdays and Fridays, they packed their foodstuffs in cavernous net bags and lugged them along the muddy path to the Nomad market. Even on a "good day," many women went home loaded down with the same food they had brought. And prices were low. For the equivalent of 60 cents, one could buy a large bunch of ripe bananas, a pile of shelled Tahitian chestnuts, and a bundle of cooked bamboo shoots. Even at that, few people aside from government workers and pastors had money to spend, and their own wages were small and undependably paid. But local women kept bringing food to market, twice each week. At least their activities gave them a small place in a cash economy.

Wanting to understand this, I tried to ferret out just how much food the women sold, how much they took back or gave away, and how much they earned. As my encounter with Bosap taught me, however, this was tricky. Women hardly wanted to disclose their many failures and even

Women from Gasumi Corners selling food at the Nomad market, 1998.

their few successes—for fear of jealousy. Only a few of them could actually count the combined value of the coins they received, and they shoved their proceeds quickly into tightly wadded bundles. When transactions did occur, they were typically shielded from view; a buyer would have exact change ready, saunter by the table, and quickly sweep the food into a net back as he handed over coins and walked away. Prices were standard for each pile of food, so there was no need to bargain or, in many cases, to talk at all.

In typical fieldwork fashion, I discovered this norm by badly breaking it. It was great to see such good and diverse food for sale, and at my first market, I decided to buy some myself. I went to a woman selling fresh bamboo shoots and found after pawing through my pockets that my smallest currency was a 2-kina bill. As I handed this to her across the table, I could see the color drain from her face. Though worth only one US dollar, the bill was 10 times the price of the shoots I was buying. The poor woman had neither the arithmetic nor the coins to make change. So she was forced to initiate a confusing chain of inquiries that rippled in domino effect through all those around her. Ten-cent loans and other transfers of coins ricocheted awkwardly through the crowd. After several long and painful minutes, my requisite 90 cents in change was dutifully amassed and counted out for me, as everyone looked on. By this time, I really just wanted to let the unfortunate women simply keep all the change. But two things prevented me. First, I would be badly undermining the standards of the market, which were based on a standard and fixed price for each pile of food. And second, the transaction would advertise to scores of people my ability and intent to pay a 900% premium for all the food that I wanted to buy! So I smiled gamely and apologized pleasantly, trying not to call yet more attention to my gaffe.

How much is a dime worth at a place like Nomad? Cultural meanings, rules, and assumptions—whole worlds of understanding—can underlie the smallest of material transactions. In the United States, I walk into a store and don't think twice about buying items from a stranger while other people may see my cost tally on the checkout screen, money given, and, especially, cash given back. This presumes a whole set of market assumptions that Gebusi and their neighbors were beginning to engage. But—and this is the more important point—Gebusi men and women were more rather than less motivated to pursue market transactions even though, and in some ways for the very reason that, their knowledge and confidence were undeveloped. Notwithstanding embarrassment, the woman I bought produce from had earned not just my 10 cents but the prestige of selling to an outsider who had money. Of all the bamboo shoot piles, I had chosen hers. She and her kin now owned a 2-kina bill received very publicly. This conveyed value, as I judged from the palaver as I walked away. If I had unwittingly trampled on local etiquette, I had also unwittingly reinforced the idea that monetary exchange is public, impersonal, and prestigious.

Being either a good or a bad ethnographer (sometimes it is hard to know which), I became increasingly interested in the larger pattern of market transactions. Like the churches, the Nomad school, and the sports league, the Nomad market is an interethnic affair that attracts people from various sides or "corners" of Nomad, each of which has its own ethnic or tribal character. Women from Gasumi Corners formed only a small fraction of those at the interethnic market, but because they were from my own community, I kept them as my focus.

The first and easiest thing to discern was that most sellers were, in fact, women. Counting the sellers from Gasumi Corners on 25 different market days, I found that more than 91% (285 of 313) were female. Some men and boys also came to market, but they seldom sold anything and tended to stay on the periphery. All the women from Gasumi Corners participated, gathering their best foodstuffs and bringing them to market on average once every 10 days. In all, the market was the prime place for village women to conduct business—and be modern. Women also went to church, of course. And girls had become students along with boys at the Nomad Community School. Only at the market, however, were women the central focus of attention. Though they tended to be quiet in public, women at the market visited casually with female kin and relatives, including those from other communities.

How much money did women actually make? I couldn't easily ask them, but I found that I could count the piles of food they initially placed on the selling tables and then determine how many of these were later sold. Women who were lucky enough to have sold several items were willing to clarify, if I was unsure, how many were purchased. During my 25 market days of documentation, Gebusi women sold less than half the food that they brought to the market; the rest was carried back home or given away. A woman's average earning per market day was just 20 cents—for

Danksop
attempting to
sell pineapples and
sweet potatoes at
the Nomad
market, 1998.

selling food weighing several pounds or more. More than 20% of women who brought food to market on a given day sold nothing at all.

The challenge of the women's enterprise was underscored by the inflated price of things that could at that time be bought at the several tiny home-front stores that Nomad had in 1998. Benchmark goods were two-pound bags of rice and 12-ounce tins of low-grade fish. Each of these cost the equivalent of US $1.50. As such, an average woman's market sales from almost an entire month were wiped out by buying a single small bag of rice or a single tin of fish. Comparing the nutritional value of these against the many hours and calories required to raise local food and haul it to market, the energy cost of women's marketing was obviously "irrational"; why would anyone put such time and effort into an often fruitless enterprise? This question grew more poignant as I saw women from Gasumi Corners continually lugging food to market and waiting aimlessly to sell it.

The answer to my question was, in a word, culture. As we ourselves know, there is much more to a purchase—and more to the work that pays for it—than the trade-off between dollars spent and functional use. Why do we prefer a Jaguar to a Ford, Godiva chocolate to Hershey's, or a ring of gold to one of tin? Similarly, why do Gebusi prefer a small bag of rice to 15 pounds of potatoes? In both cases, the items of value convey refinement, prestige, and cultural status. If Gebusi marketing seems irrational, it carries the value and prestige of earning money, of being modern. And it does this for those who are most shut out of the local cash economy: village women. If men obtain occasional paid work—cutting grass on the air-strip, doing odd jobs for government officials, or acting as carriers for visitors on a trek—women earn coins at market.

I realized this in spades when I found my "banker" in Gasumi Corners. Nelep was the cleverest old woman in the settlement. On the way back from the market one day, I joked that though I had money, it was still hard to buy things, as I needed more coins. As the path turned, Nelep quietly motioned me away from the others. "I've got coins," she said. "Come to my house." We then continued to our respective homes. After stowing my things, I walked back to her little dwelling. While doing so, I remembered her personal history, which was as colorful as it was revealing. I knew Nelep well from my first fieldwork, when she had lived in Yibihilu close to our house. She was then married to the easygoing Wasep and raising two boys. A bold character, she had not only been caught having a sexual affair with the uninitiated Doliay but was the only Gebusi woman we ever knew who had dabbled in the otherwise all-male art of shamanism.

Nelep had endured much in the intervening years. The cyst on her right wrist had grown large, making it hard to use her hand. A few years before my return, her beloved eldest son was gored to death by a wild pig, and her grief-stricken husband stopped eating and died just a few weeks later. She was then left with her remaining son and a young daughter, Kwelam, who was herself seriously ill from a bone deformity in her hip. But Nelep was tough as well as smart—always ready with a witty smirk and an astute solution. She somehow finagled the medical officer at the Nomad Aid Post to have Kwelam flown to the Kiunga Hospital for an operation—along with Nelep herself. Landing in Kiunga without money or kin, Nelep rummaged in garbage heaps for daily scraps of food. Lacking a blouse, she felt the powerful stigma of going bare-breasted in town and scrounged for rags to cover herself. Amid this abasement, Nelep nursed Kwelam through recovery until they were both flown back to Nomad. Kwelam walked with a limp but was otherwise healthy and seems indeed one of the happiest women in the village. Nelep's surviving son, Yamda (Luke), assumes pride of place as the respected lay leader of the Gasumi Catholic Church; he is married with two children of his own.

As Nelep's children grew up successfully, she married a widower, Gono—the silent, wiry man who was one of our carriers during our first expedition to Gebusi-land. By middle-age, however, Gono became crotchety, and he resented his wife's feisty wit and lack of deference. In 1998, he beat Nelep on more than one occasion. As a remarkable stigma, Gono was criticized for his actions by both the men and the women of Gasumi Corners.

Though Nelep still lived in Gono's small house, she kept her affairs to herself—including her earnings from the market, which she squirreled away without telling him. The market money of most wives becomes part of the household economy and ultimately subject to decisions by men. This said, women took pride in their hard-earned funds and the fact that these could pay for prestigious tins of fish and bags of rice at community feasts, even if these were presented by men. Most Gebusi women were uncomfortable or embarrassed to make significant store purchases on their own.

Strong-minded, Nelep kept her earnings for herself and her own children. And she had wisely focused on raising and marketing peanuts, which were the item most widely and regularly sold at the market, even though it was not the splashiest or most expensive product. Week after week, Nelep quietly sold piles of peanuts from her big bag—and over time, her 10-cent sales added up. After we were safely in her tiny house, Nelep smiled wryly and carefully unwrapped several unobtrusive bundles. To my amazement, a mountain of coins tumbled out. She didn't know how much she had earned, but when I counted it up her earnings, she had amassed more than 40 kina, or US $20. This equaled 200 sales at 10 cents each—two years of market sales for the average market woman.

With easy trust, Nelep gave me the bulk of her coins in exchange for two crisp 20-kina bills. Everyone knew that bright red "pigs head" money, as it was called, was at the time the largest and most prestigious currency. That Nelep now had two of these bills seemed to give her a great sense of satisfaction. As she carefully tucked them away, we both knew she could use them to support her children or herself however she wished—and that they were easier to conceal from prying eyes than piles of coins. As for me, I had all the coins that I needed. As I walked home, I tried to carry my stash in my own net bag as unobtrusively as possible. I smiled at the thought that an economy of new money could, at least on rare occasions, benefit both a Gebusi woman and an outsider without compromising the integrity

Nelep—still active and alert well into her late 60s—snapping fingers with Bruce in 2017.

of either. The economy of money in Gasumi Corners was paltry and largely "unproductive." But its economy of culture was strong and important.

My experience with Nelep got me thinking about how women's relations with men were changing as the 2000 millennium approached. If the Nomad market underscored the hopeful if compromised role of women in a fledgling cash economy, it was complemented by their new role in other spheres. Christian churches had given women a new sense of spiritual participation, even though men were ultimately in charge. Other institutions and activities at Nomad also gave greater opportunities for women—while also allowing new forms of male dominance, especially in terms of education, sports, and, perhaps surprisingly, theft. But it was difficult for me to talk with women about these developments. For an unrelated man to talk with a Gebusi woman automatically implied sexual interest. Older women like Nelep and Bosap were easier for me to approach as they were no longer considered sexually active. But younger women were a different story. Even for married women in their 30s and 40s, a personal interview was difficult to arrange and even more difficult to carry out. I could talk to a woman if her husband or brother was present. But then the man would reinterpret my questions and answer many of them himself.

On Saturday and Sunday afternoons, though, the village men and boys were away either playing in or watching ball games of soccer and rugby at Nomad Station. For these few precious hours, women's talk became freer and more relaxed, and I could talk with them at least a bit, as long as it was a group occasion. It helped that I had brought special trade goods for women that were hard for them to get—especially dresses, bras, and costume jewelry. Shopping for these back in the United States, I can still remember the look on the saleswoman's face in the Dollar Store in Atlanta when I heaped 15 inexpensive bras into my shopping basket along with mounds of cheap costume jewelry. Sensing that I should somehow "explain myself," I had said to her, without thinking carefully, that I was buying gifts for my many female friends in the rainforest. Aghast at the implications of my statement, I guiltily guessed what she must be thinking. But it all turned out fine. The sales clerk was Malaysian, and she knew a good bit about rainforest peoples, the difficulty of obtaining trade goods in remote areas, and the politics of gift giving. In fact, she ended up advising me about which bras were most likely to fit the short but sometimes well-endowed women of Gasumi Corners. I came away with a fresh understanding about crossing cultural boundaries with women—in Atlanta as well as Papua New Guinea.

Back in Gasumi Corners, the women were drawn to the goods I had brought. With all of them looking on, I talked with each individually as primary interviewees—listening to the woman's life history and getting her opinions and reflections on various subjects. Particularly with less articulate women, their female kin and friends chimed in with helpful promptings, clarifications, and elaborations. Young women and adolescent girls remained the toughest to talk with. Even when asked by a not-so-young and weirdly acceptable man such as myself, and even with other women present, their responses were often only shuffling feet, embarrassment, and blank looks. Nonetheless, all the women, even the younger ones, maintained their desire to work with me. Partly this was because the other women were also doing it and partly because my background and interest in the community provoked a sense of obligation. But mostly, I think, they wanted the trade goods I gave at the end of the sessions.

A punctuation point to gender change among Gebusi—across developments in church, market, school, sports, and domestic relations—concern the yearnings for manufactured commodities and a modern way of life. During the latter part of my 1998 fieldwork, the high water mark of Gebusi "development," I sponsored a contest in which Nomad schoolchildren drew pictures of how they envisaged themselves in the future. I was amazed how eagerly and effectively they took up this task, not to mention the high quality of their drawings. Burgeoning on the pages were full-color pictures of their future selves in modern walks and ways of life. Boys drew themselves as heavy machine operators, pilots, doctors, a rock singer, or a newsman. Girls drew themselves especially as nurses, teachers, or housewives in nice Western dresses. Girls as well as boys drew themselves in highly modern futures. A few actually drew themselves as living in a Christian heaven. By contrast, very few students—just 6% of the boys and 5% of the girls—drew their future selves conducting traditional livelihoods such as gardening, hunting, or fishing.

Notwithstanding their optimism, the students' desires were mostly unrealistic. It seemed highly unlikely that many or perhaps any of them could achieve the future lives they envisaged; the economy of Nomad was too paltry, and education too limited. Not to mention the cratering of the Nomad cash economy that was to come in a few short years.

What happens to the inflated expectations of young people when their aspirations are dashed? If gender did not divide the modern aspirations of boys and girls in Nomad, one important contrast did emerge. Virtually

Schoolboy Tolowe's drawing of wanting to be a brave policeman who catches young criminals, 1998.

half the boys envisaged their future as gun-wielding members of the Papua New Guinea Defense Force or the National Police. That boys gravitated to images and roles of forceful power is not surprising. But in a local world where manufactured goods and commodities are increasingly expected—and unavailable—frustrated aspirations can fuel the desire to forcefully possess such items, especially for young men. Theft has been an increasing problem across most of Papua New Guinea. Back at Yibihilu in 1981, people had craved our Western commodities, but we had never feared having them stolen. Living so communally, Gebusi had made a virtue of sharing and respecting each other's property. But things had changed. Villagers were more possessive of Western goods, and money was increasingly important. Activities in Nomad entailed interaction with many strangers—and potential thievery. Families now wanted chains, locks, and metal boxes. In the Nomad police register, theft was the most frequently reported offense—almost twice as common as any other crime—and most of these cases were both brought by and targeted against men. Though theft in Nomad was only a small problem compared to Papua New Guinea's larger towns and cities, it was still a focus of real concern.

For Gebusi near Nomad as the year 2000 approached, local modern developments promised progress. Women, in particular, had more possibilities for participation than they had had before; their lives were expanding at school, in church, and at the market. And yet, expectations confronted a dearth of realistic ways to attain modern goals and its lifestyle—apart from the deferred gratification of Christianity. This was true at school in the higher grades, and at the market for women, including Bosap. But it seemed especially true of young men as they aspired to greater progress. For most young men, traditional masculinity—with its emphasis on initiation, ritual dancing, displays of aggression, sorcery, and violence—had not been replaced with viable ways to be modern. In some cases, these tensions were redirected back onto women—as was the case of Gono beating Nelep, his economically successful wife. For the most part, however, Gebusi men as well as women drew upon deeper cultural values of acceptance to simply absorb their frustrations. In any event, the attractions of Nomad seemed bright with action and possibility—and more interesting for most than life in the deep rainforest. The most palpable sense at the time was of better things to come, even if challenges were great and sometimes insurmountable.

Anne-Sylvie

One can try to imagine how local desires to have goods and money rebound back upon the anthropologist. In an area where visitors are seldom seen, a couple of Westerners show up bringing what seems by local standards to be an enormous amount of wealth. People would happily walk miles and miles to meet us, talk to us, and often present us with a request after sharing their story with us.

It seems at various points in the colonial past that a missionary or some agent of the state advised locals that if they explained their desires and needs more clearly and explicitly it would improve the chances that their request would be granted. Whatever its origin, the sentence *mi gat rekwest* (me got request) has become so common in Papua New Guinea that I have become allergic to it. Irritating in general, the phase becomes rather comical when accompanied by Christmas wish lists for bullets, a set of new teeth, or pornographic images. Whether a by-product of cargo cult beliefs or the notion that well-supplied outsiders will eventually return (Bruce being a good example), it is often expected that whites will return bringing inflated quantities of gifts and new commodities that quickly become "indispensable"—from axes to flashlights to fishing goggles. Perhaps unknowingly, Bayi's son pushed this logic a bit far during our second field season. Following our inability to gift him the laptop computer that he had requested, he wrote us a formal letter "thanking [us] for nothing."

In my experience in Papua New Guinea, asking, "requesting," is largely a male prerogative. But in my Gebusi fieldwork, receiving became an increasingly frequent female privilege. Part of this was because I worked with Gebusi women considerably more than with men; I found their company far more agreeable. As women in this remote area were far more left behind in material modernity than men, I felt more pleasure from bringing smiles to their faces by giving them things. Unfortunately, a woman will usually not be able to keep the present given by her white friend very long; invariably, a husband, brother, or father will appropriate any mark of modernity, along with the social status that accompanies it even and especially in the depth of the bush—apart maybe from food peelers. Let's not kid ourselves, it's still women's job to peel everyone's potatoes.

Gebusi women with a pile of
their peeled potatoes, 2013.

Update: The bustling energy and potential—and the subordination and challenge—of local modernity for Gebusi in the late 1990s seem, in hindsight, all the more vivid and striking. On a regular basis, Gebusi would stroll into Nomad just to "take a spin" and see what was going on. The market, school, sports leagues, and government programs were so primed with potential, who could have guessed it would all decline?

Now there is little happening in Nomad; its world has faded to near insignificance. The Nomad market, while not completely gone, is but a shadow of its former self. As described in part three, money and buyers are now so scarce that few women bother to tote produce to Nomad in a futile attempt to sell it. In a way, this is good or at least economically "rational." Even more than the market, Nomad sports games are now completely a thing of the past: the ball field is overgrown, and there have been no games there for years. So, too, the Nomad school flirts between low attendance and closure or the merging of students across grades: it is difficult to keep teachers committed to staying and living at Nomad Station. And yet, as we shall later see, Gebusi have not given up. In fact, they have rejuvenated their home-grown culture in remarkable ways.

It is sometimes too easy to assume that old traditions die out while modern changes endure. In fact, the sharpness of the new cutting edge may be blunted while older patterns reemerge or are revisited in new guises. Consider the impact of "retro" in American pop culture today.

For Gebusi, the past persists in immediate human terms. Though Nelep is now a very aged woman, she has proudly survived to see a whopping nine grandchildren survive. And her surviving son, whom she adores, has become the community leader of the Gasumi Corners St. Paul Catholic Church.

As with older traditions, the previous influence of life in and around Nomad Station has a continuing legacy. As men and women have settled back into a decreasingly modern life, the division and separation between them has continued to soften. Gender relations are not as charged or as fraught as they used to be. Though still a challenge, it is now easier to interview women than it was before. In the mix, men as well as women have largely accepted their reduced ability to engage a larger world—and to appreciate their own more fully. Theft is less of a problem than it was in the late 1990s—in part because there are fewer commodities to covet or steal. And the incidence of beating, both of women and of pets, seems less than it used to be.

Outsiders have indeed given up and left Nomad, including government officials, some teachers, and all the police. Predictably, they blamed their departure on local conditions and attitudes. But Gebusi and others do not accept this responsibility. In particular, they do not blame themselves as having been sinful or as sliding into "backwardness" due to their own shortcomings. Instead, they say, it is the government's own fault that it has gone, that it has "died." In the bargain, though a number people in Gasumi Corners still go to church, there is neither so much hope of heavenly progress nor fear of hellish decline. Peanuts, pennies, hope and success: like some of Gebusi's older traditions, these now increasingly seem like things of the past—even as they are not fully gone and may someday come back.

Note: See Gebusi video clips of and commentary on Gebusi gender relations ("Gender") in 2013 on Bruce Knauft's website or on YouTube (video #6) by searching for "Gebusi videos."

BROADER CONNECTIONS
Markets, Development, and Modern Aspiration

- **Modern institutions and activities** that are common globally, including among Gebusi, include government schooling, public **markets** at which women are prominent, practicing a **world religion**, and sports events for men.

- As is the case with many peoples, modern changes among the Gebusi included increasing interaction with outsiders as well as those from other ethnic groups.

- In contrast to indigenous gift exchange, **modern market exchange**—as reflected at the Nomad market—is relatively impersonal and involves the transaction of goods between strangers by means of money.

- Gebusi women, like women in many world areas, are highly motivated to invest time and effort in market activity. Indeed, their investment was more than what they received back in money. This reflects how modern cultural values and prestige can motivate people to give up traditional practices in hopes of success in a modern **cash economy**.

- Modern female status among Gebusi, as among many peoples, increased in the sense that women participated meaningfully in modern institutions and activities such as church, school, and the market. At the same time, gender dominance has taken on new dimensions; women's education, church leadership, and economic control are significantly less than that of men. Men continue to appropriate the fruits of female labor along with most of the modern commodities or money that come into women's possession.

- As is often the case in developing countries, **formal schooling** was important but compromised at the Nomad school, with large classes and difficulty of educational advancement, especially for girls.

- As reflected in drawings of their anticipated adult selves, children at the Nomad Community School, like in many contexts cross-culturally, desired to have successful modern futures. However, most of these desires were most unlikely to be fulfilled.

- As revealed by Gebusi in 1998 and especially since that time, hopes of modern success are often complemented by challenges and periods of decline.

- Like many peoples, Gebusi selectively draw upon or resuscitate longer-standing traditions over time, including during periods of increased stress or challenge.

Chapter 9

Mysterious Romance, Marital Choice

Wayabay was as spare with words as he was decent and direct in his actions. He was clearly troubled, so I asked him in. It was 1998. He hesitated, strong young man that he was then, until the force of his question overcame his embarrassment. "Do you have any *adameni*? I would really like some." I had no idea what this was. He stammered and continued on: "*Adameni* is something special. It has to do with an unmarried woman and an unmarried man. When they really like each other and think of coming together." I still had no idea. Whatever *adameni* was, it related to sexual desire between young people. Wayabay was the oldest of the bachelors and was actively trying to find a wife. But what was *adameni*? I wracked my brain. It was clearly important to Wayabay. I was both concerned and curious.

Could Wayabay be asking me for a condom? I knew that he had worked for a trail-clearing crew a few years back and that he had traveled to Kiunga. He had greater knowledge and experience than many. Perhaps he was in a romantic liaison and wanted to protect either himself or the girl. This would explain his embarrassment. I tried, gently, to describe a condom in Gebusi vernacular: "There is this thing that men wear when they have sex. Is this like *adameni*?" Wayabay replied, "Well, I'm not sure." My unease mounted, but I forged ahead: "This is something that a man puts over his 'thing,' his phallus. It stretches like rubber. He puts this rubber thing over his penis before he has sex. He has sex but his 'thing' doesn't touch the woman's 'thing.'"

Now it was Wayabay's turn to be uncomprehending—and mine to be embarrassed. I tried to explain that men can use these rubber coverings when they don't want the woman to get pregnant or when they worry about getting diseases from having sex. All of which sounded no better and, indeed, much worse when spoken in Gebusi. Wayabay shook his head vehemently; *adameni* was definitely NOT a condom.

In despair, we invited Sayu and Didiga into our conversation. Both spoke a smattering of English and had had more schooling than Wayabay. Yes, they said, *adameni* was something for a man. And, yes, it had to do with sex. It also had something do to with *oop*, the generic Gebusi word for "slippery, milky substance" that refers especially to semen. Sex. Men. Semen. I was stymied. Could they be referring to some custom or substance having to do with traditional practices of sex between men? This would certainly explain Wayabay's embarrassment. Perhaps he was having sexual relations with another young man before finding a wife. I took another deep breath. "Does *adameni* have to do with Gebusi traditional sex customs between men?" They looked puzzled. "You know, the sex custom in the initiations, when the adolescent strokes the man's phallus and swallows his semen—so he can grow bigger and achieve more manhood."

Culturally speaking, I had dropped a bomb. Their mouths hung in disbelief, their faces grew ashen. Sayu finally broke the silence: "Did our fathers and boys really do that? In olden times? Did they? Really?!"

Double ouch. Although they had all grown up in a world of male banter and horseplay, none of them, I now realized, had been initiated; the last initiation ceremony had been held before they had been old enough. They had never been introduced to sex relations with other men. Given their Christian conversion, it was quite possible they had never been told about the practice. Against their ignorance, I had divulged the reality of a strange sexual practice, a shocking custom that was hard to believe and disgusting to them. I felt awful. But I also felt that I had to be truthful: "Yes, that is the custom that men and initiated teenagers sometimes followed before."

Shaking their heads in disbelief, they stressed, as if it needed emphasis, that *adameni* had nothing whatsoever to do with sex between men or boys; it was for men with women. What about *oop*? This wasn't semen, they said; it was a thick liquid, but it smelled sweet and tasted good. It was something that a man would dab about his eyes. When a woman looked at him, she would be attracted. Evidently, *adameni* was a love potion. In fact, they asserted, it came from whites and not from Papua New Guineans, including at the logging camp where Wayabay had worked. *Adameni* came in a bottle and was quite expensive, but whites said it really worked. The bottles had a picture of a naked man and woman on the label, just like in the Bible.

Gracious! *Adameni* wasn't a Gebusi word. It was their pronunciation of "Adam and Eve"!—an expensive love potion. Unscrupulous traders peddled it in bottles promising biblical sex and lovely sin—which Wayabay now wanted to attract a wife.

So they asked again, "Do you have any *adameni*? And if not, can you get some?" They all believed in this love potion, almost desperately in Wayabay's case. How to answer? I had already embarrassed both them and myself. For a moment, I thought of boosting Wayabay's confidence by giving him scented skin cream to dab on his cheeks. But I quickly dismissed this as a bad idea: I had already caused enough confusion for one day, So I said I didn't have any *adameni*. Disappointed but at least in mutual understanding, we finished our conversation and they left.

If Gebusi culture had been hard for me to learn at first, I realized that it could still chew up my seasoned understandings with plenty of spit left over. I was still surprised, challenged, and sometimes at sea. During the 16 years since my first visit, Gebusi young men had gone from having sex with one another to apparently not even knowing about the practice. Could this really be? If they hadn't been directly exposed to or told about it, their knowledge would have been hazy, and in a Christian context, excluded. Compare it with our own knowledge of sexual practices among our forebears—including our typical ignorance about sexual practices our own parents may or may not have engaged in. Like many peoples, Gebusi distinguish between things that are explicitly experienced or transmitted and those that are only implied or uncertain. In this sense, Wayabay, Sayu, and Didiga had probably not known about sex between Gebusi men. Until I had told them.

As a 44-year-old, I was one of the older men in the community. It was not uncommon for me to know more about Gebusi family ancestries, based on my earlier collection of genealogies and life histories, than the younger Gebusi did. The gap between young men's knowledge and my own concerning traditional Gebusi sex practices was hence not surprising.

Beyond the shock and apparent unawareness of my companions, it was clear: as bachelors, they were far more concerned about sexual attraction with women than with other men. Before, sex between men was in part a prelude or a complement to marriage. A young man who had "become big" at the costumed initiation was attractive to women by his very presence; within a few months, all the initiates had found wives and were married. But now this custom was gone, along with much of men's social life. As I was finding out, the same seemed true of women's desire and obligation to marry through sister-exchange. Though it sometimes still occurred, sister-exchange marriage was not as *culturally* emphasized as it had been before. As such, men could no longer count on the splendor of ritual attraction or obligations of kinship and reciprocity to obtain a wife. Increasingly, young men were on their own; they had to attract a wife through more modern forms of courtship.

Wayabay had not been successful in this regard. He was several years past the age of normal marriage and was among the small minority of young men who had not taken an interest in activities associated with Nomad Station. He played soccer and rugby only intermittently and awkwardly, would not dance to Papua New Guinea "disco music," did not sing in the community's contemporary string band, and he had not been baptized and did not go to church. Instead, Wayabay honed traditional skills and spent long periods hunting in the forest and building a house in the village. He was unusually devoted to traditional customs and was proud of his ability to travel to remote feasts and initiations and dance in full costume. In all, Wayabay was a good traditionalist born a generation too late. In this context, *adameni* was a hopeful substitute for the alluring male initiation costume that Wayabay would never wear.

Gebusi men who were most successful at attracting girlfriends and brides, by contrast, were more locally modern. They could joke with some facility in Tok Pisin, had been to school for a few years, and gravitated toward the lifestyle of Nomad Station. They finagled a little money and managed to sport a jaunty baseball cap, sunglasses, or colorful shirt. Perhaps they even had a boom box on which they could play cassettes of rock music. They enjoyed playing rugby and soccer if not also dancing to disco music, and they were comfortable interacting casually with those from

Kamu [l] and Wayabay [r] dressed for a   Disco dancing competition at the Nomad
traditional village dance, 1998.   Independence Day celebration, 1998.

other communities. For Wayabay, however, being locally modern was difficult. He could kill a wild boar in the forest but he couldn't shoot the
modern breeze.

For young Gebusi men, desire for modern commodities is complicated by economic pressures to pay brideprice or bridewealth. Failing sister-exchange marriage, the brothers or fathers of young women say they
will be satisfied only with a large cash payment from the would-be groom.
In many areas of the world—including parts of Africa and South Asia as
well as the South Pacific—inflated demands for bridewealth or a dowry
cause major problems for young people who want to get married. Fortunately for young Gebusi men, the amount of money they actually pay is
comparatively low: for first marriages in Gasumi Corners between 1982

and 1998, the average bride payment was only 56 kina, or 28 dollars. But even this small amount was difficult for many young men to amass, and it has been growing and inflating ever since. By 2017 a prospective father-in-law might demand many thousands of kina in brideprice from the wannabe groom. But in fact, the father would often be satisfied with just a few hundred kina, and this was often paid over many years.

Gebusi courtship has become sandwiched between a rhetorical mandate for sister-exchange, inflated claims for bridewealth, desire for commodities, and the demands of modern styles of interaction. Bachelors in Gasumi Corners lament that they can never get married. How did they find wives in fact? In large part through the idiosyncrasies of romantic attraction. In the present as in the past, attractions between a young man and woman could lead to marriage over the objections of her father or her brothers. But now, with a reduced sense of kinship obligation, and without the display of ritual attraction, romantic marriage seemed both the primary way of getting married and increasingly stressful for young men.

The special stresses that young women in Gasumi Corners were also under became dramatically evident in one attempt to arrange a traditional sister-exchange marriage between two clans. . . .

Gami was 16, full-bodied, vivacious, and, if anything, readier for marriage than her slightly built older "brother," Moka. Her intended husband was Guyul, a cheerful, strapping 21-year-old bachelor. Guyul's sister was the comely and straightforward Kubwam, herself a mature 16-year-old prime for marriage. Much was made of the fact that Gami's "brother" would be marrying her groom's sister—a classic sister-exchange marriage.

Following spicy rumors that spread through the village, the courtship of the two young couples became official. Following Gebusi custom, each young woman was "seized" by the wrist and led away by a male kinsman of her husband-to-be. Kubwam appeared a bit forlorn, which is proper etiquette for a woman taken in marriage. But Gami could hardly keep from smiling despite her presumed sobriety. The four new spouses were made to sit together and were exhorted to keep their obligations to each other as husbands and wives. It was not simply a double marriage but an exchange among the four of them, and everything was going according to plan.

The two women, Gami and Kubwam, swapped residences across the four-minute walk that separated their husbands' respective households in Gasumi Corners. Each extended family simultaneously gained a daughter-in-law while losing a daughter. The two mothers-in-law made special efforts to ensure that the incoming brides felt welcome and at home. I paid visits to both households and gave small gifts. With her typical pleasant reserve, Kubwam seemed comfortable in Moka's household. And Gami was practically ebullient with Guyul's family; she smiled broadly and engaged eagerly with his kin.

The first crack in the arrangement surfaced after just a day and a half. Moka started spending time away from his new wife, going off with the remaining bachelors. Not yet 20 years old, Moka was still "young" to get married, and younger husbands sometimes took a while to settle into their new role. Though his marriage was not yet consummated, Moka's new wife, Kubwam, continued to live in his household. By itself, Moka's equivocation presented only a small wrinkle, not a major cause for alarm.

On the other side of Gasumi Corners, Gami's relationship with Guyul started off like a rocket. She had been the village belle—friendly, flirtatious, buxom, and with a thousand-watt smile. When Gami and Guyul went off together to garden and came back with moony dispositions and euphoric smiles, village gossip was ribald and irrepressible: they had consummated their marriage.

But this happiness did not last. Exactly what went wrong I never learned, least of all from Gami or Guyul themselves. Signals seemed to point to an abrupt U-turn in their sexual compatibility. Gami's disposition turned suddenly from sweet to sour. She wouldn't look at her husband, wouldn't work in his household, and wouldn't eat. She tried to go back to her adopted mother's home but was forced back to her husband's house. She tried again, but was again forced back. Still she refused to cooperate and returned yet again to her own family home. No entreaty made headway; no inquiry bore fruit. "Who knows what goes on in a young woman's heart or mind?!" "Gami is just stubborn and 'bigheaded.'" "She just won't be married." But why? "Just because," I was told repeatedly. "That's just the way she is."

As the hours passed, Gami's recalcitrance fueled increasing anger against her. It is a serious matter for a Gebusi woman to consummate her marriage and then repudiate it. That a woman could have sex with a husband she had publicly accepted and then reject him after a few days of romance struck against the heart of Gebusi morality. Not only was Gami's virtue on the line but also the manhood and self-esteem of her husband, Guyul. The stakes were yet higher because the marriage was a sister-exchange; Gami's rejection of Guyul also compromised the union between her "brother," Moka, and Guyul's sister, Kubwam. If her marriage dissolved, her brother's union would also be forfeited.

In short order, everyone turned against Gami. Her new husband disdained her, and her mother-in-law was incensed. Her adopted mother was even more furious, as was Moka. Her "mother" slapped her, her "brother" beat her, and she endured a barrage of verbal abuse. "What is WRONG with you?!" "You are good for NOTHING!" "Guyul is a fine man!" "You think you can just 'open your skirt' and then say you won't be married?! Huh? HUH?" "Don't you care about your 'brother'?" "Don't you care about your 'mother'?" "No one in this village will protect you." "Where are you going to find a new husband? Do you think any man would want you now? Huh? HUH?" "You are alone, no one cares about you." "You can't stay here. You have no home here. You are finished."

Gami never once explained and never argued back. But she wouldn't budge, wouldn't go back to Guyul. As the hours mounted into a second day, the tension worsened. Women from other households took up the banner of village honor. Senior women badgered Gami in every way they could think of. Finally, Moka had had enough. He grabbed Gami and dragged her bodily out the door of his house. She shrieked and screamed, refusing to leave. Heavier and at least as strong as he, she held her ground. But as Moka grabbed one of her arms, his mother and another man took hold of the other. Gami was dragged screaming and crying, feet trailing and flailing. By the time they had hauled her 15 feet from her house, she was covered in mud and bloody scrapes. Still she refused to cooperate. They pulled her by the hair, but she would not give in. Panting and screaming, they told her she could lie there and rot.

Then a senior woman came over. She was someone, here nameless, whom I otherwise liked and admired, but whom it was hard to forgive. She silently walked up to Gami, leaned down, and talked to her in low tones. Watching from my doorstep, I had a sinking feeling that I knew what she was saying, and my suspicion was later verified. It was terrible to have seen Gami hit and dragged. But it is almost unimaginable for a young woman to be threatened with a public stripping, to be seen naked by everyone in the village. For Gebusi, this idea is so deeply shameful as to be a kind of social death—never forgotten, never expunged. And it is triply so for a nubile young woman. It was true that Gami had badly misjudged the game and the stakes of her marriage. Her girlish flirtation and mature body had led her into the four-sided vice of sister-exchange. At first, she had complied enthusiastically, but then realized her decision was an appalling mistake that she would now risk everything to repudiate. But the threat of being stripped in public made her resistance too costly. After a minute or two, Gami got up and walked lifelessly back to Guyul's household.

I assumed that would be the end of the story, that both unhappy marriages would stay intact. But I was wrong. Though Gami stayed in Guyul's household, she would not respond or cooperate in any way. She stayed defiant, a living dead person. In exasperation, her relatives took the matter to a higher authority, the Nomad police. As chance would have it, I was at the station studying the police register when they trooped in. The village men and a Nomad police constable sat Gami down in a chair, surrounded her, and began their inquisition. "Why won't you marry this man?" "Why did you have sex with him and then refuse him?" "Do you really want to reject your own family?" "What are you going to do if you don't stay married to Guyul?" "We can bring charges to put you in jail for immoral conduct." I thought Gami would certainly crack. Alone, she faced the most powerful men not just in the village but at Nomad Station. But she refused even to speak. Her only words were "I don't know" and "I don't want to." She hung her head and sobbed. Fortunately, the men did not touch or strike her. I don't know if my presence deterred them. But I was knotted up, frustrated at not being able to intervene. Ultimately, they gave up in desperation and returned Gami to our settlement. A public meeting was then held in Gasumi Corners. The invective again started as people debated what steps to take next. They also aired opinions about the morality of young women in the village in general—how shameless and loose they had become.

I had never made a speech at a Gebusi public meeting; I had never felt it my place to do so. And my mastery of Gebusi language was never good enough to wrap myself in their rhetoric. But this time I felt I had no choice. I knew I couldn't change Gebusi customs, alter Gami's predicament, or impose my will on theirs. Still, these were people I had lived with.

They were my friends. And I thought what they were doing to Gami was wrong. As I got up to speak, I started to tremble. It was like that first speech you make in junior high school when you can't remember the words and you know your voice and bearing betray your fear. But I had to continue. What I said, or at least what I tried to say, was that those in the village had to respect their own custom—the custom that no one can ultimately force a woman to be married. Even in the old days, I said, some women had refused to be married. No matter what anyone had done, and no matter even what the women themselves had done, they had simply refused. I alluded to some of the failed first marriages of the people sitting around me, including some of the older women who had berated Gami. I reminded them that they, too, had ultimately refused the men they had been pressured to marry. The police, I said, respected the same custom, following the laws of Papua New Guinea. People could try to persuade a woman to marry, but they could not force her. That was all.

I don't know if my words had any effect. I was too nervous to judge people's reactions or to recall things clearly afterward. I wasn't saying anything heretical but merely putting into words the reality that I hoped they would accept—and that they were grudgingly beginning to accept anyway. Then I did something else that I had never done before. After the meeting was over, I asked to talk with Gami. Alone. Of all the things I have intentionally done with Gebusi before or since, this was the most awkward. An unrelated man simply does not talk with an unmarried woman alone—especially one like Gami, who bore the stigma of sexual impropriety. In addition, Gami had been a flirtatious and endearing young woman. Anthropology is littered with tales of well-meaning White men who scheme to help attractive women of color only to unwittingly leave them worse than they were to begin with. So I had to be very clear about my motives.

My request related to Gami's family situation. Her father had died and her biological mother had remarried. This woman was now living near the town of Kiunga with her second husband; she was the only woman in the community to have left the Nomad area. Without money for the airfare, Gami had been left behind with her adoptive mother. Now, however, Gami's true mother was the one person who might have cared enough to help her. I knew Gami's mother from before and thought she was a good person. Because Gami could not read or write, I thought she might like me to write a letter to her mother in Kiunga—to communicate with her and solicit help. This practice is not unusual in many parts of Papua New Guinea. When I had previously visited male inmates at the national prison in Port Moresby, many of them had immediately accepted my offer to write letters on their behalf to send to their families back home. In some ways, I thought, Gami was now a prisoner in Gasumi Corners.

Apart from this, there was something else that I wanted to communicate. I wanted to tell Gami that I didn't think she was a bad or wicked person. Many young women struggle to find a man they can live with. I wanted to tell her I thought she had courage to stand up for herself. I knew I was on cultural thin ice. I had no idea if these words would make sense or if they would backfire. But I had to try. And there was no way I could talk to her with other villagers intervening.

In the village clearing, I told Gami's adoptive mother and the others gathered there that I needed to talk to Gami, alone. They looked at me, and I looked at them back. I told them not to worry, that I was only an "old man" and that we wouldn't be long. My excuse was that Gami had never shown me the abandoned spur settlement, just 200 yards away, where her true mother had previously lived. I thought this might be a good place for her to think of her mother and to tell me anything she wanted me to write in a letter. I was touched that the villagers trusted me enough to let Gami go off with me. Gami herself had been through the wringer already, and who knows what she thought now. She had every reason to be scared of any new development, and she was, in culturally appropriate fashion, reluctant to go with me. To my distress, her relatives now yelled an order that she accompany me to her mother's old settlement.

As I walked slowly out of our hamlet, Gami trailed a good 15 feet behind. My first thought was to wait for her and say something innocuous. But when I slowed, so did she. It got worse when a 12-year-old boy crossed paths with us. Gami and I were the spitting image of a married couple—adult man up front and younger wife coming behind. The boy was incredulous. I mumbled that Gami was going to show me her mother's house and that her adopted mother had said it was okay. As we neared the site, a second boy appeared. I repeated the story. But he was too captivated by the sight of Gami with me to be easily deterred. Even as I told him to move along, I could see him scurry away and watch from the bushes.

My conversation with Gami took place close to the main path and was very short. We stood about a dozen feet apart—as close as we ever got.

Both of us looked at the ground or anywhere except at each other. I said that I was sorry for her. I said I thought she was not a bad person, but a person who had much inside that was good. I said, without repeating the obvious, I knew she had "worries." Then I said I had known her mother and I knew she was now living near Kiunga. And I asked her if she wanted me to write a letter to her mother—to see if she or other members of her family could help. Nervously, Gami said simply, "No." I continued, "Is there anything else you would like to say? Is there anything you would like to talk about or that I might do?" She replied again, "No." I responded, "That's fine. I just wanted to ask. We'll leave it go." Then we walked directly back to the village. Gami took the lead, walking much faster than she had before.

I will never know if my awkward attempt to help Gami was an abject failure or merely a nominal one. Perhaps the idea of telling one's long-lost mother about one's moral indiscretions and predicament wasn't that appealing. Perhaps I was guilty of cultural insensitivity or of taking license against Gebusi norms of gendered interaction. I could not know and could only hope that some part of Gami sensed, amid my indiscretion, that I was trying to help her. The best of intentions can sometimes have the worst of results. But I had to try.

What conclusions can we draw? On a personal level, my engagement with Gami and also with Wayabay led me into the uncertain territory of trying to help or intervene with Gebusi. In addition to being researchers, anthropologists are people who can feel compelled to act on behalf of those they are studying. But we can't know the consequences of our actions or even if good intentions will be recognized. It seems as important as it is difficult to balance our positive intent against the specter of unanticipated outcomes. Western intervention among foreign peoples has often spawned unfortunate results, even when the intent was noble. Beyond the colonialism of the past, many large and expensive international aid projects around the world have created little long-term benefit. Sometimes they have done greater harm than good to local people. As a caution against this potential, a sense of humility and an awareness of our own limitations—as researchers, as advocates, and as human beings—remain important.

In ethnographic terms, Gami's case and that of Wayabay illustrate the challenges Gebusi faced in trying to find marriage partners during a period of heightened modern influence, personal choice, and potential risk. In many parts of the world, personal options are expanding, including for women. Relative to unions arranged or pressured by kin and relatives, "marriage by choice" or "companionate marriage" is generally on the rise. Gami's and Wayabay's plights illustrate this larger pattern in Gasumi Corners from complementary male and female perspectives.

As opposed to marriage arranged by kinship, obligation, or exchange, modern ways of choosing a partner accentuate the determination, physical attraction, and romance that women and men have for each other, even as the risks of personal choice are ratcheted up. Who can say if women or men are happier as a result? But in a world of modern alternatives, the lives of young men and women are increasingly shaped by the intended or unintended consequences of their own actions, beyond those of family and kin.

Amid the clash of choice and constraint, some predicaments work out better than one might have imagined. This was finally the case for Gami and also for Wayabay. Despite their respective trials, each of them ended up finding an acceptable spouse after I left the field. In each case, their partner carried a history of difficult choices in the village that complemented their own. In December 2001 I received the following in a letter from Gasumi Corners written on behalf of Sayu: "Wayabay got married already to Gami. And ready to deliver baby." Long live their lives together. Long live their resilience.

Wayabay and Gami have stayed married, and as of 2017 they had seven children. Since the time of their marriage, the world of the Gebusi has surprisingly come back, at least in part, to that which Wayabay was more comfortable to begin with; Gebusi have been reorienting more to the rainforest and away from activities associated with Nomad Station. Sister-exchange marriage also seems to have changed in emphasis. In 1998 men were primed to receive material compensation for sisters or daughters given in marriage. But due to the decline in the local monied economy, expectations and demands of brideprice have been enhanced by possibilities and plans for marriage by sister-exchange.

Male camaraderie and sexual joking have certainly rebounded since
the 1990s and are now alive and well in Gasumi Corners, but male–male
sexuality still appears vestigial if not completely absent among Gebusi; it
seems unlikely to reemerge. With the continuing absence of spirit séances
and initiations, the ritual structure and cultural impetus for sexual relations between men is absent. The sexual emphasis and orientation of
Gebusi men has always included if not emphasized heterosexual desire,
and this pattern now continues amid male joking in the absence of male–
male sexuality per se. Whatever sex does take place between Gebusi men
occurs not as a social norm but as a private individual practice.

Finally, the tenor of courtship seems to have mellowed. Though begging
more information, it seems women and men now have neither the traditional mandate of ritualized attraction, from the 1980s and before, nor the
heightened expectation of money and modern allure, from the late 1990s.
Young men and women continue to wrestle with issues of "exchange" or
"compensation" as they become attracted to each other and get married.
But on the whole, the stakes and their stress seem less than they did before.

Anne-Sylvie

Pelap can't have been older than 20. She always carried a bush knife
and dressed in shorts, could alternately be really serious or very jokey,
and understood Tok Pisin but would not speak it. At least not with
me. She spent a lot of time around our house helping us with chores,
but there was something that never clicked between us. While I was
easily making friends with other women in her age range, especially
women who were not following the expected path their parents and
more largely their culture had set them on, Pelap was the odd one
out. Perhaps it was because she was a strong-willed woman in a family of men, bullied by them and ordered to be someone she was not,
but ultimately acting only as she saw fit.

While I cannot say I identified with her situation, I did sympathize
with her. But she was not accepting of that sympathy. I think the cultural gap between us was too large for her. She did not care that I
wanted to hear her story, to know how she felt, to bond and commis-
erate with her over the very visible hand men had over Gebusi
women. I think she saw all the privilege I came from (correct), pre-

Pelap, 2016.

sumed I was not there to stay (also correct), and concluded I would never fully get her (absolutely correct). She did not have time to engage in this "bonding" effort.

She was basically holding up to my face the distorted mirror I've so often looked into when I was in the field, glaringly showing me just how much of a gap can exist between two realities. Tok Pisin was a delusion, a reassuring tool ensconced in my mind to make me believe I was gathering data, understanding stories, comprehending social facts, and embracing them within a reality that made full sense at both ends—mine and others'. Yet how could I possibly fathom what any of this meant? How could I feel in my flesh and in my mind what it meant to grow up as a Gebusi woman, carrying firewood and bananas and siblings in a second net bag that weighed heavily on one's back and was trussed across the forehead; obeying the long-standing sister-exchange logic to share a bed and a life with someone not of my own choosing; prematurely leaving school to spend long hot days harvesting sweet potatoes and feeding an ever-growing family? I can barely understand people in my own culture who decide to embark on paths radically different from mine, but in the name of science I sometimes delude myself into thinking it is possible for me to collect stories and provide in-depth analyses about them.

My previous long-term field experience among the Baruya had taught me that I was ill-prepared to welcome otherness—busy as I was, back then, trying to make it fit into my own categories. Now that I was aspiring to do better, I also had to understand and accept that empathy and decentering could only take you so far. Not to say that all my Gebusi connections were superficial, or mere illusions, but it was up to Gebusi, ultimately, to welcome *my* otherness.

Pelap displayed a half-smile, always the same, whenever we exchanged a few words, a barrier blocking any other expression that may have yielded meaning. I had to respect her boundaries, and so I stopped trying to read her. But social scientists can at least do one thing, even when so many dimensions of reality elude them: observe and gather facts and write them down.

I learned Pelap had given birth to an illegitimate child, a little girl born less than a year before our arrival, whom she gave up for adoption within the village. She had "gone to the bush" with Dugam's brother, Weka, a young and attractive lad who later married another woman. Much as I wanted to, I could never get Pelap's version of the story. Yet the young woman in me craved details at least as much as the ethnographer did. How acceptable were Pelap's actions? How frequently did actions like these occur among Gebusi? In my previous fieldwork I had never felt so close to the reality of unmarried women (who in large parts of Papua New Guinea do not have much margin to navigate their own matrimonial fate, and rarely have sex before marriage). Among Gebusi, I discovered that if you liked someone, you could have sex together, but you would presumably hide that from your parents if you were still living at home. Maybe you and the young man would date for a bit; maybe later you would find someone else you liked better, until one day, maybe, you would decide to settle. This land of "maybes" and possibilities delighted me, as it opened up a whole world of what might be called "strategies." If I was guilty at that stage of essentializing the people I lived with, it was not because I wanted to reify them into the "good savage" category but rather because I wanted to bring them closer to the reality that made sense to me, which was not the rationale of the arranged marriages I had observed and analyzed until then. But I quickly came to realize that both logics, mine and theirs, coexisted there. Sometimes violently.

Pelap was Bayi's daughter, and Bayi as *consol* of Gasumi did not care much for the rumors circumventing his daughters—especially when said rumors turned into growing bumps and then into babies. Pelap's younger sister, Gote, gave birth to an illegitimate child during our time there. She was swiftly kicked out of her parents' house and forbidden from returning for as long as she was not married. As she did not want to give up her baby, her clan only saw one solution to this mess: forcing the presumed father to marry her.

Bayi accusing Weka of making his daughter pregnant and not paying brideprice to marry her, 2016.

In the golden light of one late June afternoon, we heard shouting from the heart of the village. Bayi and his eldest son, Tobias, were furious and red-faced, one draped in dignity and the other armed with a pole. They were angry with various clansmen who had positioned themselves at cardinal points around the longhouse. Bayi and Tobias were demanding thousands of kina in compensation from the kin of bush-lover Weka. They were yelling that this "bastard of the road" could simply not be. Bayi, never short of ideas to make a bit of extra cash, had set the brideprice for Pelap ridiculously high, which I thought was poor strategy if he wanted to get his adversaries to shake on it. I wondered whether his number one grievance was his daughter's "defilement" by the lad, and whether her well-being was his main objective, or if he wanted to profit monetarily. Maybe I could make room for the fact that such feelings are often nuanced, and that everywhere actions are overdetermined. A self-serving calculus, after all, is something we understand well in the West, where logics of "individualism" were born and flourish while communities have become less of a driving force in our daily lives. Still, Bayi needed his own clansmen to support his position, and he was facing rather unhappy men who had to support Weka for clan-based reasons (and maybe because they enjoyed pissing off Bayi a bit, too). They were not exactly delighted at the prospect of shelling out the hefty sum the *consol* was demanding.

Far from defending principles, all these men seemed to be knocking their "strong will" against each other to save their own interests. Whatever the two young people were feeling did not seem to matter.

The freedom of "going to the bush" still came at a cost, and mostly for women. That was a reality I could fully comprehend and embrace within my own.

Pelap did not have it easy either. While her family had been less irate with her than they subsequently were with her sister, this partial forbearance was predicated on Pelap's decision to not keep her baby. That happened to align with her own inclination to stay single (I later found out she turned down Weka's proposal of marriage). But this did not mean she was quite so free to roam around the village. As I learned quickly, Gebusi women still very much had to fit into the strict housewife category in order for things to be deemed harmonious by others in the village.

That same afternoon, another fight exploded, this time between Sayu and his wife, Danksop. Her loud recriminations against him had gone beyond the thin walls of their house and were now invading everyone else's. We all quickly heard that she was accusing Sayu of cheating on her with Pelap. In his 40s, married twice, and with seven children, Sayu was notoriously flirty, the epitome of the eternal teenager. He engaged most of all with the cohort of unmarried men, smoking and drinking various substances while chatting for hours into the night to the sound of 90s disco music (when the boom box would work, that is). As Bruce's "adopted son," he would come to our place most days, and there he would interact with Pelap. I never saw anything beyond banter and pleasant teasing between them, but it is not for me to judge what is considered "innocent" or "acceptable" in another culture. The fact remained that being loudmouthed and provocative did not mean they were sleeping together. It possibly didn't help matters that Sayu had engaged in serious relations with "Danksie," his wife, back when he was still married to someone else— a fact she herself confirmed with a giggle, admitting that they had "gone to the bush" at the time.

That afternoon, things got pretty heated, culminating in a surreal scene in which verbal fighting quickly gave way to antagonists chasing each other around the village. This also involved Bruce, who intervened to stop his adopted son from throwing a punch at his wife by tackling him to the ground. It went without saying that the community at large could always butt into marital affairs and that, in the bargain, Sayu was not right simply by virtue of being a man. Still, those events reminded me that despite the widening of their horizons beyond the domestic sphere, despite larger access to school, the market, and contraceptives, Gebusi women were always first and foremost someone's daughter, sister, or wife and, as such, could not be fully in charge of their own destiny.

What happened to Pelap's illegitimate daughter? Little Josephine was adopted by Didiga—a very decent man in all respects (even though he fervently believed in the justice of accusing people of sorcery). He did not hide his rationale from me, or indeed the fact that welcoming this little girl into his home was a calculus. His wife, Sam, had given birth to three sons and one daughter. One baby boy had died toward the end of his first year, leaving the parents with two boys and a girl. Hence, when this little baby girl showed up, Didiga saw the opportunity to even things out: two girls as well as two boys. Sam was only mildly happy, as she was not even done breast-feeding her lastborn. It sounded to me like she was not consulted on the matter. "You see," Didiga explained, "now I have two boys and two girls, so I can use the girls in exchange for brides for the boys when they get married later on."

I should probably feel some solace at the thought that in this nook of the Pacific, unlike in many other areas of our world, girls are not victims of infanticide; they are useful to help ensure that their brothers can in turn find someone to marry. Such phrasing, however, would be reductive, misleading, and far from doing justice to the multiple ways in which Gebusi women can nowadays influence their own matrimonial destiny (at least compared to the old days). Paradoxically, with the introduction of money into matrimonial arrangements, women are not used as monetary compensation like they were in the past. Instead, their presence or absence, can now be compensated at least to some extent by the exchange of cash.

Note: As also for chapters 5 and 8, see Gebusi video clips of and commentary on Gebusi male–male social and sexual relations ("Sexuality") and gender relations ("Gender") in 2013 on Bruce Knauft's website or on YouTube (videos #6 and #7) by searching for "Gebusi videos."

BROADER CONNECTIONS
Ethical Challenges, Agency, and "Companionate Marriage"

- Like cultural anthropologists generally, Bruce invariably confronted **ethical challenges** during fieldwork with the Gebusi.

- Among Gebusi, as in many societies, young people have adopted modern customs that place increased emphasis on marriage based on individual desire, agency, and romance.

- Bruce's response to Wayabay's request for *adameni*, and his interaction with Gami, reveal:

  — Anthropologists may be surprised and ignorant even when they think they know a culture well.

  — Good intentions in fieldwork can still lead to awkwardness or misunderstanding.

  — Local people are often forgiving of an anthropologist's unwitting mistakes.

- As in many societies, marriage among Gebusi came to rely on personal attraction and modern courtship rather than on traditional gender roles or ritual association.

- The attempted sister-exchange marriage between four Gebusi young people in 1998 reveals changes in courtship and marriage across the world, including:

  — The modern difficulty of **arranged marriages**

  — Increasing female choice

  — Resilience of women against others' opinions

  — Increased emphasis on mutually acceptable **companionate marriage**

  — Continuing moral stigma against sexual misconduct, especially for women

- Bruce's actions with Gami illustrate:

  — Anthropologists sometimes feel compelled to act as members of their field community.

  — It is important to use caution and be humble when intervening.

  — It is vital to ask local people for their own opinion/s.

  — Creative solutions by local people—such as the Wayabay and Gami's marriage described in this chapter—often work better than interventions by outsiders.

- Changes regarding Gebusi sex and marriage since 1998 suggest that Gebusi:

  — Continue to have male social bonding and homo*social* camaraderie

  — Seldom if ever engage in sexual relations between men

— Are somewhat more flexible than they were in defining marriage as an "exchange" between wider groups of kin

— Have somewhat less stress and anxiety than they previously did concerning modern forms of courtship and marital compensation

- The story of Pelap from 2017 illustrates that younger generations of Gebusi women:

    — Have greater flexibility of individual choice in sexual and martial relations than they did in the traditional past

    — Continue to be under the influence and domination if not control by Gebusi men

    — Presently expand on a long-standing tradition in which some women are highly self-willed, notwithstanding negative consequences for themselves

    — Are not used as compensation. Money now helps mediate disputes over women and sexuality, at least between men. Ironically, this reduces to some extent Gebusi men's perceived need to outright control women's bodies, sexuality, and reproduction.

Chapter 10

The Wider World of Influence—and Its Limits

If initiations were the biggest and grandest spectacles of Gebusi culture, the celebrations of National Independence Day at Nomad Station had by the late 1990s not just supplanted them but galvanized the power of outside influence into Gebusi culture itself. The festivities now included more people than just Gebusi, and they put issues of ethnicity, colonialism, and racial notions of blackness and whiteness at cultural issue. Along with Gebusi dancing, athleticism, music, and dramatic skits were those of other ethnic groups that ringed Nomad Station and that Gebusi had little peaceful contact with prior to colonial intervention: the Bedamini, Kubor, Samo, Oybae, Honibo, and even distant peoples such as the Pa and the Kabasi. Nomad has been the administrative center for some 9,000 people scattered across 3,500 square miles of rainforest; many of those within a two-day walk came to attend Independence Day at Nomad Station in 1998. No white persons except for yours truly were present. Yet the specter and impact of Australian white colonialism was prominent if not prevalent, including the local adoption and modified inculcation of colonial and racial assumptions. These concerned modern notions of enlightened progress, Christian salvation by a God-head authority, and the administrative machinery of white colonial organization, judgment, and aspiration. As such, the local celebration of Papua New Guinea's political independence from colonial Australia on September 16 was not just marked but permeated by assertion of Western values bequeathed from colonialism and racial domination. In the bargain, Gebusi culture was now presented as folkloric reenactment, a small part of a large regional interethnic festival replete with performances that both denied and selectively acknowledged or appreciated the region's cultural past.

I realized at the time that my sense of Gebusi culture had to expand to include a host of wider identifications, meanings, and institutions. Anthropologists often look to public celebrations and rituals as key expressions of a culture's values and history. As cultures interconnect, these associations increase—and the lines between them can blur. Gebusi meanings, identities, and values of culture had become regional, national, and even international in scale. Anthropology not only acknowledges these dynamics but takes them as a pivotal if not axiomatic to the workings of contemporary cultures.

Ultimately, Independence Day at Nomad in 1998 featured a whole week of festivities and celebrations. Well more than 1,000 people attended. Ceremonies began with two days of team sports on the Nomad ball field, focusing on soccer, rugby, and to some degree basketball. These were all sports that white colonial officers had introduced to Nomad in an attempt to channel aggressive energy from local warfare into organized and ostensibly nonviolent competition on the ball field. For Independence Day, the long series of sports matches pitted different groups and erstwhile enemies against each other. The contests escalated through several rounds and climaxed in all-star games that pitted the best players from opposing ethnic groups or "tribes" against each other.

For Gebusi, their key matches were against the Bedamini—the much larger ethnic group next door that had raided and decimated their villages. Though pacification had stopped Bedamini raids, they retained a reputation for fierceness. But Gebusi had the advantage of close proximity to Nomad, where they could practice and play league sports on a regular basis. They were also playing on their home field. At the end of the competition, the headline could have read, "David beats Goliath!" In an amazing coup, Gebusi won all but one game against the Bedamini. Their defeated rivals were so frustrated and angry as to accuse Gebusi of sabotaging them with magic, for which they ominously suggested they would take revenge. Fear of Bedamini actually attacking our village and stealing things led selected men to stay back and keep watch on the goods in my house and in the little store that I had helped them set up at Gasumi Corners—while I and almost everyone else were at Nomad Station watching the festivities. When I first worked among them, Gebusi played soccer as much as possible until a tie score was reached, so no one would gloat as winners or be humiliated as losers. But those days were long gone as the millennium approached, even as Gebusi, mindful of Bedamini antagonism, stayed even-keeled and sportsmanlike.

As Independence Day unfolded, I struggled to keep up. There was excited talk of "dramas." What could these be? As dusk turned into night, a large performance area was roped off next to the government station. Many hundreds of people from different tribes amassed to watch the performances. And when they started, what a shock! Most of them were spoofs, farces, and parodies of local traditions acted out by villagers themselves. In one prominent skit, a local man dressed as a white colonial officer—wearing spotless long white socks, a cowboy hat, sunglasses, and sporting a Western-style haircut—tried with generous pride to give a can of tinned fish to an "ignorant savage." The latter was coated in dark black charcoal, painted with clumsy and uneven white stripes, and adorned with a tattered headdress that was all askew. The "savage" could make only grunting noises. Ostensibly not knowing that the tin of fish was a prized gift of food, the traditional bumpkin went through hilarious slapstick antics as he tried to figure out what this strange object was. He tried to open it with his hands and teeth, banged it on the ground, and stomped on it, all in a futile attempt to discover what was inside. It was all enormously funny, and the audience erupted in howls of laughter. To underscore the message, its "meaning" was shouted out to all through a battery-operated bullhorn: "In the old days, we were ignorant. White people tried to give us good things, but we didn't realize how good they were, and we destroyed them in our ignorance. Now things have changed. We have given up our bad ways and become good."

The moral connotation of this message was driven home in other performances. In one, a man in random black paint and wearing an old cassowary headdress and loincloth groaned buffoonishly as he tried with clumsy effort to hack down a tiny tree using a traditional stone adze. Though his efforts were futile, his antics were riotous. The man's sardonic companion sat smoking a traditional pipe and refused to help until they got into a fight. Then came the "meaning": "In the old days, we didn't know about steel axes and how good they were. We tried to chop trees with stone axes, but it didn't work and we got angry and fought with each other."

In skit after skit, one or another traditional practice or belief was skewered for audience delight. Many customs portrayed were ones I had seen quite genuinely in 1980–1982. Rites once performed with dignity and grace—magic spells, origin myths, fish poisoning rituals, spirit séances, divinations, and dances—were transformed into farce. What bittersweet comedy! As an anthropologist, it was sad to see such a mockery of rich local traditions by the very people who used to practice them—in favor of colonial-cum-modern progress. And yet, the skits *were* very funny, sometimes uproariously so. I fought back tears of laughter even as I felt pangs of nostalgia for customs I had witnessed "for real" just 16 years before.

For me, the most dramatic skit was performed by friends from Gasumi Corners: a spoof of sickness, death, and sorcery divination. The opening performer was Mora—the teenager who had tried to be my romantic partner during my first fieldwork, and who was now a senior man with several children. He was caked with mud and wore a large fake phallus strapped about his waist. Smoking continually from a traditional tobacco pipe, he wheezed and coughed loudly until, in a spasm of sickness, he toppled over with a loud thud. This attracted the attention of a spirit

Mora [l] and Yamdaw [r] performing the Gasumi Corners skit at the Nomad Independence Day celebrations, 1998.

medium, played by Yamdaw, the son of Nelep. Yamdaw's costume was absurdly traditional, including an upside-down cassowary headdress and a bark belt that was so oversized that it slid down whenever he got up. Mora then cried that he was going to die. This prompted Yamdaw to scream directly into his ear—a traditional way to forestall a friend from losing consciousness or dying. These efforts were futile, and Mora quickly "died." After farcical wailing, a sorcery suspect was paraded up to Mora's corpse. The suspect was Kawuk, a senior man of Gasumi Corners and staunch supporter of the Catholic Church. (During the early years of colonial influence, Kawuk had, in fact, killed a family of three—a husband and wife accused as sorcerers, plus their son.) In the skit, Kawuk was made up with black paint, white body markings, leaf strips, and feathers. Now it was his turn to be the "victim." As he was forced to wail over Mora's corpse, the body gave a dramatic "sign." A fishing line that had been tied to the tip of Mora's fake phallus was surreptitiously pulled. As Mora dramatically arched his back and moaned, this large organ raised up in a monumental erection. The audience exploded with laughter. Needless to say, the corpse had indicated that Kawuk was "guilty" as the sorcerer responsible. Kawuk was then interrogated, cried like a baby, and was summarily "killed," after which everyone ran off.

To conclude their act, the performers distanced themselves clearly from the roles they had been playing. Marching solemnly back into the performance area, they lined up in a neat row and stood at attention in front of the judges. Formally and soberly, they bowed in unison to each side of the audience that encircled them—left, right, rear, and front. Finally, with military precision, they marched out, to the cheers of the crowd.

What was I to think? The richness of Gebusi spirit beliefs, the poetry and aesthetics of their spirit mediumship, and even their concern for the sick and dying were turned into farce. Their very ethnicity and race were debunked in favor of white colonial intervention and modern intrusion. And yet, the skit presented a stinging critique of sorcery beliefs, inquests, and fights that had killed many Gebusi in the past. That persons such as Kawuk could play lead characters in this mocking retort—themselves having killed suspected sorcerers in years gone by—underscored this rejection. The skit was very funny, very smart, and very well performed—even as Gebusi continued to believe very deeply in sorcery (!). I was left with much to ponder.

During two nights, a total of 42 dramas were performed. Most, like those described, were spoofs of tradition while values of outside influence and modern progress were trumpeted. This theme was thrown into relief by the remaining acts. Many of these were Christian morality plays, with large posters upon which verses from the Bible were written. In one performance, a villager dressed, in a full white costume and a peaked white crown, assumed the role of Jesus. He was accompanied by a second white-clad man who held a large "trumpet" and played the part of Angel Gabriel. Across from them and from the rest of their white angelic retinue were a dozen or so bare-breasted village women dressed in neotraditional garb, dancing and cavorting lewdly with flowers in their hair and their hands thrown above their heads. As the force of Jesus and his angels grew closer and more powerful, the dancing women became fearful and started to tremble. Eventually they were overcome with shame and guilt for their smutty behavior; they writhed in spasms on the ground and died. The meaning was clearly given from the Bible passages that were then read: traditional expressions of women's allure and sexuality, such as had occurred in female dancing at initiations, had been sinful and were now fully replaced by Christian morality and chaste propriety. I was left wondering how much men's gender domination in the traditional past was being countered in the modernizing present as opposed to simply being reinscribed in new guises. Certainly there were some Gebusi traditions that I was glad to see disappear. But much that was beautiful was lost in the bargain. And the new inequalities that Gebusi were experiencing—in church, school, and the market—did not always seem preferable to the practices they replaced.

The remaining skits, though few in number, suggested a more ambivalent view. These enacted the traumas and foibles of locally modern life. Some of these portrayed the challenges of living in town at Kiunga—scrounging medicine for a sick child from a pompous official, and coping with children who drift into trouble after school. In one poignant little play, an impoverished city youth stole and ran off with a suitcase full of money. The owner then returned, pulled out a gun, and shot dead the two security guards who had failed to guard his wealth. Here, the hungry boy escaped as a criminal, but worse, the powerful boss had become a murderer. Indeed, the skit echoed the life of the provincial premier, who had recently been charged with attempted murder. Despite the seriousness of such themes, the skits maintained a humorous tone. In this way, they played flexibly with alternative outcomes rather than asserting foregone conclusions.

Although local traditions were lampooned at night, they were honored at least in part in the full light of the following day. While a thousand people looked on, villagers in meticulous costumes danced in full traditional fashion. Diverse ethnic groups displayed their dances and initiations: Bedamini, Kubor, Samo, and even the Pa from across the Strickland River. Their performances were spectacular, a photographer's dream. Gasumi Corners was represented by Halowa, Yuway's married brother and an Evangelical Christian, who drum-danced with a traditionally dressed Gebusi woman from another settlement. The performance that stole the heart of the audience, however, was by dancers from the distant Kabasi peoples, who lived three days' hard walk southeast of Nomad. With slow, dignified dancing and haunting songs, they performed both standing and sitting for over half an hour. At traditional Gebusi feasts, dancers visiting from distant settlements were often given pride of place. Here, on a larger scale, many in the audience were visibly enthralled, appearing to have never before seen the Kabasi style of performance.

Though with some traditional elements, these performances of cultural history were now staged in a wholly new and newly controlled neocolonial ethnic and racial context. Rather than being performed as all-night rituals in a darkened longhouse for kin and friends, dances were now reenacted at Nomad Station for a thousand strangers in the glaring heat of day. Even a member of the National Parliament of Papua New Guinea was present. The performances were not designed to initiate a young man, cure a sick person, celebrate a local accomplishment, or embody the spirits. Rather, the pageantry was organized and structured by government officials—and performed on the government parade field by the flagpole at the center of Nomad Station. The dancing was not done as a spiritual celebration but staged in the competition for nominal amounts of prize money doled out to the winning performers. The performances were rated and judged not by locals but by Nomad government officials who did not come from the area, did not know any of its local languages, and knew little of the area's distinctive cultures. Carrying clipboards to write down their evaluations, they later publicly announced and paid the performers they had chosen to "win." This was consequential. Indeed, the small purses of prize money were a major if not prime motivation for

A woman and man from Gasumi Corners perform
traditional dancing for a crowd of hundreds by the
Nomad Sub-District Office at the PNG Independence
Day celebrations, 1998.

many performers to stage their dances at Nomad Station in the first place.
Many villagers were dressed up for presentation regardless of whether they
were otherwise qualified to wear the costume, including young boys in
initiation garb who were not in fact being initiated. For most of those
present, the displays did not reflect current practices, beliefs, or rituals in
their own villages. Indigenous culture was here being reenacted as folklore
for neocolonial consumption and monetary reward.

If the Independence Day festivities both spoofed and celebrated traditional practices, they also enacted games and customs introduced or associated with Australian colonial influence, in addition to competitive
sports. This included competitions such as drinking quantities of hot tea,
pillow fighting while sitting on a beam, blindfolded women trying to split
papayas with a bush knife, and climbing a greased pole—for which the
winners received very small amounts of prize money from government
officials. The atmosphere was that of a Western county fair, with hundreds

of people milling about. Villagers sold cooked food from stalls as music blared from boom boxes. Tables of ring toss and gambling games were set up for those willing to risk 5 or 10 cents in a game of skill or chance. The final afternoon boasted a lively disco contest, at which the dance ground was thronged with bodies gyrating to the throb of Papua New Guinea rock music. Although a few brave women participated—mostly mothers dancing with their daughters—the dance ground was dominated by older boys and young men. All dancing appeared to be same-sex: guys with guys, and girls with girls. The dancers' outfits presented a mélange of styles ranging from traditional costumes to spiffy modern shirts and jeans or hip-hop clothes. A couple of young men dressed up and danced buffoonishly as women in modern dress.

What was I to make of this hodgepodge? Ultimately, the Independence Day festivities were a smorgasbord of cultural diversity. If rituals reflect and symbolize the structure of people's social life, as Émile Durkheim suggested long ago, then Nomad Independence Day celebrations in the late 1990s reflected lives that included a tapestry of different, multifaceted influences. Within this mix, indigenous customs were alternately taken out of context, parodied or debunked, and reperformed with modern honor. For Gebusi at the time, the festivities seemed to symbolize the diverse opportunities and many challenges of living so near to the government station. On the whole, these challenges debunked customary traditions and relegated them to a foregone past while foregrounding and valorizing "modern" ways of life associated especially with the legacy of colonialism and with its white racial influence and domination.

The question of how people do or don't resist and repel the legacy of colonial or racial domination, as opposed to simply internalizing it, looms large in contemporary anthropology. This issue is made more poignant by that fact that dominance and oppression are "influential"; they are often internalized to at least some extent by those who are subordinate or subordinated, and this internalization occurs at the same time that oppressed traditions recede into the deeper past. In religion, politics, language, and culture itself, historical dominance has a continuing influence in the present, even when this influence is recognized and resisted. In the American civil rights movement, for instance, the power and influence of Martin Luther King Jr. drew more strongly on Southern Baptist Christianity, evangelicalism, and articulate modern American oratory—features that originally developed through dominant white American culture—than they did on customs bequeathed directly from Africa.

It is important here to gauge different degrees and measures of disempowerment, dispossession, and abasement; that is, we cannot assume domination and oppression to be uniform across cases. For their part, Gebusi have been largely appreciative of white Australian colonial intervention and its legacy. Though Australian officers were intimidating, no Gebusi lost their lives as a result, and colonial pacification provided the huge benefit of stopping further decimation if not extinction of Gebusi by the raids of their Bedamini neighbors. The Bedamini, quite predictably, have not been so positively disposed to the heavy influence of Australian colonialism on their indigenous culture. But even this is at a huge distance from the depredations, for instance, of the trans-Atlantic slave trade, whereby millions of Africans were dragged from their homes and ended up dead or enslaved for centuries in the United States or in other parts of the ostensibly New World. The legacy of slavery—however much white American culture and values have since become influential and/or internalized by African-Americans themselves—remains deeply with us today. It is little wonder that the killing of Blacks by white policemen in America carries such deep and pernicious messages of virulent racism and disregard for Black lives. As such, it is important to critically recognize histories of ethnic dominance and racial oppression and to critically assess their impact under contemporary conditions.

In the aftermath of Independence Day, the Nomad area seemed to relax. Having worked and played so hard, people unwound in a kind of collective morning-after. In Gasumi Corners, respite lasted several weeks before gradually giving way to plans for another occasion that was especially poignant for me: the feast to commemorate my own departure in 1998.

As my time to leave Gebusi inched gradually closer, my days became bittersweet. My friendships had been so deeply rekindled, and new ones had taken root. How could I go? It ended up as an incredible finale, and I wasn't the reason for its success. Village celebrations have always served several purposes. And Gebusi are the first to keep anyone from getting a big head. But it was hard not to cry when I first heard the song that the Gasumi string band composed to thank me for having come back to them.

With their typical casual gusto, the village buzzed with preparations. Firewood and cooking leaves were stockpiled, sago was processed, and game was hunted deep in the forest. As a contemporary twist, profits were pooled from our local store to buy a large stock of tinned fish and rice. Added to these were my own gifts to the community, both to individuals and for our collective feast. These included further cartons of store-bought food and a score of coveted shotgun cartridges, which Wayabay and other young men used to hunt a large slew of wild pigs and cassowaries.

During several weeks of preparation, everyone was so busy in the forest gathering food and materials that I started feeling lonely in the village. I longed to be with Gebusi in their timbered hideaways, and I was nostalgic for the rainforest. So Sayu, Didiga, and I set off to visit the makeshift forest camp at Harfolobi. We canoed up the Kum River under the stately canopy of the towering trees that lined the banks. Climbing up the bluff at Yibihilu, my lip quivered to see our former village and even the site of my first house. It was all overgrown, not just with weeds but with trees turning into forest. Gone as well were so many friends from my first fieldwork, reclaimed by nature. Up at Harfolobi I visited the grave of Sayu's wondrous mother, Boyl, and it was hard not to weep. I sat in crystal waters of the waterfall where I had bathed years before. I enjoyed once again the easy rhythm of rainforest life—husbands, wives, and children relaxed and peaceful, and I at home among them.

After several days, obligations drew us reluctantly back to Gasumi Corners, where the festive buildup continued. Though I knew the general contours of the event to come, its specifics remained a mystery to me. On the day of reckoning, visitors came from near and far. This included those still living whom I had known so well, others whom I had seen only occasionally, and a few who knew of me just by reputation. For several days in advance, piles of coconuts, a ton or more of sago starch, mounds of dried game, and stashes of rice and fish had spawned a veritable village industry of cutting, cleaning, wrapping, and cooking. Now it was time to pull it all from the cooking fires, divide it up, and give it away. Hundreds of visitors had come. Amid our shouts of laughter and whoops of celebration, the gift giving continued long after dusk turned into night. By now I was no longer a bystander but a primary host. I tried to make sure that my friends and acquaintances, the government officials, and even the hangers-on each got their appropriate share.

Then came the entertainment. Would this be a traditional dance, an appreciation of historical customs? Or would it be modern? Instead of choosing a single option, my friends let all the flowers bloom. On one side of the hamlet, in the dim light of a darkened house, a visiting dancer in traditional costume performed in full dignity. Older men and women were especially drawn to this proud display of days gone by. Mothers held their smallest children, some of whom were possibly seeing a fully traditional Gebusi dance for the first time. On the other side of the settlement came strains of a visiting string band with guitar and ukulele, playing wonderful songs I had never heard. In the middle, the settlement's central clearing, was a modern disco. My friends had finagled a big boom box and a set of speakers from workers at Nomad Station and lugged them all the way to Gasumi Corners. With light from a bright lantern, their music poured forth. As older folks looked on, youngsters picked up the beat. Within minutes, they were grooving in ways that would have passed tolerably in an American disco.

In the moonlight and gentle breeze, the joy and sadness of nostalgia blurred together. For me, it was the modern Gebusi equivalent of old *fafadagim-da*—the wistful enjoyment of strong, unfathomable longing, of being together while thinking of loneliness and loss. Swaying to different beats from one end of the settlement to the other, the village became a three-ring circus of bittersweet pleasure. I shuttled between the traditional dance, the string band, and the disco in the middle, delighting in each for their part. Together, they formed a fugue of cadences that were discordant yet strangely harmonious. No one minded this jumble of aesthetics and experiences, and neither did I. Perhaps I had learned something new after all—not just to accept the fragmentary nature of Gebusi culture as it now was expressed, but to enjoy and revel it. I thought back to Sayu's first traditional dance and all the years of ritual splendor that preceded it. Was Gebusi ritual life now a past tradition, or a spirit of new things to come? I realized the answer could not be one or the other; it was both at the same time. Outpacing my understanding, the people of Gasumi Corners had become modern in their own special way. On the eve of my departure, I contemplated again what they had given me. Their gift had gone beyond their past or their present: they had shown me the discovery and surprise of continued human connection.

Anne-Sylvie, on our departure from Gebusi, 2016

That afternoon, the whole village smelled of cooking. Everywhere people were roasting stuff, and small groups gathered around fuming heaps of embers. Gradually smoke joyfully conquered every little space. I was given the full treatment during a fun dress-up gathering, during which my female friends and I all donned traditional attire, *bilas*. I had paint all over my face and body, and feathers and neck-laces were paired with a fluorescent bikini top—all in all, enough to make people laugh for a couple of generations (see color insert photo #12). When the moment came to share the food, men endeavored to appropriate women's labor and claim the paternity of the great results displayed in front of us. There was much happy yelling that adver-tised how they had organized the alignment of plates and bowls and the distribution of their contents. For a second, one might have believed the men were actually in control of this vast cooking affair.

Then we got ready for the dance. Two parallel universes dilated into the hot air of the night. Quickly a "disco" was set up in front of the longhouse. Shy women formed a large circle in the middle of which alcohol-soaked young men were gesticulating and laughing. Inside, under the longhouse's thatched roof, a man was silently get-ting ready to dance; he was decorated with black and ochre paint all over the body, a crown and necklaces of feathers, and, in his train of dried grass, a long "tail" made of crayfish claws. Around 3:00 a.m. came the first sound of his drum. Suddenly his steps imprinted their own cadence onto the structure of the longhouse, vibrating beneath the gravity of his frail frame, grown heavier under the weight of tradi-tion. Before my eyes, under the flickering light of the flame and with the backdrop of a hypnotic female chorus, the metamorphosis from human to bird of paradise happened. The skinny man with a high-pitched voice was entirely absorbed by the spirit of the healing bird. His each step enjoined the air to make his feathers move, like the tick-ing of a clock that would not go anywhere and would instead freeze time. His identical and mesmerizing movements made, by contrast, the dance steps of the young people congregated outside resemble a frenzy of jumping jacks; the youths were too drunk to really jump anywhere, their muscles galvanized and trapped in a tune they had already heard too many times.

On one side of this parallel universe was the enclosed space of the longhouse, the shrunken perimeter where all the solemn force of

Male dancer, Halowa, at our final feast.

ancestors was allowed to deploy itself under the stunned gaze of children and old people. They sat in silence, their calm faces caressed by the flames. On the other side was the ever-growing space outside, occupied by a loud and jolly crowd of loosened up bodies moving to the sound of instruments that condensed all the seductive power of modernity. Toward the entrance of the longhouse, a few middle-aged men sat chewing and spitting kava roots before leaching and drinking their juice. I fell asleep on the rough ground of the longhouse, Papua New Guinea disco and the bird of paradise merging into a hazy ochre dream as the night got less and less dark.

At an early hour, my silently sobbing companions walked me back to our house. The place was etched into my flesh, in all the fibers of my being that had once rejected it as much as they now loved it. I raised my eyes to the coconut trees, toward the sky where I had so often raised my hand, holding an expensive cell phone hoping to connect with my distant world back home. This time my hope was the same—but reversed: that the place, this place, would stay connected with me, beyond time and space.

Men dancing while holding bottles of homebrew at our final feast.

[Left] Female dancer, Dohayn, at our final feast.
[Below] Male dancer, Halowa, at our final feast.

Update: Where does it go, the past? In the late 1990s, life at Nomad Station and in Gasumi Corners seemed so locally modern, so vibrantly diverse, so hopeful. Almost as much as spirit séances or sorcery inquests in 1980, it was hard to believe that their more modern world would ever really change—yet it has. At Nomad Station, almost nothing is now happening; aside from the struggling local school and a dismal market, there is little reason for anyone to go there. I have not had the occasion to be at Nomad for Independence Day in recent years, but I can only imagine how small and restricted its celebration must be, with no government, the station shut, and little economic livelihood.

The Gebusi, however, have neither stayed still nor regretted their modern decline. Sayu now has seven children. He still sings in the local string band and dances disco with the best of them. Other Gebusi have similarly thrived with their families and their local life in Gasumi Corners. Against the hopeful opportunities that ramped up to the Gebusi millennium, they remind us that progress is not inevitable, that downturns are inevitable, and that adapting to them is necessary, one way or the other. While I was in the field, the United States had its own recession, followed later by the crash of 2008 and then the Great Recession. The Gebusi's economic downturn is lasting longer than our own. Perhaps because of this, its lesson seems all the greater: adapt not just to a world of hoped-for growth but to one of unforeseen challenge and ultimate limitation while drawing on deeper and longer-standing cultural resources.

BROADER CONNECTIONS
Nationhood, Ethnicity, and Folklore

- Expressive or **popular culture**—including dance, music, public display, and major celebrations and festivities—reveals much about contemporary conditions of culture and culture change.

- Many peoples feel conflicted or ambivalent about some of their traditional beliefs and practices. At the National Independence Day celebrations, old-time customs such as sorcery divinations, spirit séances, warfare, and even indigenous material culture were spoofed and mocked, though there was also nostalgia for indigenous costuming and dancing.

- In many societies, including the Gebusi, some indigenous practices are taken out of cultural context and enacted as historic **folklore**.

- Independence Day revealed and symbolized how Gebusi, like many peoples, grapple with and internalize the previous impact of colonialism, including its influence on national culture and identification with the modern **nation-state**.

- Gebusi sports competition against Bedamini, and the threatening Bedamini accusations of attack, reflect how historical enmities inform modern ethnic conflict.

- As occurs in many world areas, the Nomad Independence Day commemorations reveal and express the continuing impact of preceding colonial and racial domination.

- Like events of **public culture** in many developing societies, Independence Day festivities often reflect and symbolize diverse alternatives and values that inform society and culture.

- Following the theories of Émile Durkheim, the rituals and festivities of Independence Day at Nomad Station reflected the prevalent pattern of Gebusi social life leading up to the 2000 millennium.

- The cultures of many peoples mix-and-match modern or contemporary practices and beliefs with long-standing or indigenous ones. The combination is sometimes called **syncretism or hybridity**. Syncretism among Gebusi was evident in the combination of different dress styles at feasts, and more generally in the combined activity of traditional dancing, "dramas," and modern sports and games at Independence Day festivities.

- In long-term or longitudinal fieldwork, anthropologists often form strong personal relationships and become closely associated with the people they study. At the final feast to commemorate his departure in 1998, Bruce was not just an observer but a primary participant and host. In 2016, Anne-Sylvie was dressed up in costume along with other Gebusi women.

- Decline of activities at Nomad Station in the 2000s underscores that progress and development are not inevitable; people must also adapt to conditions of economic downturn or limitation.

- Modern change often also brings challenges and problems—such as Gebusi men's drunkenness at some feasts and ceremonies.

- Gebusi taught Bruce that older and newer patterns of culture do not need to oppose each other. This fuels our continuing surprise and discovery in making human connections across cultures.

Making do with little: A boy plays with a cardboard box hat, 2013. →

Part Three

Blurring the Past in the Present

Chapter 11

Closer, Closer, Further Away
Revival, Independence, and Government Absurdity

I had tried to send word ahead about my return in 2008. This would be a briefer visit than the one in 1998, but no less important for that. Ten years later, what had changed? Would my Gebusi friends be yet more engaged in an outside world, their old customs further gone, their rush to be modern yet more intense?

My first inkling of the answer was the challenge of getting there. Back in Atlanta, I looked in amazement at the Mission Aviation Fellowship's (MAF) e-reply to my request for a plane ticket: the Nomad airstrip was closed. How could this be? For 45 years that airstrip had been the lifeline for Gebusi and their neighbors to the outside world. With no roads in the area, what did this new isolation mean? Had Gebusi become more remote? How had they responded, given all the change they had already experienced? These questions haunted my plans. My sinking fear was that I wouldn't see Gebusi at all. With no air transport, the overland trip to Nomad from Kiunga takes up to a week on foot, tramping across swamps and fording the large and dangerous Strickland River. I was tempted to try this, but luckily, the MAF agent had a better idea. He suggested I land at a tiny mission airstrip at Honinabi that was open on the Gebusi's side of the Strickland River—and then hike from there to Nomad and on to Gasumi Corners. Maybe the Nomad strip would be fixed and reopened by the time I arrived in the country. If all else failed, I would just stay in Kiunga and make contact with whichever Gebusi happened to be residing in the corners of the town.

On leaving Atlanta, I didn't know which option would come to pass. Twenty-eight years after my first trip, I was still in suspense.

After the grueling trip from Atlanta to Los Angeles to Australia to Papua New Guinea's capital of Port Moresby, and then to the rainforest town of Kiunga, I finally got word about Gebusi. Though none of my messages had gotten through, Father Eddy at the Kiunga Catholic mission recognized my photo of Sayu. He said Sayu was now married with several children. My appetite whetted; I was all the more eager to see my Gebusi friends. But first I had to get there.

The challenges that afflict infrastructure in outstation areas of developing countries are socially and culturally crucial. The present backstory, which I discovered later, was that the Nomad government had run out of money to pay Gebusi and others for cutting and clearing grass on the local airstrip. Eventually, laborers gave up and stopped working. As grass shot up, the airstrip degraded until incoming planes could barely land. Nomad's officials, hailing from other parts of the country, flew out on the last planes. They did not come back. Sadly, politics and cronyism allowed them to continue collecting government pay while in Kiunga or elsewhere—without living or working at Nomad Station at all. So government presence shrank to almost nothing. The grass continued growing, and the airstrip was closed. When infrastructure works, it is easy to take it for granted. But when it fails, the consequences are grave.

After months of cajoling and diligence, two local men who had been associated with the government managed to raise enough money to get the airstrip partly repaired. By the time I arrived in Kiunga, the strip had been closed for nine months. Using me as a test case, MAF asked me to pay full fare for a charter flight but take little cargo, lightening the weight of the plane. The seasoned bush pilot, Nick Swaim, said we should wait for a dry day. When the weather finally cleared, I loaded my few things and we took off. Lifting up, I marveled again at the full magnificence of the rainforest, horizon to horizon. Awe and sorrow shook me as I realized how rare such an unbroken vista of rainforest has become on our planet.

Almost before I was ready, the Strickland River passed beneath and we approached Nomad Station. Nick circled and careened us down to just six or eight feet above the ground—so he could carefully inspect the strip. I looked across anxiously as he pulled up suddenly to get us back over the treetops. He gave me the thumbs up: we would try to land. My pulse raced as the plane circled in for a final descent. On touching down, we caught a rut and skidded right and then left. But Nick got us calmly straightened out and brought the plane to a gentle stop. It was only later that I learned the greater risk—that if we had hit a deeper rut, the plane would have catapulted forward. If the lone front propeller hits the ground, its powerful torque flips the rest of the plane to disaster.

But, oh, to be safely back! I gazed out eagerly as we taxied, remembering the same experience in 1980 and in 1998. Who and what would I find? Each time was so new.

Word about my arrival had finally gotten to Nomad that very morning, and Sayu and Didiga had rushed to the airstrip—arriving in time to meet me! I could hardly believe it. We hugged and hugged and snapped fingers. At first, we could barely say anything, overcome by joy of simply being together again. Their faces were now middle-aged, but their smiles were as bright and deep as ever.

As I got my bearings, I realized that the clothes on those around me were plainly ragged, unlike before. Looking up across Nomad Station, I saw that it, too, was ragged. Houses had deteriorated and most were boarded up. The Nomad school, so full of boisterous students the decade before, was empty, closed to students. Even the schoolyard grass was burned and charred black. The Nomad ball field, having seen so many rivalries and triumphs in years past, was now overgrown with two feet of grass. Gebusi themselves were smiles all over. But what was their circumstance?

Not wanting to linger at Nomad Station, we gathered up my few supplies. As the Cessna quickly taxied and took off, we trotted off in high gear to Gasumi Corners. I apologized to everyone that I had not been able to bring many supplies or gifts, since a heavier plane couldn't have landed.

Reassuring me, my friends understood but hardly seemed to care. My questions deepened, though, when I arrived in the village and saw that people's possessions were few, their clothes torn, their pots battered, and their knives and axes worn out.

My first priority was simply to see who was still alive. To my huge relief, most of my closest friends had survived; a surge of welcomes came from Kilasui, Mosomiay, Hogaya, Wayabay, Agiwa, Yokwa, and my great old friends Yuway, Keda, Kawuk, and Hawi. Among the women, Mus, Dohayn, Dasom, Tabway, Kuni, To'ofun, Towe, Hahap, Oip, and Nelep were still living. Complementing the adults was a bounding gaggle of children born since my last visit; I struggled to record and remember their many names. As my tabulations showed, the work of time had been kind to the people Gasumi Corners: through natural increase, their numbers had grown by 38% between 1998 and 2008—from 122 to 168. Among the additions was one new "Knauft": Didiga's first son, to whom he gave my last name.

Among some peoples of the developing world, a swelling tide of children presents major problems: too many mouths, poverty, poor health,

Children in Gasumi
Corners, 2008.

and lack of education. But given Gebusi's extensive tracts of land, their surge in numbers was more a vibrant replenishment than a crisis.

How else had the community changed? Back at Nomad Station, with the airstrip virtually closed, the government was gone, the offices vacant. There was no Nomad school, no effective medical clinic, no sports leagues, no development projects, and—in the absence of a cash economy—the Nomad market was poorly attended, with just a few sellers offering paltry goods to nonexistent buyers. Against this, Gasumi Corners itself was a different story. Its biggest change was also the most obvious—a great new longhouse in the center of the community! I knew immediately what this meant: a whole new generation of Gebusi had been initiated since I had last been there. Their transmission of indigenous culture across generations had been rekindled and maintained. What a joy! Given this, I suspected I would soon learn of other traditions that were also reemerging.

When I first entered the longhouse, as if there were any doubt, I was besieged by a flurry of traditional welcoming. My fingers were snapped again and again, my gift-exchange names were called out, and the floor swept clean. After being begged to sit down, I was offered water, bananas, and, most significantly, round upon round of strong sweet tobacco from traditional bamboo pipes. In short order, festivities were punctuated by waves of good-natured sexual joking, as I had remembered from 1980. In marked contrast to a decade earlier, men were delighted almost to tears that I could joke with them in traditional style. In the mix, beyond the more strident patriarchy of the past, social relations between men and women had over the years become more casual than they had been during my early fieldwork. Men and women, even unrelated, might talk pleasantly and without particular suspicion—though if they got too friendly, a watchful spouse or sibling would take caustic note. Even so, there was an easier flow of interaction between women and men than had previously been the case, and many or most of the previous sexual and pollution taboos had been dropped or greatly softened. For the most part, however, men still tended to sleep in a separate room in their family houses, apart from women and young children, and they still occupied center stage at meetings and in ritual festivities. The gender divide was also still highly evident in matters of political and other public decision-making.

As my conversations became more earnest with the men, I found that my long-standing interest in Gebusi customs was not as marginal to them as it had been before. Alongside the resurgence of traditions was new curi-osity about the Gebusi's past, including the life stories and genealogies that I had brought with me. I gave a full copy to of these to Didiga, who could read and recite the information as a kind of community history. That night, I stumbled to bed astounded: Gebusi were reclaiming their past in ways I could not have imagined. The decade before, I had tried hard to respect and document Gebusi desires for change and the forces that had underlain them. But I had also wondered how Gebusi could ben-efit from outside influence without losing the richness of what was already theirs. Now they seemed more self-determined and more able to balance modern desires with appreciation of their cultural past.

To my delight, this balance now included traditional dancing. Within three days of my arrival, a dance with full regalia was held in a large house just five-minutes' walk from Gasumi Corners. In good classic style, the dancer was from a distant village; in this case, his dance helped cure a man who was regaining strength following illness. In style, form, and costume, the dance was similar to those I had seen so many years earlier (see color insert photo #7). Indeed, men's chewing and drinking of kava, the local root intoxicant, were more pronounced than they had been before—and the upcoming younger men were the most active drinkers. (Fortunately, in my opinion, alcohol had not yet made its way into Gasumi Corners.)

By and large, I found that Gebusi had continued to accommodate with remarkably good spirit—and with good result—their continuing iso-lation and lack of money or goods. Added to the ongoing closure of the Nomad airstrip and government office has been the decline of other mod-ern institutions, including even the local Catholic Church. With the departure of the previous parish priest, the St. Paul Catholic Church at Gasumi had ebbed in influence, attendance, and local significance, though it still labored on.

Left on their own, the people of Gasumi Corners have reoriented increasingly to the abundance of the deeper rainforest. Indeed, their nutri-tion and health seem better than ever! Rather than amassing prized foods to sell to government workers, Gebusi now grow and harvest these fully for themselves. They have retained and expanded their use of peanuts, pineapple, corn, pumpkins, beans, manioc, and several root crops—adapting their cultivation to local conditions. Of particular importance is sweet potato, which was indigenously raised as a rare and scrawny tuber.

Now, by contrast, sweet potatoes are grown abundantly by using mounding techniques and ingenious means of keeping away pigs. As such, sweet potatoes have become a major food staple alongside plantains and sago—and are much more nutritious than either of these.

This time I had the luxury of making deeper travels into the forest with Gebusi than I had in some years. And I quickly realized how adept and effective they had become at using canoes. Historically, living near a riverbank left a settlement vulnerable to attack; for defensive purposes, Gebusi preferred their houses perched on ridgetops. Even then, settlements were easily uprooted by raiding, killing, and accusations of sorcery. Under such conditions, it hardly made sense to invest heavy work in carving hand-hewn canoes from tree trunks—not to mention doing so with stone adzes. And canoes once made could be stolen by enemies. In 1982 the community of Yibihilu was at the downstream juncture where the Kum River became fully navigable; Gebusi had two or three canoes but mostly traveled overland. The neighboring community lived a good distance from any major river and had no canoes at all.

Now, however, rivers are routes of connection rather than barriers of separation. With increasing years and then decades of peace and stability, many Gebusi have gravitated increasingly downstream along their large and most easily traveled rivers. This includes those further downstream at

Canoeing on the Kum River, 2013.

Gasumi Corners, whose waterway to the Kum River is just five minutes' walk from the main settlement. Their neighboring community, Yehebi, has relocated entirely from its ridgetop to a bluff along the large Sio River. Every family has a canoe or two, and these are easily shared. Gebusi are now skilled oarsmen (and women!) and are quite comfortable spending from dawn to dusk on the river. Fishing is at once relaxing, productive, and a great supplement to nutrition. Further, Gebusi now cut large gardens along the banks of their rivers. Some stretches of riverbank boast one large food-producing plot after another. Rather than trudging through the forest and hauling produce back laboriously, Gebusi now rely increasingly on canoes to easily ferry themselves, supplies, and food directly to and from their garden settlements. In reorienting back to the rainforest, they have now, to a significant extent, become "canoe people."

In all, Gebusi seem to benefit greatly from increased nutrition, diet, and good health. And this despite the collapse of medical services (apart from infant inoculations, which thankfully continued at Nomad Station due to the heroic efforts of two Catholic nuns). In concert with the low rate of violence and the continued absence of killing, Gebusi enjoy increased fertility and a burgeoning rise in population. By 2013, as I discovered five years later, the population of Gasumi Corners had grown to almost 200 persons, marking an annual increase of about 3.5% since 2008 and, similarly before that, since 1998. Along with this has come greater longevity. In the deeper past, most people died by what we would consider middle age; it was unusual or rare for a man to live long enough to see the birth of a single grandchild. Now, however, enjoying grandchildren is not

Tabway with five of her grandchildren, 2013.

just cherished but commonplace. Kawuk has lived into his 60s and has 12 grandchildren while he himself is active and vibrant. And amid their other changes, land for Gebusi still remains a plentiful rather than a limited or contested resource; there is plenty of it to go around. Thankfully, I also determined that though Gebusi still believe in sorcery, the violence associated with it has been minimal, and no suspected sorcerers have been killed.

Gebusi said that with the closing of Nomad Station, the government died (*gamani golom-da*). But Gebusi have reasserted their own cultural vitality, which increasingly informs their understanding of, ambivalence toward, and rejection of government intrusion. This attitude stands in contrast to their passive acceptance and submission to government officials and their authority just 10 years earlier.

Anne-Sylvie

Amid the stupefying and sometimes tragic stories that unfold among Gebusi on a regular basis are those that have less to do with traditional practices than with recent political retooling. These stories are no less interesting to the anthropologist who has come to try and understand all the dynamics that create the sociocultural universe of this small patch of the world. Yet that is where I most often failed as an ethnographer; that is where my most deeply rooted annoyance manifested, as well as my reticence to accept that "another logic" was at play, dictating what appeared to me as absurd. I most often and most flagrantly lost all patience when faced with administrative snafus.

Supervised quagmires, overly meticulous and "under control" confusion, seemed to be a norm of sorts among the government officials who rarely but pompously visited Nomad. Grotesquely buttoned-up, in contrast to the raggedly clothed Gebusi, these men (for they are invariably men) displayed the distinction their government afforded them. Typically they insisted on being greeted by name prefixed with a "title" that made their status clearer (or not) to the world, and like former US presidents, they would forever keep the title. Yet turnover could be high, and the mushrooming of honorific labels and verbal accolades made biweekly greetings around the marketplace an hour-long affair. Some of these men were elected every five years, while others enjoyed an obscure longevity in office, which seemed to be self-attributed but was never questioned. Whether that came with prerogatives or not, or with a salary or not, was always hard to establish: when asked by us or by the community, "officials" tended to downplay and fudge how much they earned.

In any event, titled men arrived with annoying—or comedic—linguistic mannerisms. Not only did they love to speak in convoluted Tok Pisin and administrative English jargon, they used it to make any set of circumstances look like they were strictly in charge and under control—especially when our queries verged on the discovery that the officials' mastery over a situation had clearly run amok. We often asked the wrong (or right?) questions.

"Of course, it might," as an official responded when I asked why an airplane charter announced the previous day had not come, and whether it would show up the following day. "Of course, it might": the new motto of the place, perfectly conveying that we are ensured of the possibility of an event, nothing more. That is for sure!

I did not think I would see the Gebusi "bush hillbillies," as they were perceived to be, come head-to-head with the most powerful person in the province: the governor. It all started in 2015. The climatic phenomenon known as "El Niño" had devastated the South Pacific that year and was particularly tough on parts of Papua New Guinea; it caused record droughts with disastrous consequences in subsistence-based areas. By August it had been four months in a row that Gebusi had not seen a drop of rain. The "rainforest" was barely even a "forest," as leaves lost color and fell from the trees.

By October, due to the absence food, most villagers had deserted Gasumi Corners and gone deep into the forest. These former semi-nomads have retained aspects of that lifestyle and can still disappear into the bush for months on end. Though the Baruya, with whom I worked before, are horticulturalists, the Gebusi are more practiced at hunting, fishing, and gathering. But even Gebusi could not harvest hope from their dried-up patches of land: no bananas, sweet potatoes, or taros; no corn or pumpkin; no water nearby to process sago palm starch, not even any greens left from their former gardens. Not a single breadfruit or nut. Under the blazing sun everything had burned, and the jungle crackled under foot. Gebusi fell ill, since their streams and sources of pure water had dried up, and they had to drink brackish water from bigger rivers, where unhealthy sediments were rife. On one lucky day, an intrepid squad of young men saw seven huge turtles at the bottom of the Sio River. Usually such protein-rich treats dwell in deep water, making them impossible for anyone to catch. But the river's bottom was now near to its surface, and one of the men spotted a glimmer of shell under the sun; he wondered why this fossil was moving. At the height of the famine, they captured these turtles, floated them back alive to Gasumi Corners, and held an all-night feast. Here is yet another illustration of the triumph of good company among them, a cultural resource they would not lose in the midst of natural chaos.

Rain came around Christmastime, much earlier than any whiff of governmental help. The government's bragging, though, reached the depths of the rainforest much faster and circled the country many times over—and with it, the confirmation that the Papuan state was gangrenous to its core and incapable of organizing substantial relief efforts. With postcolonial bravado, Papua New Guinea refused to accept food aid from Australia even as the former's population suffered. It was a matter of pride: food relief would come from within.

In June 2016, right in the middle of our fieldwork, bags of rice did get to Nomad. But their arrival had nothing to do with the government. The development fund generated by the interests from the Ok Tedi mine, an open-pit copper, gold, and silver mine located 100 northwest of Gasumi Corner, (the mine had incidentally closed down during the drought) paid for the food; Digicel, the most important telecom company in the country, paid for its transport; and the whole thing was coordinated by the UN World Food Programme, notably by Sally Lloyd, an Australian lady who is considered a local by the locals, having grown up the daughter of a missionary in the area. There is nothing like emotional and personal investment in a community to ensure things get done. The plan was to distribute 10 kilos of rice per person—so all the adults and children registered in the district would get their share. That same plan had arranged for the rice to be delivered in 20-kg bags.

The airstrip in Nomad—which at least for the moment was made to function—became the convergence point of many villages around the area and was populated by different tribal groups. Within a few days, according to our own census, some 6,060 kg of rice were delivered by plane, but each charter brought only 80 bags at a time (which amounted to approximately 6 kilos of rice per person). Nothing could be distributed until all of it arrived, but nobody knew exactly how many bags to expect, how many planes were still scheduled to land, or when people could finally get their rice. At this point in time, people had long stopped starving and their historic drought had

Food-relief rice bags being
unloaded at Nomad, 2016.

turned into a distant memory. But rice is rice, a rare and prized food-
stuff no matter what nature otherwise yields or not.

Hundreds of bags of rice had to be stashed somewhere while waiting for the rest to arrive, and someone had to keep an eye on them.
How would such guards be compensated for their time? If they were
given more rice, there would not be enough for everyone. The old
floorboards of a former school broke through under the weight of all
the small grains in big bags. A blackboard welcomed chalk-scratched
counts and recounts: the bags that arrived, the bags to be redistrib-
uted, the bags counted twice, the bags deducted, the bags forgotten
about. The chalk marks became faded and smudged in places, and
intermediary and final counts were lost. Numbers that corresponded
to no reality were shouted around, and in the end, 42 bags were left
unaccounted for after all the planes had gone, along with the guards
who finally got their extra share.

Each village received a fixed amount. Groups gathered around,
each near a sign with their village's name on it and a depiction of
white pyramids of Trukai rice. Around the sign that said "Gasumi,"

despite the official guidelines that blasted through megaphones, a handful of men decided how to allocate the village's rice; that is, they would supervise their own distribution. It was decided that each family would get two bags, and that was it. No matter the size of the family—a widow or a couple with seven children, everyone would leave with 40 kg of rice, end of the story. All leftovers would go into a collective feast. "That's our own sense of justice, you know! (?)" Of course there was little we could say against this, but it did not stop us from rolling our eyes. The senior men finagled the rules to their own personal advantage just the same.

Gasumi men deciding rice distribution to families, 2016.

Gasumi women and children look on while men decide rice distribution, 2016.

The rice relief distribution came with yet stricter directions from the UN Programme Coordinator. She repeated many times over: do not eat only rice; do not eat over 300 grams of rice per person per day; continue tending your gardens and growing your own food; eat greens. In other words: eating only rice is not healthy, and further-more, you cannot count on this kind of rice distribution for your long-term survival. Although the villagers usually heeded her instruc-tions, because she spoke the local language and because they had loved her father, they hesitated this time. The problem was, after people had been suddenly gifted heaps of riches deposited from the skies, they believed it could happen again—and the gifts could get larger. A cargo cult was looming closer, because nothing from the outside world was rational—not the rice-carrying planes that landed after the drought was over and not the sudden distribution of the prized white grains. One thing local children would learn, however, is that this starchy godsend should not be relied upon when famine did in fact strike.

Bruce: In many world areas, social or religious movements have devel-oped to address frustrated desires to be or become modern. For many years in some parts of Melanesia, so-called "cargo cults" sprang up, whereby rit-ual means were developed as hopeful ways of attracting or magically creat-ing Western wealth and commodities. Outsiders saw these cults as superstitious and irrational ways of mimicking or aping Western produc-tivity—without producing anything of value. From the perspective of those living in remote areas, however, these terms can seem somewhat reversed. Who can explain why so much money from the outside world comes to some places and people, at some times, and not at all to others, or at other times? Who can explain the vast riches and resources of multinational energy corporations like ExxonMobil, how they bet billions of dollars on the global price of natural gas? How can stock market algorithms make and break gargantuan fortunes in the flash of an eye? And how should all this impact some group in rural Papua New Guinea whose future will be radi-cally influenced by either the presence of a pipeline or its absence?

Not just from the perspective of those living in the rainforest but from the larger perspective of human experience, the ideologies, beliefs, and practices of modern global capitalism—including the multinational min-ing, logging, and petroleum projects that mightily impact the island of New Guinea and so many other world areas—can seem as idiosyncratic, counterintuitive, and irrational as traditional religions seemed, on first blush, to Western colonialists. Imagine the reaction of highlanders when explorers first ventured in so laboriously and looked so insistently for little pellets of this useless yellow substance—gold—that they sometimes had put in their teeth. How seemingly irrational! In both directions, the notion that "they just don't understand" can seem equally valid.

Among Gebusi, attempts to engage the modern world—and also to accept their ultimate inability to do just that—seem not just understandable but creative and effective. Gebusi provide an insightful example of how people manage a local modernity under conditions that, as Karl Marx put it, are not of their own choosing. Against this backdrop, our common tendency to polarize the advanced against the backward, the civilized against the undeveloped, can all too easily obscure—and reinforce—the huge difference that continues to separate the earnest activities and meaningful engagements of economically poor and disempowered people from those with enormous wealth.

Anne-Sylvie

Papua New Guinea is plagued by corruption, and everyone knows it. The Western Province is full of stories about officials who cared more about being reelected than relieving hunger in their constituency, such as how they would often organize mistimed food relief distribution. There were stories of food deliveries getting to places that did not need them and of food deliveries that were three-quarters empty, having been gradually siphoned off along the way by corrupt politicians needing to pay someone back, pay someone forward, or pay themselves. Half-hearted actions, promises phrased but never fulfilled, gifts given at the wrong time, for the wrong reasons, or not at all. The worst thing about all these stories is it is virtually impossible to document the failures, and the successes are at best half-truths. One thing is for sure: it all cost mountains and mountains of government money—to get nothing done. Once, I was seriously warned of the sanctions awaiting those who investigated the scheming done in high places. I was told that nobody ever remembered anything anyway. As my Italian friends say: "You were not there. And if you were, you were asleep."

Amidst this dysfunction, the same officials were the first to rejoice when a good PR stunt made them appear righteous. They would show up in the bush to take credit for something they had not done.

This is why the governor of Papua New Guinea's large Western Province did not pass up the chance, in June 2016, to go to Nomad to take credit for the rice relief distribution. He was certainly hoping to get a misdirected splatter of prestige and reinforce his chances to win the next election in the process. He had never been seen in Nomad. People thought until the end that it would not happen; among the people scheduled to pay a visit was not just the governor but also his vice president, the president of the local government, and a few other dignitaries whose titles were as inflated as they were obscure. In the skewer of meticulously dressed men we could find a certain number of people elected "locally," meaning they should have had their residence here. In reality, many of them had long since left the place and lived in town, where it was much easier to receive their biweekly stipend. The advanced state of infrastructure dilapidation at Nomad Station is by and large the responsibility of these men, who are said to get richer as they are further from their district. At Nomad Station, people decided not to cut the grass on the airstrip for the occasion, not to hide any disrepair, not to clean up anything, and to put their government representatives in front of the blatant reality of decrepitude that the officials themselves had created.

We did not know at that stage that some villagers had arrived early to hide their bows and arrows under the houses around the place where visiting dignitaries' speeches were going to be given. I had not yet taken the full measure of the rancour that fueled local discourses. Instead I had put it on the same level as what can be found all over the world: irritated people lamenting the fact that their politicians are not doing enough and do not relate to the lifestyle of those who elected them. The meteorological irony of that moment caused torrential rains to flood the area for a few days, submerging even the log bridge we had to cross to go into Nomad.

The officials landed at Nomad Station in an Ok Tedi bimotored plane, already underlining the collusion between government entities and the richest private company in the country. A fat policeman armed with a Kalashnikov opened the way for the flock of potbellied men, solemn in their neat white shirts. Facing them were skinny villagers in rags and bare feet. The dignitaries sat under a porch roof while, opposite them, the locals stood in the rain, taking in the lies thrown at them. The governor gave his speech in English, in front of an audience that could at best speak Tok Pisin. He talked about an unprecedented economic crisis and the somber affair of bureaucracy

The Western Province governor (center) and his aids listen to villagers' accusations, 2016.

A visiting policeman armed with an assault rifle watches the villagers disputing with the governor, Nomad 2016.

and corruption: "My dear friends, I am fighting to access the millions of kinas the court has blocked because of corruption by my predecessors. I cannot help you. I want to help you, but my hands are tied. During my four and a half years as your administrator, I was on trial. Our enemies are numerous, but God is testing us, so we get closer to him." This speech lasted for roughly two hours. His calculated splutter reaching us carefully spun out the bitter irony of a story where corruption itself comes out with a glorified halo, justifying in passing the political inaction people were angry about.

The governor stood there and told us with emotional quavers that he wanted to access the blocked funds, which would allow him to do so much good in the region, but he could not do so: "And listen to me, good people, this is why . . . " I forget the intricacies of his tales; he lost the audience in the complex history of the mine, dropping acronyms, speaking office jargon, and referring to unfamiliar government departments, and sprinkling in patchworks of summaries whose meanings escaped us all. He did, however, give birth to a pretty neat mechanism, allowing him to come out as if the whole debacle of his administration somehow magnified his loftiness. "I make it a point of honor to pay all the civil servants first—teachers, hospital staff members, all those who do so much good in the field." But the rest of the funds could not be accessed, so nobody else can be helped. Bruce was not impressed by the governor's claims and remarked that the funds had been sequestered so they could go directly for services to the people—like buying the rice—and not be siphoned off by politicians like the governor.

I learned later from a member of the local dispensary that during the 2015 drought, when the Ok Tedi Mine closed, his own pay was frozen; for a few months, nobody got paid in the province. Which means that the funds, normally allocated to each province during the drought and that should have been used to keep the services' machine turning, were somehow allocated elsewhere—to deep pockets, by any chance? As for the millions of kinas that the governor could not access, they came from the interests generated by the mine and were being held by a foundation precisely to prevent shady politicians from putting their chubby little hands on such money. If these funds were unblocked and up for grabs, they would vanish into the aforementioned bottomless pockets. Meanwhile, officials were blatantly misusing the funds that should have allowed the province to run.

As people's questions got more aggressive, the governor's answers got more confusing. Hazy sentences flew into the murky air under a

A villager accuses the Western Province governor of neglect and malfeasance, 2016.

thick layer of unattackable vocabulary. Suddenly tension moved up a notch among the locals. Anagi, a quick-tempered man of prime glory from Gasumi, confronted and harangued his interlocutor: "Why have you come here then? Why? Why would you come here today, to do what? Give us the money and f . . . k off! And if you haven't brought any extra money, just empty your pockets and go!" Women joined in. Civil servants were accused of not being here in Nomad, their wasteful use of funds pointed out, their corruption booed. The officials looked stoic, all in all waiting for the crowd's anger to pass, and probably wondering if lunch would be catered on site. Intermittently their smooth voices tried to reassure the crowd, while arguments and facts seemed to desert their speeches. The air got both hotter and much colder. In the last instance they all referred to God, the only one who could probably see clearly in this mess.

So why did they come exactly? Probably to hijack credit for the rice distribution—planned and executed by others, without the smallest contribution from the government. They were hoping to be crowned with usurped laurels, but all they received that day were invectives. People seemed embarrassed for them, because the obvious manoeuver blatantly failed but could not hide itself. In the general condemnation, in all the accusations flying around, the main issue of fixing up the Nomad Station, which they briefly promised, seemed to be forgotten. Saved by the rain, the dignitaries made a quick return to

their plane and flew back to Kiunga, earlier than scheduled and without even visiting the main government office, which they claimed
they would reopen; the medical dispensary; or the school. They also
avoided the arrows that were intended to be shot at them.

Shortly afterward, the Nomad airstrip closed for good, failing government funds to pay people to maintain it.

In June 2017, with no official reopening of the airstrip, air traffic
was suddenly revived, because the government needed a way to get to
Nomad—to hold general elections. The elections were all people
talked about for weeks in advance; at the biweekly market, mega-
phone announcements were made and orders were given—on June
24, like in the whole country, we would be voting at Nomad Station.
Or not. While the local-level elections I had seen among the Baruya
seemed rather fluid (the various liberalities included that my then-
partner and I, both non-Papuan citizens who had resided in the
country less than six months, were allowed to cast votes), in Nomad,
the process left me speechless.

Many charter planes—and helicopters, which were much more
expensive to rent and use—landed, dropping off material and people
in the smallest of installments. These frequent flights casually signaled
to villagers that the many hundreds of thousands of kinas that were
not getting to them could be burned into thin air right above their
heads within a few hours. For the first time in months, since the governor's visit of the previous year, government representatives set foot on
the land they were supposed to administer—"Say, maybe this could do
with a bit of maintenance . . . ?" On June 24, a chopper arrived to
unload the ballot boxes and voter registration papers, but the team left
the electoral roll in Kiunga. Oops. In Gasumi we did laugh a lot.

The infamous electoral roll got to Nomad about two weeks later,
the day people actually voted. In Gasumi, only six names appeared on
the electoral roll, including that of a dead lady. This despite the fact
that a meticulous and double-checked local census had established
that 96 adults could vote (and that the dead lady was already dead).
But these scrupulous registration rolls compiled by trained recorders
were not consulted—or if they were, nobody in authority flinched
when the total number of registered voters jumped from 96 to 6.

Women look at a poster
of candidates nailed to a
coconut tree on election day
in Gasumi Corners, June 2016.

Officials diligently copy vote totals at Nomad Station, June 2016.

Election day itself did not lose an inch of solemnity: Long sentences describing the official procedures were broadcast through megaphones; after all, the show of a well-oiled and neatly staged proceeding has a higher chance of deception. With all the administrative rigor still fitting into tight, ironed trousers and starched shirts, the officials formally read out and repeated for each other several times the serial numbers stamped on each of the ballot boxes that were officially closed and then sealed with great ritual flourish. These procedures were supposed to vouchsafe the boxes from fraud. I later learned that each of those boxes was opened up in each new village that would vote, and that a whole box would have to be discarded from the final count as it seemed odd that it contained 200 ballots after about three dozen people voted. However, at each level of the chain of command, everyone was congratulated for doing such a good job.

Note: See Gebusi video clips of and commentary on "Gebusi Underdevelopment" in 2013 on Bruce Knauft's website or on YouTube by searching for "Gebusi videos."

BROADER CONNECTIONS
Cultural Survival, Development, and Engaged Anthropology

- Problems of **infrastructure** and **government** are common in rural areas of developing countries.
- Like people in many world areas, Gebusi facilitate their **cultural survival** by rejuvenating selected older practices and, in the process, **reinvent culture**.
- In formal economic terms, Gebusi live in **poverty**—they earn less than a dollar a day. But they are arguably richer now in cultural meaning and social quality of life than when they were more "developed," including in terms of locally sustainable food subsistence.
- With passage of time, Gebusi, like many peoples, take increasing interest in their own cultural past, including ethnographic documentation, books, and other information given to them by anthropologists who have worked among them. This process of giving back to local people is sometimes called **cultural repatriation.**
- Peoples undergoing **cultural loss** do not recoup the full range of their previous beliefs and practices, including during periods of **cultural rejuvenation**. Gebusi have not reestablished spirit mediumship or shamanism, séances, sorcery divinations, or other traditional practices that escalated violence.

- The homicide rate among the people of Gasumi Corners continues to be zero since the late 1980s. This illustrates that (1) violence is not innate or inevitable but is strongly shaped by social and cultural influences over time, and (2) culture change on its own terms can have positive results in managing and quelling conflict.

- Gebusi illustrate the importance of complementing our understanding of large-scale changes, including **globalization**, chronic **poverty**, and challenges of **development**, with a human appreciation of how people adapt and find meaning and value in their own culture.

- Though devoid of **economic development**, Gebusi have intensified their use of traditional rainforest resources and newly introduced crops to enrich their subsistence livelihood.

- Based on self-reliance, Gebusi now appear to have better nutrition, better health, higher fertility, and longer life spans than they did previously.

- Like many peoples, the economic future of the Gebusi is difficult to predict, highly uncertain, and could result in long-term **underdevelopment**.

- Among Gebusi as is the case among many marginalized people, government graft and corruption degrade local infrastructure and sap the ability of local people to establish positive economic relations with a wider world.

- Poor peoples like the Gebusi typically have very little influence over larger political and economic conditions—the broader **political economy**—that may radically change their lives.

- The visit of the Western Province governor to Nomad in 2016 revealed how political resistance and opposition by local people can send signals of warning and discontent to officials—even if these signals are not effective or productive.

- Gebusi reveal that despite poverty and disempowerment, **culture change** can be surprisingly productive over time. And connections with anthropologists have the potential to facilitate such positive changes. (In 2016–2017, Bruce and Anne-Sylvie set up a support fund for qualified school children from Gasumi Corners to attend high school in Kiunga.)

Chapter 12

The Larger Future

As they wrestle with continuing hopes and long-standing frustrations of modern underdevelopment, Gebusi may in some ways be ahead of our own 21st-century curve rather than behind it. Amid our own hopes for continuous economic growth, uncertainty and significant downtowns—economic, political, ecological—are almost certain over the course of time. Against these, the adaptive responses and even the seemingly quaint enchantments that we richly find among people like Gebusi may help us learn as we confront our own futures. Gebusi illustrate the ability of people to create dignity and meaning amid conditions of challenge or crisis as well as those of incremental change. Here we are encouraged to rely on personal and local resources to find meaning and value even and especially when times are tough.

Back in Gasumi Corners, life goes on. The government may have "died," along with the general cash economy, but Gebusi do not blame themselves for lack of outside support. Rather, they develop and assert their own local customs and beliefs. In the process, they muster their own responsibility and initiative, drawing on cultural resources and their environment to shape their destiny, if not under conditions of their own choosing.

Around the world, traditions fade. But important parts of them are rediscovered, reinvented, and expressed in new ways. This pattern continues for Gebusi. On the one hand, they face deepening challenges of marginality, isolation, and poverty—at least as measured in money. At present, the

Nomad airstrip remains closed, the government departed, the cash economy moribund, and the area more remote than even—even as ExxonMobil, the world's largest energy company, could be tapping on their doorstep
(but, more probably, not). No Gebusi have yet graduated from high school,
and though the Nomad elementary school has reopened, it is poorly and
inconsistently staffed. Gebusi still have no roads to anywhere. On the other
hand, they are buoyed by the vibrant resources of their own traditions, the
good fortune of access to their indigenous lands, a keen sense of humor and
vitality, and the benefit of having shed the violence of their deeper past.

As our 21st century connects the world more tightly, Gebusi are no
more accessible, and in some ways more remote, than they were when I
first met them in 1980. The breathlessness of our current digital world
easily hides the spotty and uneven nature of global development. Some
people and some places get richly "developed," at least temporarily, while
others get relatively poorer. Amid the rush to the future, our integral connection to and exploitation of those in less-developed areas remains as
poignant as it is underemphasized.

Gebusi's regional context has been greatly and unevenly impacted by
outside influence. This includes colonial pacification and the introduction
of steel tools in the 1960s and 1970s and the advent of Christianity, schooling, and the Nomad market during the late 1980s and the 1990s. These latter changes have been ultimately hinged to government royalties from the
huge Ok Tedi gold and copper mine, some 100 miles to their northwest. In
operation since the 1980s, the mine supplied a whopping 32% of the
export earnings of the entire country of Papua New Guinea by 2010.

The long and complex story of Ok Tedi need not concern us here
except to say that over the years it has had a seismic influence on the economic fortunes of Gebusi, and, indeed, almost everyone in Papua New
Guinea's vast Western Province. Since the country's independence in 1975
until the early 2000s, royalties from this enormous mine, which none in
Gasumi Corners have ever seen, supported the infrastructure of the Western Province, including at Nomad Station—its airstrip, government officers, school, health post, and so on. During this period, despite graft,
corruption, and inefficiency, a trickle of the funds from the Ok Tedi
Development Fund kept Nomad Station—and the tiny market cash economy of the Gebusi—afloat and gradually rising. In the late 2000s and
since, however, this basic supporting revenue has declined if not

stopped—and the Papua New Guinea government has not effectively supplanted or replaced its loss. This funding collapse is due to several factors, including the enormous ecological catastrophe that the mine itself has caused along the huge Fly River system downstream from it; the inability to fix this problem; the declining profitability and dwindling ore reserves at the mine itself; and the inability and unwillingness of the Papua New Guinea government to shut the mine down due to their economic dependence on it—even as the mine's proceeds are diminishing and will eventually cease. In the mix, the paltry government wages and service funds that came to Nomad during the 1980s and 1990s have since "evaporated"—but not "for real." While copious funds are still allocated for the Nomad Sub-District, they do not result in services or on-site personnel that actually support Nomad Station and its surrounding peoples. Rather, they support government workers who stay off-site at Kiunga and other places where they simply collect their continuing pay. These were the deeper issues that underlay the angry local response of Gebusi and others to the governor's visit to Nomad in 2016, as Anne-Sylvie describes in chapter 11.

The larger point for the Gebusi, and for anthropology, is that larger and broader features of political economy—of money, profit, and governance at encompassing structural levels—inform and deeply influence local development and inequities that might otherwise seem far removed from them. The uneven nature of capitalist development makes it is difficult to generalize about the impact of globalization on society and culture, and we are provoked to probe more deeply into specific patterns that both connect and divide people in different world areas. But in general, money tends to make more money for those who have it and, over time, increase the level of inequality. Unless, that is, change to the contrary is effected by a progressive government, by popular demand, or by rebellious social movements. Because these developments are dynamic, they caution us to avoid either rosy assumptions of global development or pessimistic ones of unmitigated catastrophe or degradation. Challenges are great but so, too, are local abilities to respond with insight and dedication. From my own perspective, a combination of scholarly and engaged anthropology is needed to determine both how patterns of development and exploitation occur and how these can be more progressively managed and changed. Within this process, culture is not simply a passive bystander to economic development, political control, or manipulation. Rather, cultural identity—including ethnic or racial identity, national history, class identification, and religious affiliation—is often at the heart of the matter, including how and why benefits are unequally apportioned and distributed.

In some respects, social and economic developments converge globally to make people more similar across the world. Modern institutions of schooling, health care, government, development projects, local markets, and churches or their equivalent are influential in almost all world areas, as they have been for Gebusi. But against such international influences, the resurgence of local cultures cannot be discounted. Arguably, in fact, the reemergence of new forms of cultural diversity is now as great across the world, if not greater, than it has ever been.

Through culture, the paths of the past fertilize those of the present, even if the latter seem increasingly well trodden. People like the Gebusi experiment continually with this mix. As an ethnographer and as a person, engaging this process has been an intellectual challenge and also an emotional one. Addressing the dynamics of culture change requires a balance and sometimes a healthy tension between the analysis of our minds and the ethical principles and humanism of our hearts. Where would we be without both of these in our lives and in our work?

Over the years, I have come to view Gebusi as emergent, vibrant in their present. Gebusi themselves have negotiated their challenges better than I could have imagined. The same is true of peoples in many parts of the world today. For Gebusi, I think they have managed well in part because of their abiding flexibility, on one hand, and their sense of playfulness, on the other. My Gebusi friends might embrace new events and activities as if they were separate from their past, or they might rediscover older customs in a new light. But in either case, they convey strong awareness—through humor, irony, play, and performance—that developments are neither as fixed nor as serious as they might otherwise appear. Even as some of their beliefs or practices are left aside and in some cases actively abandoned, others are reinvented.

Gebusi still desire money, modern goods, and more contemporary styles of life. But they are no longer as subordinate to outside authority figures—pastors, teachers, government officials, and buyers at the market—as

Good company in
the rainforest, 2013.

they were during the 1990s, when they identified so closely with developments taking place at Nomad Station. Since that time, the people of Gasumi
Corners have reasserted their own social world and have reinforced the
integrity of their own community, including in relation to the rainforest.
How and how much this pattern will continue remains a continually open
question. Like the mixed vocabularies of their vernacular language and Tok
Pisin that pervade their current language, contemporary life for Gebusi cannot be framed solely in terms of external influences or indigenous dispositions; rather, it is a product of both. This rich tapestry is now their culture.

In their own context, Gebusi are especially fortunate to have the continuing bounty of their land. They retain the land of their villages as well as
the gardens and pristine forests that provide them with abundant food.
Many peoples who experience so-called modernization are not so lucky. By
contrast, Gebusi have not had to endure violent subjugation, land alienation, punitive taxation, exploitative wage labor, slavery, depletion of natural
resources, or degradation of their immediate natural environment. This history has provided them the flexibility to orient toward outside activities or
to thrive on their own, including their livelihood in the primary rainforest.

I have been fortunate as well. I have had the rare opportunity to know
the Gebusi, to be part of their lives, and to share in their customs across a
rich spectrum of traditional, modern, rediscovered, and hybrid orientations. These have spanned remarkable diversity over four decades, making
my fortune all the greater. Gebusi in 1980 were neither pristine nor fully

"traditional," but their history gave them a special opportunity to develop their culture, in significant part, on their own terms. By 1998 the Gebusi's path of cultural development had not just taken off but run circles around its previous scope and scale, including changes in subsistence, economy, religion, marriage, politics, aesthetic life, and even their sense of time. Due to these changes, Gebusi will never be as independent or remote from outside influence as they once were. During the last 15 years, a negative turn of the economic wheel has slammed Gebusi; their lack of money and services has now become chronic. In the mix, Gebusi traditions are more fully reasserted and more fully combined with newer developments. These are resurgent not as simple replicas of older history but as cultural resources that deeply enrich the present from their past.

No matter how often I return to the Gebusi, their story is always fresh. Each time, my expectations of who they have become are wonderfully recast. In the process, my life as well as my understanding become richer. Gebusi have taught me that our understanding of peoples and cultures—across the world and around the corner—is never finished. Today's new finding may be changed tomorrow. This does not mean our efforts to understand are either inadequate or doomed to be history. It simply means our work, like our lives, continually engages new realms of experience that can inspire both our minds and our hearts.

Since my first fieldwork, Gebusi culture has been transformed for me from an alien world to one of powerful value and then to one of friendship and deep connection. Reflecting their openness, the Gebusi warmly welcomed me from the start. They have given me the greatest gift that people can give and that we can all appreciate: sharing life across differences of culture. Across the miles and the years, what more can I ask?

BROADER CONNECTIONS
Globalization, Political Economy, and the Future of Culture

- As Gebusi illustrate, **globalization** affects all societies and cultures but is also highly uneven in its impact and effects. Globalization can intensify poverty and inequality at the same time that it informs economic growth.

- For Gebusi and virtually all peoples today, **political economy** includes interconnected economic and political forces, interests, and institutions that are regional, national, and ultimately international in scale and influence. The ability of local people to influence or change these larger forces is often minimal.

- Amid globalization, some traditions fade while others are rediscovered and expressed in new ways. This reflects the **reinvention of culture.**

- **Economic development** does not always move "forward." In significant ways, Gebusi are more remote now than they were in 1980: the local airstrip is closed, schooling and health care are minimal, and police and government presence is absent.

- For Gebusi, like people in many developing countries, the larger political economy is strongly impacted by hard-to-predict patterns of **resource extraction,** including by multinational corporations. For Gebusi, this is illustrated both by the Ok Tedi gold and copper mine, and by the building of a large liquefied natural gas pipeline through nearby territory by ExxonMobil.

- The Ok Tedi mine illustrates how exploitation of natural resources can be at once an economic benefit and also a **resource curse** that causes conflict, corruption, and environmental degradation.

- Culture informs key features of personal and group identity—such as ethnic, racial, national, and religious affiliation—that strongly influences how regional and global forces affect local conditions.

- Basic services of the **modern state** and its government—activities and functions that the state is supposed to carry out (but may not, in fact)—typically include **education, health care, infrastructure,** and **security.**

- As Gebusi illustrate, including with respect to historic patterns of violence, local initiatives are often better at instituting positive change than those envisaged or directed primarily by outsiders.

- Many peripheral peoples in the world today have a history of having been subject to **colonialism,** which includes coerced labor or slavery, tribute or taxation, land alienation, out-migration, and indebtedness due to reliance on cash crops or commodities. Gebusi are fortunate to have not suffered greatly so far from such negative impacts.

- Like other peoples, Gebusi are becoming contemporary or locally modern in their own distinct way. Gebusi's flexibility and playful creativity are especially useful and effective in this regard.

- Both personally and professionally, cultural anthropologists are fortunate that during **fieldwork** people often share their lives across differences of culture with those who come to study with them.

- Over time, **cultural anthropologists** and the people they study may become closely connected personally as well as professionally.

- The vibrancy and creativity of **cultural change** are irrepressible; they cannot be easily suppressed or denied.

Farewells

Anne-Sylvie

As the end of a fieldtrip looms near, so does the moment we must disassemble what took so long to assemble. Clearing, inventorying, and packing our belongings become our main task as we dismantle the precarious scaffolding that helped support our daily life. We revisit the thousand little steps we took, unstitching the carefully woven daily moments, and in this trail of our embodied experience, we find the density of lives nestled there—at the bottom of a Soco bottle, in the illegible words of a drenched notebook, in a case containing a rusty nail clipper and a bottle of lavender essential oil, in the cockroach-eaten Kissing Bridge wine labels. I marvel at so much life accumulated in such a short amount of time. I see smiles and faces behind objects now that I have shared them with people, now that relationships are incorporated in them.

Moving out of our house—dismembering our home—must be organized in advance. The rainforest will not eat the structure, but we know its contents will go through the big digestive tube of the people in Gasumi Corners. All these objects will be gifted and will integrate invisible cycles of exchange elsewhere—down to the last nail, and not forgetting the house itself. This makes me feel a tad better, as I contemplate the mountain of plastic, fabric, and metal that has already been introduced into the jungle.

Playing Santa Claus in flip-flops must be carefully planned, as the distribution of goods might create a larger sense of injustice and resentment than it would "spark joy." For in the colorful batch of our possessions, everything does not perfectly line up on the local scale of values. As Bruce learned from his previous visits, the increase in gifts over the course of the years had not matched up with the dramatic increase in Gebusi family size. At the end of each visit he wondered which system of giving things away at the end is best, or, failing that, which is least bad.

After completing our inventory list, we make a list of all the adults and then cross-reference it with a map of the village to identify who lives in which "corner" (and thus who would lend what to whom if need be). We start ticking items off of our inventory list and link these up with names—all the while trying to remember which corner or family had received which gifts in the previous years. Measuring the utility of an object in the rainforest among Gebusi is not always easy, just like measuring the depth of a relationship. There is a whole world of in-between items that we will have to allocate arbitrarily.

In the West we like constructing the notion of "pure relation," detaching it from the material world we so often revere. As if the object, liked if not loved for itself, too, could cast its own shadow on the feelings people have for each other. Among Gebusi, as well as among the Baruya, I felt closer to women, who were never phrasing as many "requests" as the men were. Far from being the indicator of a radically different kind of relationship between them and me, it was rather the sign of a world where women were used to receiving less than men—and would request less often as a result. It always reinforced my willingness to give them things they would not ask for.

Preparing to leave the Gebusi was precisely the moment when we wanted to take our time, to be together, to acknowledge silently and sometimes tearfully the beauty of everything we now have to leave behind. I hugged my narrow-shouldered "pumpkin." My "banana" lifted me up in her large arms. I cried with my "coconut." I cried with my dearest "Soco."

Bruce: On the day of departure, 1998, I had no shame. The morning started rainy, and I hoped it would continue so the plane wouldn't come. I didn't care that my few boxes were already sealed and that everything else had been given away. Eventually, though, the rain let up, and I trekked in sorrow with everyone else to the airstrip.

Anne-Sylvie with Tinagoyl.   Bruce with Sayu.

I started choking up well before the plane emerged on the horizon. I knew it would happen, as it had before. I fought back tears, but they kept coming. I have known the people of Yibihilu and now of Gasumi Corners for so many years, first when they were young, now with their own children as well. There is always the question of when and if I will see them again. Their place is remote, the logistics are hard, and the tropics grind hard on my body. My Gebusi friends know this. Those who are older know I may never see them again; each time, more of them have died before I can return.

Instead of taking photographs at the end, I take mental pictures that are more indelible. I move down the sorrowful line of those gathered to say good-byes, and I force myself to peer in the face and gaze in the eyes of each man and woman, each boy and girl from Gasumi Corners. Snapping their fingers in the best and most forthright manner, I burn into my mind the living image of each of these unique persons so as never to forget their exquisite humanity. Their tear-streaked faces mirror my own as we fight

Yuway with his wife, Warbwi, and two of their children, 2008.

the impulse to turn away. I cry, oblivious to onlookers, a six-foot white guy bawling with a crowd of villagers.

I remember Yuway. He was my most sensitive and caring helper when I was first learning the language, and he was my best friend. When I last left him, I looked into his eyes and blurted out, "Friend. Oh friend. When will I ever see you again?!" With a weepy and yet dignified smile, he told me, "I'll see you later, in heaven." My last sight of Yuway was at the edge of the Nomad. He waved me a final goodbye as my plane soared off. As I sailed toward the heavens, Yuway awaited his own. He died on June 16, 2009.

Fast-forward to 2017. With the Nomad airstrip closed, we had to trek and go by canoe across the full tilt of Gebusi land, up the Sio River to Yehebi, where a small airstrip was still maintained. The trip with our gear was arduous, and the sun blazed down on our long trip by canoe on the unshaded river. By nightfall, the rashes and infections on my skin covered much of my body. I was already on antibiotics and Benadryl and Prednisone and pain killers. But none of these turned the tide; I really needed to leave the field. The Yehebi people were nice, but many of them didn't know me very well. When the plane didn't come for several days—the pilot was sick—I had to do something. For the first time since 1998, I ended up either having or staging a Gebusi anger display, in this case targeted against the guy who for a few scant minutes had daily radio contact with the MAF plane service out of Kiunga. It was not his fault, but I screamed and yelled at him just the same. The plane came the next day. By that time, weary of waiting, most of my Gebusi friends had left and gone back to Gasumi. They needed to attend to their lives and their children; they couldn't wait day upon day just to see us leave. As we finally flew off, I was beyond exhaustion. My final hugs to remaining friends were, what? All that they could be.

Since then, I've realized that I may not be able to go back to the Gebusi; my contact with them may be finished. I never say never, but I also face the odds. The Nomad airstrip can't be reopened; it is now overgrown and rutted by pigs. The cost of a helicopter is prohibitive, tens of thousands of dollars, plus difficult and uncertain to arrange, and with little place for cargo. And robust as I otherwise am, I have to admit that ignoring physical risks now would be rash for me, beyond skin deep.

It's common for experiences and relationships to be marked by their end, judged by the terms of their conclusion. The end of my own recent time with Gebusi was not as uplifting as I had hoped or expected. Does this matter? As a teenager, I recall reading a passage, I think by Aldous Huxley, which asked what difference it would make if the very last thing you happened to do in this life, the very last thing, was to pick your teeth or to pick your nose. Would it really make a difference, a difference to the life you had lived? As I wrote in my afterword to Howell and Talle's wonderful book, *Returns to the Field*, the end of fieldwork cannot be branded by its conclusion, not judged against the standard of a rousing finale. The end of fieldwork, like the end of a relationship, works its own designs in conclusion. And, as among Gebusi themselves, things of the past may always turn out differently than one expects, arising anew in unexpected guises. You never know.

The deepest and most authentic thing I have learned with and about Gebusi is how much they have enjoyed life in the face of privation and suffering. During my first fieldwork among them, their lives were amazingly short, poorly nourished, ravaged by disease and plagued by both the imagined horror of sorcery and the real horror of killing each other. And yet they were the happiest people I have ever known. Their collective bonding and joy and festivity—yes, primarily among men, but among women, too—were simply breathtaking; I have never experienced anything like it. Though tempered since by the upturns and downturns of their local modernity, Gebusi have weathered the cost and the stigma of being left behind in their ever-more remote corner of the New Guinea rainforest. Not just their fortitude but their sense of meaning and value continue to be uplifting. There are worse things in life than trying to attest to that. And to render it authentic.

Bruce leaving the Gebusi.

Index